THE
UNKNOWN
PAUL

THE UNKNOWN PAUL

Essays on Luke-Acts and Early Christian History

JACOB JERVELL

AUGSBURG Publishing House • Minneapolis

THE UNKNOWN PAUL
Essays on Luke-Acts and Early Christian History

Copyright © 1984 Augsburg Publishing House

Scripture quotations unless otherwise noted are from the Revised Standard Version of the Bible, copyright 1946, 1952, and 1971 by the Division of Christian Education of the National Council of Churches.

Library of Congress Cataloging in Publication Data

Jervell, Jacob.
  THE UNKNOWN PAUL.

  Bibliography: p.
  1. Bible. N.T. Acts—Criticism, interpretation,
etc.—Addresses, essays, lectures.   2. Paul, the
Apostle, Saint—Addresses, essays, lectures.
3. Bible N.T. Luke—Criticism, interpretation, etc.—
Addresses, essays, lectures.   4. Church history—
Primitive and early church, ca. 30-600—Addresses,
essays, lectures.   I. Title.
BS2625.2.J47   1984   226'.606   84-24605
ISBN 0-8066-2119-2 (pbk.)

Manufactured in the U.S.A.

APH 10-6815

1   2   3   4   5   6   7   8   9   0   1   2   3   4   5   6   7   8   9

Contents

Abbreviations 7

Preface 9

1   The History of Early Christianity
    and the Acts of the Apostles 13

2   The Mighty Minority 26

3   The Unknown Paul 52

4   Paul in the Acts of the Apostles:
    Tradition, History, Theology 68

5   The Signs of an Apostle: Paul's Miracles 77

6   Sons of the Prophets: The Holy Spirit
    in the Acts of the Apostles 96

7   The Center of Scripture in Luke 122

8   The Circumcised Messiah 138

9   The Daughters of Abraham: Women in Acts 146

Notes 158

Abbreviations

ASNU	Acta Seminarii Neotestamentici Upsaliensis
ATANT	Abhandlungen zur Theologie des Alten und Neuen Testaments
BETL	Bibliotheca Ephemeridum Theologicarum Lovaniensium
BEvT	Beiträge zur Förderung christlicher Theologie
BHT	Beiträge zur historischen Theologie
BWANT	Beiträge zur Wissenschaft vom Alten und Neuen Testament
BZ	*Biblische Zeitschrift*
BZNW	Beihefte zur ZNW
CBQ	*Catholic Biblical Quarterly*
EvT	*Evangelische Theologie*
FRLANT	Forschungen zur Religion und Literatur des Alten und Neuen Testament
HNT	Handbuch zum Neuen Testament
HTKNT	Herders theologischer Kommentar zum Neuen Testament
HTR	*Harvard Theological Review*
KEK	Kritisch-exegetischer Kommentar über das Neue Testament
NovT	*Novum Testamentum*
NTANF	Neutestamentliche Abhandlungen, neue Folge
NTD	Das Neue Testament Deutsch
NTS	*New Testament Studies*

NTT	*Norsk Teologisk Tidsskrift*
RB	*Revue Biblique*
RNT	Regensburger Neues Testament
SBT	Studies in Biblical Theology
SE	Studia Evangelica
SEÅ	*Svensk Exegetisk Årsbok*
SNT	Studien zum Neuen Testament
SNTSMS	Society for New Testament Studies Monograph Series
ST	Studies in Theology
STANT	Studien zum Alten und Neuen Testament
StTh	*Studia Theologica*
TDNT	*Theological Dictionary of the New Testament*
THKNT	Theologischer Handkommentar zum Neuen Testament
ThLZ	*Theologische Literaturzeitung*
ThR	*Theologische Rundschau*
UNT	Untersuchungen zum Neuen Testament
WMANT	Wissenschaftliche Monographien zum Alten und Neuen Testament
ZKG	*Zeitschrift für Kirchengeschichte*
ZNW	*Zeitschrift für die neutestamentliche Wissenschaft*
ZThK	*Zeitschrift für Theologie und Kirche*

Preface

What happened in the early church? Where is its true history to be found? In dealing with such questions the information found in the Acts of the Apostles is indispensable. Nevertheless, due to skepticism regarding Luke's reliability as a historian, the history of the early church is usually written with an outline completely different from that of the author of the Acts of the Apostles.

The following essays serve to outline the history of the early church as it is reflected in the Acts of the Apostles and to demonstrate, among other things, that Luke's idea of what happened is more to the point than the notions generally held by modern exegetes. This is the special emphasis of Chapter 1, "The History of Early Christianity and the Acts of the Apostles."

Above all, our concept of the history in question has to do with the role of Jewish Christianity, which in modern exegesis is often de-emphasized and held to come to an end within the church at least by A.D. 70. In Chapter 2, "The Mighty Minority," Jewish Christianity is understood as a great power in the church during the whole of the first century. It is in the process of establishing itself theologically after the apostolic council and understands itself to be the very center of Christianity, thus functioning as an influential minority between A.D. 70 and 100.

The other main source for the history of the early church is Paul. Here, however, we face the problem of the difference between the Paul of the Pauline letters and the Paul of the Acts of the Apostles. In

9

"The Unknown Paul" (Chapter 3) it becomes evident that we are aware only of fragments of the historical Paul. This has to do with the very character of his letters, mostly written in polemical situations and determined by a few controversial questions in Paul's dealing with some of his churches and his Jewish and Jewish Christian opponents. The other, unknown Paul is the irenic, noncontroversial, and nonpolemical apostle and missionary with the same preaching and practice as the other parts of the church. The unknown Paul can be found mostly in marginal remarks and allusions in his letters, often overlooked in presentations of Paul's theology. But this Paul dominates the portrait in the Acts of the Apostles, whereas Luke plays down the polemical Paul (so in Chapter 4, "Paul in the Acts of the Apostles").

In this connection the miracles are important; these are too often ignored in Paul's theology. To Paul as well as to Luke the miracles are "The Signs of an Apostle" (Chapter 5). Acts portrays Paul as a miracle worker in order to demonstrate his preaching as the divine word. Paul as a miracle worker is a historically correct image of Paul, who considers his own miracles an indispensable part of the gospel itself.

Luke found the early church to be a charismatic community guided by the Holy Spirit and thereby legitimated as the true people of God. In "Sons of the Prophets: The Holy Spirit in the Acts of the Apostles" the idea is that the Spirit for Luke is the Spirit of the Holy Scriptures which prophetically contain the gospel, word for word. The Spirit as the prophetic Spirit has always been there in the history of God's Israel, but serves now to identify Jesus as the true Messiah. The people of the Spirit keep the law, whereas the other Jews oppose the Spirit and therefore are in conflict with the Scriptures and the law. And so for the "rationalistic fundamentalist," as we may characterize Luke as exegete, the very midpoint of Scripture is the prophecy of the suffering and resurrected Messiah of the people of God. So "The Center of Scripture in Luke" shows that this prophetic gospel is presented in the synagogue, the house of the Scriptures, by years of reading, but *received* only in the church.

This prophetic Messiah, as the only true Messiah, coming now from the long sweep of history to the church, has to be circumcised, an idea important for the understanding of the character of the church and found in the New Testament only in Luke's gospel ("The Circumcised Messiah," Chapter 8). Finally, the question of the role of women according to Luke is raised in "The Daughters of Abraham." Luke sees the place of women in the church according to his main concept of the church being the true, reconstituted Israel, heir of the promises. Together with the men, women constitute the church, but in subordination and without leadership positions.

Two of the essays in this book, "The History of Early Christianity and the Acts of the Apostles" and "Sons of the Prophets: The Holy Spirit in the Acts of the Apostles," are published here for the first time. The others have previously appeared in the following journals and books:

"The Mighty Minority" in *Studia Theologica* 34 (1980): 13-38.

"The Unknown Paul" as "Der unbekannte Paulus" in *Die Paulinische Literatur und Theologie*, ed. Sigfred Pedersen [Skandinavische Beiträge] (Aarhus: Forlaget Aros, and Göttingen: Vandenhoeck & Ruprecht, 1980), pp. 29-49.

"Paul in the Acts of the Apostles: Tradition, History, Theology" in *Les Acts des Apôtres*, ed. J. Kremer [Bibliotheca Ephemeridum Theologicarum Lovaniensium 48] (Gembloux: J. Duculot and Leuven: University Press, 1979), pp. 297-306.

"The Signs of an Apostle: Paul's Miracles" as "Die Zeichen des Apostels: Die Wunder beim lukanischen und paulinischen Paulus" in *Studien zum Neuen Testament und seiner Umwelt* 5, ed. A. Fuchs (1980), pp. 54-75.

"The Center of Scripture in Luke" as "Die Mitte der Schrift: Zum lukanischen Verständnis des Alten Testaments" in *Die Mitte der Schrift* [Festschrift für Eduard Schweizer zum 70. Geburtstag], ed. U. Luz and H. Weder (Göttingen: Vandenhoeck & Ruprecht, 1983).

"The Circumcised Messiah" as "Den omskarne Messias" in *Svensk Exegetisk Aarsbok* 37-38 (1972-73): 145-155; and as "Die Beschneidung des Messias" in *Studien zum Neuen Testament und seiner Umwelt* 2 [Theologie aus dem Norden] (1977), pp. 68-78.

"The Daughters of Abraham: Women in Acts" as "Die Töchter Abrahams: Die Frau in der Apostelgeschichte" in *Glaube und Gerechtigkeit* [in Memoriam Rafael Gyllenberg] (Helsinki: Schriften der Finnischen Exegetischen Gesellschaft, 1983).

The essays as a whole raise anew the question of the history of early Christianity and constitute a call for the partial rewriting of that history.

JACOB JERVELL

1

The History of Early Christianity and the Acts of the Apostles

The history of early Christianity[1] is currently written using the Acts of the Apostles as the main source. But as a rule when we write that history we sketch a pattern of development, the *Entwicklungslinie*, totally different from the pattern presented in Acts. This is true of theologians of all persuasions.

There is to some extent a consensus on the evolution of early Christianity, namely, that there was a line of development from Palestinian Jewish Christianity through Hellenistic Jewish Christianity, to Paul and Gentile Christianity, ending with the total victory of Gentile Christianity about A.D. 70. This trend of development is still to a great extent dependent on F. C. Baur. In spite of all criticism of Baur, especially with regard to Jewish Christianity after A.D. 70,[2] his categories are still determinative—and rightly so. But this pattern of development is not the one we have in Acts. The dilemma of current exegesis dealing with Acts as a historical source can be seen from the interpretation of the Hellenists in Acts 6–7 and 11. Nearly all exegetes find in Luke's references to the Hellenists[3] evidence for a segment of early Christianity[4] that was highly critical of the law and the temple and so they locate here the origin of the Gentile mission. That is to say, we use as historical sources accusations that Luke attributes to the Jews. According to Luke the same charges were brought against Paul as against the Hellenists (Acts 21:21,28; 26:8). At the same time, our problem is that Luke labels the charges as false, stemming from false witnesses (Acts 6:13). It is no accident that we find the reference to false witnesses here, and in nothing that can be ascribed to a source, because it agrees with what Luke otherwise tells us about the loyal attitude of the church to temple and law (e.g., Acts 21:15ff.). So we base our concept on accusations that are groundless—from Luke's perspective. There is, of course, nothing to prevent us from looking upon such charges as true in spite of Luke. We here leave out of account the many curious attempts to understand the words of Luke about the false witnesses as not being too false.[5] It is a fact already observed by F. Overbeck that almost no exegete takes Luke's word here seriously.[6]

Our problem and my starting point is to ask why Luke labels these charges as false in spite of their being partly confirmed in Acts 7,[7] especially the criticism of the temple.[8] Whether the relevant parts of the discourse are to be understood to mean that Stephen regards the temple as a place where God cannot be worshiped, or views the temple as a temporary place for worship on God's way to the nations,[9] it is under any circumstance a saying critical of the temple, that is, from a Jewish perspective. What situation makes it possible for Luke to brand the charges as false?

This is a puzzle when we conceive of Luke as a spokesman for a universalistic Gentile Christianity that has replaced Jewish Christianity—Gentile Christianity that has inherited the traditions but found no meaning in the election of Israel and the sacrifices of the temple.[10]

Such a concept replaced the one of F. C. Baur, but his was far better because ours seems unable to account for the Jewish material in Luke-Acts. Actually, even F. Overbeck is far ahead of us, as he saw clearly the Jewish Christianity in Acts but understood it as a part of Gentile Christianity[11]—a point of view that makes sense. What our concept of the total victory of Gentile Christianity can lead to A. v. Harnack illustrates. The good historian Harnack saw the Jewish elements and the Jewish Christian thoughts in Acts. And so he was forced to a very early dating, that is, in the beginning of the 60s, because, as he thought, the ideas in Acts were not possible in the church after that time.[12]

We will now try to concentrate on the trend of development[13] that Luke gives in his description of the progress of the church from Jerusalem to Rome from two points of view:

1. What does the church look like, how is it made up, and what is its way of thinking at the end of Acts? That is, where has "the way" from Jerusalem to Rome led the church?

2. How does the church look at the beginning of Acts, in the initial phases?

It goes without saying that it would not be possible at all to write the history of early Christianity without Acts. We would lack so many decisive data that there would be even more guesswork than we already have today. Not least, our picture of Paul would be altered, as we would have a Paul based on the Pauline letters, on his own words.[14] And so we would not get at the historical Paul. This is not only due to the fact that we would have nothing but fragments of the history, but also that we would have a very different image of Paul from the one the church in general saw, not only at Paul's own time but even when Luke wrote Acts. These are good reasons to remind ourselves of that fact, because it is above all Paul's portrait in Acts that has occasioned much of the criticism of the historical trustworthiness of Luke's work.[15]

The church which was the outcome of the work of the Spirit beginning in Jerusalem on the day of Pentecost consisted mainly of Jews. We find this in the many reports of mass conversions[16] which deal mainly with the conversion of Jews (Acts 2:41,47; 4:4; 5:14; 6:1,7; 9:42; 12:24; 13:43; 14:1; 17:10ff.; 21:20). If Luke, when writing Acts, had had the idea that the church was mainly for Gentiles, we should expect something quite different from this. The last notice with a description of the church's composition (Acts 21:20) gives us "myriads" (so in the original Greek)—ten thousands—of torah-abiding Jews. The next group consists of "Jews and God-fearers," that is, Jews and non-Jews, but as one group, because the God-fearers are Gentiles with ties to the synagogue (13:43; 14:1; 17:4,12). Gentiles without connections to the synagogue are mentioned twice in reports of mass conversions, but the references are not totally clear (11:21,24; 18:8). Nothing is said in general about the Gentiles in the reports of mass conversions, and we have local and specific mass conversions in only two places, namely, Antioch and Corinth. Quite different is Acts 21:20 with regard to converted Jews in general; they are innumerable in the church over the whole world. As for the Gentiles, we find mentioned occasional and unsuccessful attempts to bring them the gospel, as in the mission of Paul to Lystra (14:18) and to Athens (17:32ff.). Our typical modern image of the Gentiles always accepting the gospel promptly and willingly and the Jews in general rejecting it is not correct, according to Acts. Both Jews and Gentiles accept the gospel, but the Jews are the great majority. Our impression that it is the other way around does not come from Acts, but from our common conception of the history of early Christianity.

The church consists mainly of Jews, and this conclusion from the reports of mass conversions is confirmed by the description of the Pauline churches. The church as a whole consists mainly of the Pauline congregations,[17] in addition to which there are chiefly the churches in Jerusalem and Antioch. Luke knew quite well that there was an expansion of Christianity independent of Paul, but Luke gives us nothing but hints of this. The church outside Palestine, the worldwide church, above all in Asia Minor and Greece, is the outcome of Paul's work. The picture is clear: members of the church are with some exceptions Jews. There are in addition some Gentiles who are not members of the people of Israel, but attached to it (13:43,48; 14:1; 16:33; 17:4,12; 18:4, 8,24; 19:8,10). Only 14:21, about Derbe, gives us no information about the composition of the congregation. And it is clear that no churches are mentioned where the members are only non-Jews.

We thus have a church determined by a more and more influential Jewish Christianity. The Jews of the church have not left Judaism. They have not become Gentile Christians in their way of thinking, and they do not think in a non-Jewish manner, as Luke understood "Jewish." This is clear from the portrait of Paul,[18] who in Acts primarily is a missionary to the Jews. And the church in Acts is, at least after Acts 15, in the main a Pauline church. Preaching takes place almost exclusively in the synagogues. This has nothing to do with tactics or *Anknüpfung* (linkage); Luke did not know about such things. The reason for the preaching in the synagogues is a simple one: Christianity is for Luke the religion of Israel.

The synagogue scenes do not signal the transition from mission among Jews to Gentile mission. This is not the case even in 13:46 and 18:6. But the rejection of the gospel in one synagogue leads to preaching in other synagogues. And even in the scenes where the gospel is being rejected we have mentioned a number of Jews coming to faith and living in the congregations that accept Gentiles (so 13:43 and 18:7-8). In 18:7-8 even the chief ruler of the synagogue becomes a believer, that is, after the scene in which Paul leaves the synagogue. There is even here a mission among Jews, that is, when Paul preaches outside the synagogue. And there is not one, single, definite transition from mission among Jews to mission among Gentiles. But the preaching goes on in a way that shows that mission among Gentiles is connected with the mission among Jews; it is taken for granted that there is no mission solely for Gentiles.

The outcome of the preaching in the synagogues is that a considerable number of Jews are converted, and they constitute the core of the congregations even outside Jerusalem (Acts 20:21). And the Christianity of this church is determined by the preaching of a charismatic scribe and Pharisee, namely, Paul (23:6; 24:14ff.). He has strong ties to the traditions of Israel. In Acts, Peter and James, the brother of the Lord, are more liberal than Paul. You find no criticism of the law in the Pauline churches in Acts. The very existence of the book of Acts shows us that Paul is not forgotten at the turn of the century, even if the authentic Pauline character is weakened. Neither Acts nor the Pastorals can claim to represent the Paul we know from Galatians, Romans, and 1 and 2 Corinthians. But the Paul we have in Acts is surely to a great extent also the Paul known to the church around the turn of the century.

We have in Acts a church primarily of Jews and for the Jews, in Palestine and in the various parts of the Roman empire. There is in Acts as a whole not one Gentile Christian missionary, because the mission of the church is throughout Acts a mission to the Jews. Timothy, the only uncircumcised missionary, is circumcised by Paul (16:3). Titus, who was a Gentile, is not mentioned in Acts (if 18:7 is an exception, it refers to him not as a missionary, but as a God-fearer in whose house Paul is preaching). We know that most, but not all, of Paul's co-workers were Jews. But the non-Jews are not mentioned in Acts. There are some Gentiles attached to the great number of Jews, but no quantity is specified, and these Gentiles do not represent any specific theology.

In Acts the Gentiles have to adapt to the Jews, and not the other way around. There is no thinking in Acts dissociated from Israel and the history of the people of God. There is no tendency to overlook the meaning of the election of Israel. There have been attempts to interpret, for example, the speech of Peter in 10:34-43, especially verses 34-35 in such a way.[19] But if such thoughts perhaps lay in the material Luke had at his disposal, verses 41-42, which are genuinely Lukan, make it impossible to find here some sort of a Gentile Christian universalism. And the Gentiles in Acts know that the Scriptures are the Scriptures of Israel, first and foremost for worship in the synagogue. The only exception in Acts could be the Areopagus speech in Chapter 17, which gives us the idea of the creation of humankind and the nations instead of the history of Israel as the prehistory of the people of God. But this speech is more or less a foreign body within Acts, not a typical missionary speech, and from the point of composition and structure no lines lead from this speech to the other parts of Acts.

The third part of the picture is the church in Jerusalem. At the end of the book this congregation is decisive for the church as a whole.[20] It is noteworthy in the composition of Acts that Jerusalem is mentioned in the last part of Acts. If Jerusalem, and the church there, were a thing from the past, Luke could have ended the Jerusalem section in Chapter 7. But we have also Chapter 15, and in Chapter 21 the history of Paul is connected with and "enclosed" by Jerusalem. It is not necessary, at least from a literary point of view, to tell about the arrest of Paul or to mention Jerusalem in Chapter 21. And the content of the speech of James (21:20-25), among other things, the apostolic decree (21:25), is far beyond what is necessary for the literary context, the purpose of which is to show why Paul is being arrested.

The development of the Jerusalem church in Acts is typical as this church in the beginning was more complex and variegated than it was later. In it there were Hellenists (Acts 6–7). There was Peter, who opened the door for mission among the Gentiles and table fellowship with the uncircumcised (Acts 10–11). There were varying degrees of strictness in the demands to the non-Jews in the church (Acts 15).

In Acts 21 this is different. There is no tendency to criticize law or temple. The main feature of the church is now that it consists of "zealots for the law," people who adhere to Moses and circumcision (21:20,21). And this has to do with the ritualistic aspects of the law (21:23ff.). Everything that conflicts with that is apostasy. This congregation decides for the church as a whole. So it was already with the mission in Samaria (Acts 8) and at the conversion of Cornelius (Chapters 10–11). The decision about the apostolic decree was made by Jerusalem (15:6,19,23ff.; 21:25). And the influence of Jerusalem continues, as can be seen from Acts 21:15ff.: Jerusalem gets reports on the mission among the Gentiles (21:19); Jerusalem is kept informed about Paul's preaching among Jews in the diaspora (21:21); Jerusalem can impose ritual acts on Paul (21:23ff.); Jerusalem decides how the Gentiles shall live insofar as this church maintains the apostolic decree (21:25).

The Paul of Acts—and especially of the latter part—is not a private individual. He is not a paradigm of the ideal missionary, so that the demand here given refers to all. Rather, Paul is the representative for all the churches he has founded, a fact first clearly to be seen in his farewell speech in Miletus (20:18-21). This speech is his parting from his missionary work and from all his congregations (20:18,21,25,28). Further, this is evident from the meeting with the church of Jerusalem in 21:18-26. According to Luke, Jerusalem has authority over all the

Christian churches. There is no church disconnected from Jerusalem and so from Israel. The false charge that Paul taught apostasy is denied (21:21-26). And it is not necessary to tell how the congregation reacts to Paul's ritual act. What is important is that the readers get information about Paul's relation to the leaders of the church. And so the church in Rome has received no letters from Judea accusing Paul (Acts 28:21). The scene in 21:15-26 tells us that the important affairs in the church are the Jewish ones, for example, what the church teaches the uncircumcised Christians (21:21ff.). The Gentiles are more like an appendix (21:19,25). And there do not seem to be any problems with the Gentiles in the church at this time.

So at the end of Acts we find a church with very many Jews and some Gentiles. The "theology" is Jewish Christian within a church headed by the church in Jerusalem. And the church is for a great part the outcome of Paul's work.[21] The picture differs heavily from our critical concept according to which the author looks back, as if describing past situations that have no direct relevance for the new situation of his readers. In this view many years lie between the events narrated at the end of Acts and the totally different church we have at the time Luke is writing. So 28:28 would mean that Paul looks into the future to a church which has left Judaism and Jewish Christianity behind. Now, in the author's time, the church consists of believing Gentiles who have replaced the Jewish Christians. And Luke knows very well what Jewish Christianity is; it is no strange phenomenon to him. He knows well the need to distinguish between "those of the circumcision" and "the believers from the peoples." Luke would then see the church as the church for the Gentiles without ties to Israel.

I do not find such an understanding probable. Luke is certainly a historian, but at the same time he is a preacher and a theologian describing past situations with relevance for the situation of his own readers.

The history Luke has written would not, according to this understanding, lead up to his own situation. Important and decisive things altering the character of the church for Jews and Gentiles would have happened without Luke telling about them. This is especially relevant if he deals with a church in which the election of Israel no longer makes sense.[22] The reason why Luke did not give the last phase of the history could be that this was not necessary because the development was evident to Luke's readers, important things like the loss of meaning

in Israel's election as God's people. We would have such an understanding if at the time of writing there existed something like an establishment in the church looking back to the initial stages before any
"law and order" came to the church. But such an establishment did
not exist, and is nowhere to be found in the New Testament. For Luke
the future is still uncertain. No history of salvation is evident, manifest,
and easily read. This is why prophecy means so much to Luke, and
this is a prophecy which partly has not yet been fulfilled.[23]

Judging from this modern view, the composition of the church in
Luke's time would have been very different from the one Luke describes in Acts. If he has described the way of the gospel from Jerusalem
to "the end of the earth" (1:8), it is hard to see how this history would
continue.

The final description of the church in Jerusalem would then have
been antiquated and it could be looked upon as a failure. The problems
in Acts 21:15-26 would not be of current interest.[24] And how would
the enjoining of the apostolic decree at the end of Acts be understood?
We here have the decree for the third time in Acts, revealing a presupposition that the life of the Gentiles in the church is regulated in
relation to the Jewish Christians. It is thus taken for granted that Jerusalem is important for the church as a whole.

I see no reason to hold that the church we see at the end of Acts
was different from the church in which Luke lived. When Luke is
writing, he deals neither with a dead Jewish Christianity, or a Jewish
Christianity without any significance for the church as a whole. I would
say that the Hellenization of Christianity took place later than we think,
and that Gentile Christianity became dominant first in the second century.

We will now turn to the other part of Acts, namely, the shape of
the church in the beginning, as Luke sees it. We have here three
elements: (1) the congregation in Jerusalem, (2) the Gentile mission,
and (3) the life of the Gentiles in the church.

Jerusalem is even here in the center, but the church differs from the
description of it in other parts of Acts. Throughout Acts the Jerusalem
church is one with very many Jews. Most of the reports of mass conversions have to do with Jews (2:42 [47]; 4:4; 5:14; 6:1,7). The church
does not consist mainly of people from Galilee. The family of Jesus,
his disciples, and some followers from Galilee are a part of the church
(1:12-14), but they seem to Luke to constitute but a modest part (1:15).
Above all, inhabitants of Jerusalem constitute the church: according
to 2:41, 3000 were added to the church; in 4:4 we have 5000, and in

6:7 "a great many of the priests." They all live in the context of the temple and within the Jewish institutions.

The church in Jerusalem was originally of a "mixed" composition, partly "liberal" on questions of law and temple and open-minded regarding to uncircumcised. Later we find a theological severity on these points. A strongly Jewish imprint on theology and ethics is not there from the very beginning but develops later. This is not so much a part of Luke's concept but is inherent in the material which he treats in a faithful manner.

The church is mixed: there were "Hebrews" and "Hellenists,"[25] two groups, depicted in Acts 6. But only in this part of Acts is there a "mixed" church in Jerusalem. The description in 21:15ff. shows a far more uniform congregation. And now there is no reason to rebuke the church for criticism of temple and law, as there was in 6:11,13f. Now only Paul is accused (21:21), and we have the same charges as in 6:11,13f. The problem for the church in subsequent parts of Acts concerns Paul. The Hellenists disappear from Jerusalem in Acts 8, and they never return. Now the church as a whole is reputed to be "zealous for the law" (21:20). The criticism against Stephen for the negative attitude to temple and law comes from outside the church and is labeled "false" (6:13). In Chapter 21 the criticism comes from the church itself, which takes the reports of Paul's "heresy" seriously—at least such is the case for many members of the church. In Chapter 21 there is no temple criticism at all, but the church is throughout positive towards the temple (21:23ff.).

No matter how we evaluate the charges against the Hellenists, it seems clear that there was in Jerusalem from the beginning a church with law-observant members as well as those critical of the law and the temple.[26] Interpretations of the theology of the Hellenists have been thus far unsuccessful. It is unlikely that the language as such involves a certain theology.[27] That the "critical" theology stems from the phenomenon of Jews in the Hellenistic diaspora is no explanation. What reason do we have to think that the people in the diaspora were less observant of the law than the ones in the native country? We would thus create difficulties in explaining the diaspora as a phenomenon. The Jews have resisted assimilation and preserve their distinctive stamp and peculiarity through generations. When Luke mentions criticism of law and temple in connection with the Hellenists, and when the discourse in Chapter 7—against Luke's intentions—confirms the temple criticism, this is explained by the simple fact that criticism of temple and law actually took place in this part of the church in Jerusalem, and we are unable to give any ethnic or cultural-sociological explanation. Luke is probably right in maintaining that the resistance to and the charges against the Hellenists came from Jews from the diaspora now living in Jerusalem (6:9-13). And the Jews in the diaspora and the "God-fearers" (σεβόμενοι) were the strongest opponents of Christian preaching (9:1,20ff.,29; 13:45ff.; 14:2ff.,19f.; 16:19ff.; 17:4ff.; etc.).

The next question is that of the origin of the Gentile mission. Even here we find in Luke's writing a remarkable double-facetedness. On the one hand, the Gentile mission is traced back to the congregation in Jerusalem; on the other hand, this mission is problematic and is being resisted.[28]

In two ways the Gentile mission goes back to Jerusalem.[29] The first is that the expelled part of the church, the Hellenists, start preaching to Gentiles in Antioch (11:20). It is not said that the Hellenists are responsible for this undertaking, because we have mentioned "those who were scattered because of the persecution that arose over Stephen." According to 8:1 this is the whole congregation in Jerusalem with the exception of the apostles. We have only a short notice telling us about this undertaking among the Gentiles and it is told without report of controversy. The story about Cornelius (Acts 10–11) is not used as justification. This mission is, in other words, carried out by Christians whose law-observant life no one can deny. And Jerusalem accepts this mission unconditionally (11:22ff.).

The second way is depicted in Acts 10–11,[30] where the connection is more direct than in 11:19ff., where we find that the expelled Christians have settled in Antioch. Peter, however, all the time resides in Jerusalem.

The mission of the Hellenists is depicted as totally unproblematic, whereas the Cornelius story is quite different. The conversion and admission of Cornelius to the people of God is resisted by Peter and among those in the Jerusalem church (10:9-16, 28; 11:1-3). It is obviously correct to read the story so that God must force the Gentile mission against the will of the church in Jerusalem. This is a somewhat peculiar report about a church that is meant to be an ideal, because the Gentile mission is traced back to Jesus and the Scriptures (Luke 24:47; Acts 1:8; 10:20; 13:47; 15:16ff.; etc.).

It is important to consider why Luke depicts the Gentile mission as having had such a hard birth, and why it is met by skepticism at the time when Luke is writing. It is noteworthy that Jerusalem is connected with the Gentile mission only in the first part of Acts. Chapter 15 refers to the Cornelius story, and in 21:15ff. we have no mission among

Gentiles carried out by Jerusalem, but only reports of such a mission being carried out by others.

We get throughout Acts the notion of a Gentile mission which from the beginning was accepted, but gradually surrounded by skepticism. And this corresponds to the gradual hardening of the demands to the Gentiles.

We notice this first in the Cornelius story. After the obstacles for the admission of Gentiles to the church were removed, the church unconditionally accepted the idea that non-Jews have been "granted repentance unto life" (11:18). And, accordingly, the Gentiles gained by the mission from Antioch were accepted. Barnabas, sent from Jerusalem, affirmed the grace of God shown upon them (11:22-24). Finally, Paul was unconditionally accepted by Jerusalem as preacher of the gospel (11:26ff.).

In Chapter 15, however, we have a different situation. Here there is no unconditional acceptance of the Gentiles, but the question of what is to be demanded from them. The demands come from circles in Jerusalem (15:1,24), even if verse 24 maintains that the people in question had authority neither from the congregation nor the apostles.

The question has been raised why Jerusalem would have to deal with the problem of the conditions for admitting Gentiles into the church if in fact this matter had been resolved long ago. How is Acts 15 possible after Acts 10–11?[31] The answer is very simple. Actually, a hardening of Jerusalem in its attitude to Gentiles took place. And it is no accident that the name of James is mentioned especially in connection with the decree of 15:13-21. The Jewish-Christian church, which to an increasing extent saw Paul and his preaching as a great problem, is the result of the work of James in the decades after the founding of the Gentile mission.[32] At the meeting in Jerusalem Peter laid no demands on the Gentiles. And the speech of Peter in 15:6-11 as well as the one in 10:34ff. indicate that nothing at all was imposed on the Gentiles. James is the one who put forward the decree (16:19), even if it is clear to Luke that Peter agreed to James' proposal (15:22).

Luke testifies deliberately or unwillingly that the church in Jerusalem developed from an "open multiplicity" to the tightness described in Acts 21 and even mentioned in Paul's references to his relation to Jerusalem (Gal. 2:1ff.; Rom. 15:30-32). No matter how we value the apostolic decree it imposes demands on the Gentile Christians, demands which were not there from the beginning.

We return to the question we posed at the beginning: How can we understand Luke's assertion that the charges against the Hellenists are false?

It is not understandable from the common notion of Luke as representative of a Gentile-Christian theology within a Gentile-Christian control of the church, because Luke would then theologically be in line with the thinking of which the Hellenists were charged. But the branding of the accusations as false is easy to understand from the description of the conservative church Luke gives in the end of Acts. From the account in Acts 21 and from the idea of a dominating Jewish-Christian part of the church based upon the Pharisee Paul, the accusations are evidently false. The loyalty of the church to the law is beyond doubt, and this loyalty is that of Jewish Christians and the circumcised. There are different obligations to the law for Jewish and Gentile Christians. And these obligations stem from the church in Jerusalem, which never has criticized the temple or the law.

The same applies to the Gentile mission. It is the object of a certain skepticism when Luke is writing. And this skepticism would prevail if the Jerusalem church is described as not carrying the responsibility for the Gentile mission. This skepticism does not stem from Gentile Christians. We could imagine that Gentile Christians would indicate that their admission to the people of God came by God's own will. The point, however, in the story about Cornelius (Acts 10–11) has to do with the impurity and uncircumcised status of the Gentiles. Why is it that throughout Acts the mission to Israel is taken for granted? It tells us about a church in which Jewish Christianity dominates. When you can trace back the Gentile mission, not to Antioch, not to Paul, but to Jerusalem, Jewish Christians can approve of it.

It is probably historically correct that the Gentile mission goes back to the church in Jerusalem.[33] That does not mean the Gentile mission in general, because even the Jews until A.D. 70 had a very lively mission among Gentiles.[34] We have to do with the mission which does not demand circumcision:

First: The Hellenists undertook such a mission from Antioch. Whether the Hellenists even in Jerusalem admitted the uncircumcised to the church and baptized them, we do not know.[35]

Second: One presupposition for the mission to the Gentiles lies in the fact that in Jerusalem there was a Christian group critical of the law,[36] namely, the Hellenists. But this group could not remain in Jerusalem for long.[37]

Third: Paul says that his missionary activity, which from the very beginning was aimed at Gentiles, was favorably accepted by the church in Jerusalem (Gal. 1:23-24). The history of the first phases of Paul's life as a Christian shows that opposition against him came in time, but that he from the beginning was welcomed by Jerusalem.[38]

Fourth: Peter had, at least in one period, a "liberal" attitude to the uncircumcised Christians (Gal. 1:18; 2:9,11ff.).

Fifth: From the perspective of a Gentile mission undertaken from the church in Jerusalem we get an explanation of Paul's activity as a persecutor of the church. It comes into Acts in a somewhat abrupt and strange way (8:3). But it is not strange if we have to do with a persecution of the Hellenists caused by their attitude to the temple and law and thereby to the Gentiles. A persecution of a strict law-observant church in Jerusalem is inexplicable.

Acts is most valuable and indispensable as a source for the history of early Christianity, not only for diverse information on specific topics, but also by showing the course of history in the first century. I would say that the false witnesses in Acts 6 are not too false, because Luke writes the history of the church from the situation of the church at the time of writing.

The narratives in Acts do not cover the end of what may be called "early Christianity." Things have happened since Luke finished writing. We do not know how much time Luke thought was still left before the consummation. He obviously thought that he was living in the last days, although the end was not yet. It seems that he means that the prophecies as a whole have been fulfilled, apart from the great, last one, namely, the coming of Christ with "the times of the Gentiles being fulfilled" (Luke 21:24). It is, of course, for Luke the times of those Gentiles who are outside the church. The time of Israel never comes to an end.

With this element of uncertainty in mind we ask: How representative is Luke? He does not cover all opinions in the church, but I see confirmed in the New Testament the fact that his understanding of what has "happened among us" (Luke 1:1) is shared by the greater parts of the church of his time. This applies above all to the course of history he presents to us, which seems more historically genuine than our modern consensus referred to above. And it gives us an impulse to rethink the question of early Christianity, not least the role played by the Jewish Christians.

2

The Mighty Minority

1

More than 90 years ago Adolf Hilgenfeld stated in his *Ketzergeschichte des Urchristentums*[1] that Jewish Christianity in the first century should be considered "a great power" in the Christian church. In my opinion Hilgenfeld was right even if we have forgotten him. Nevertheless, Jewish Christianity was a minority, and we usually do not consider ethnic religious minorities to be great powers. In our context the word *minority* points to Jewish Christianity from a numerical point of view. In the second part of the first century Jewish Christianity—or the group of Christians of Jewish background—gradually became a minority. We do not have exact figures. It is still true and a commonplace to say this. There were no great numbers of Christian Jews, not compared to the increasing numbers of Gentiles in primitive Christianity, and not in relation to the non-Christian Jews. The early Christian mission to the Jews was a failure. This is true even when listening to the many reports in Acts of mass conversions among Jews,[2] and to parallel reports in the gospel of John.[3] Acts tells us that a greater part of the population in Jerusalem became Christians (μυριάδες, 21:20).[4] Luke is, moreover, generally reliable, so that his great numbers signify the spiritual, theological, ethical, sociological, and cultural Jewish Christian dominance in the church of the first century.

By saying this I have partly unveiled my thesis, but it is too early for that. I will at this time only say this much: The minority, that is, Jewish Christianity in the second part of the first century, remained in the church throughout the century, not *a* but *the* great power, determining the thinking, the theology, and the preaching of the Christian church.

The decisive argument against F. C. Baur and his concept of the history of early Christianity used to be that Jewish Christianity played no part in the last 30 years of the first century, that is after A.D. 70, and so no synthesis could possibly have taken place between Jewish and Gentile Christianity after 70. This has never been proved and is nothing but a thesis, and we have done wrong to Baur, at least when we deal with Jewish Christianity after the year A.D. 70. If Hilgenfeld is right, and I think he is, and if we have done wrong to Baur, and I think we have, we will have to reconsider or rewrite the history of primitive Christianity. This is not a question of details, but of the outline, the structure.

I will here point to two things:

First, it is commonly held that the Jewish influence in church, at least from a literary point of view, reached its climax in the third generation of Christians in the first century,[5] that is, at the same time as Jewish Christianity according to a multitude of scholars completely outplayed its role in the church. Second, the study of Acts has started afresh. We have seen more than one new analysis. Allow me to point to G. Lohfink, *Die Sammlung Israels*,[6] and my own study, *Luke and the People of God*,[7] followed by many others.[8] Common to the new approaches is, above all, that Acts does not fit into the dominant scheme when dealing with the history of the primitive Church.

I am not going to anticipate, so let me return to the minority as the great power. I am in this context above all interested in the time from A.D. 70 to 100, that is, the years in which nearly all parts of the New Testament, with the exception of the Pauline letters, were written. For these years we can give more than guesses when dealing with the historical problems. The year 70 is chosen due to the fact that a great number, a majority of scholars, maintain that the fall of Jerusalem meant the destruction of Jewish Christianity—apart from small Jewish sects in the following centuries. In any case the year 70 is a decisive one, but perhaps we should consider it in the following way: From the year 70 a strengthening of Jewish Christianity took place. For nearly all scholars, however, the year 70 is significant insofar as from this time Jewish Christianity is an insignificant and weak sectarian part of the church (according to scholars like Harnack, Lietzmann, Cullmann, Schoeps, Danielou, Munck, Lindars, Brandon, and others—to mention only a few). Some scholars held the apostolic council of 48 to be the beginning of the end, as Jewish Christianity from that time supposedly became numerically very weak.[9] If we stick to the year 70 as the end of Jewish Christianity in its role within the church, we have the aporia: How do we explain the fact that Jewish influence in the church, that is, Jewish literary material embodied in the church, reaches its climax in the third generation? This question seems to force Bo Reicke to talk about mass conversions among Jews near the end of the century.[10] I can find no evidence for that, but Bo Reicke is correct on this point: this influence cannot be understood unless we take Jewish Christianity into account.

We have on the one hand the year 70. I mentioned above the year A.D. 100, which has to do with the approximate *terminus ad quem* for most of the writings of the New Testament. In this essay I am not going to deal, as is usual when considering Jewish Christianity, with postcanonical and noncanonical early Christian documents to get information about early Jewish Christianity. This is usually done because we consider the New Testament to be a document of Gentile Christianity. And of course we must act so methodologically when dealing with the so-called sectarian and heretical Jewish Christianity which we connect with diverse names or groups and sects from the second to the fifth centuries A.D. I do intend to consider the more—*sit venia verbo*—"liberal" and cooperative Jewish Christianity from the first century, and above all, the one we find in the last three decades of that century.

As mentioned above, some scholars are inclined to think that the council in A.D. 48 is the beginning of the end for Jewish Christianity,[11] and that in any case its history ends by the year A.D. 70. Then after 70 the Jewish Christians join with and "disappear" into the Gentile Christian congregations and become in doctrine, dogma, and observance like Gentile Christians.[12] This means that postapostolic Christianity is in the first century almost exclusively Gentile Christianity. And the New Testament is, with the exception of some Jewish-Christian "remnants," a Gentile-Christian document. I have always found it peculiar, and a riddle connected with this opinion, that the only main group involved in the story of the Jewish war which did not survive should be the Jewish Christians. We find after A.D. 70 on the one hand the birth of rabbinic Judaism or the continuation of Pharisaism, and the flourishing apocalypticism in Judaism and Christianity. On the other hand we have the Gentile-Christian church, liberated from Jewish Christianity. So the Gentiles in the church survived, but the Jewish Christians, or more precisely, Jewish Christianity, died. Were they more nationalistic than other Jewish groups before 70 or more one with the nation than other groups?[13]

The common concept of the history of early Christianity is roughly taken as follows:

Christianity was in the beginning (Palestinian) Jewish Christianity. After that came a period where we find side by side Hellenistic Jewish Christianity, Gentile Hellenistic Christianity, and Paul—with Palestinian Jewish Christianity somewhere in the background. In this period, the second one, Jewish Christianity was forced back and acted solely in defense. In the third period Gentile Christianity triumphed, whereas the Jewish Christians returned to the synagogue or lived as Gentile Christians or settled as an isolated and sectarian Christianity or Christian Judaism, half Jewish, half Christian. This last phenomenon later became "Jewish Christianity." And the final result is *Frühkatholizismus*[14] (early catholicism)—with the main witness being the Acts of the Apostles.

If we operate within our subject in numerical categories, this concept of the evolution from Jewish to Gentile Christianity in the first century Christianity is obviously correct. But what kind of picture do we get if we attempt to understand Jewish Christianity from a theological, cultural, and sociological point of view?

Jewish Christianity is a multifarious phenomenon, in itself a theological spectrum, and in the first century probably consisted of different parties. Jewish Christianity remained such a phenomenon as long as it ever existed, even in what may be called the sectarian period. And this is not the least peculiar if we understand it from the background of Jewish orthopraxy more than orthodoxy. The manifoldness of Jewish Christianity is no less true of Gentile Christianity, which is far more difficult to define than the former. In spite of the multifarious phenomenon, we have sufficient common denominators or features in the divergent theological modes of expressions to use the term Jewish Christianity as a meaningful reference to a theological entity.

I would like to question some parts of our concept of primitive Christianity. Has not the time come to ask for a revision of the generally held opinion that early Christianity is an uncomplicated, one-way development and movement from Jewish to Gentile Christianity? Moreover, is it true that Jewish Christianity as a theological entity always represents the beginning, the origin, in the oldest church? I do not have in mind such ideas as the concept of more than one *Urgemeinde* (primitive community) and that the first congregations differed in many ways. It goes without saying that Christianity from the very beginning was considered as determined for Jews and carried on by Jews, some sort of a Jewish "revival movement." Decisive, however, is what early Christianity looked like theologically and how it developed theologically.

And now my thesis.

First, Jewish Christianity did not develop into a theologically active, articulate, and conscious entity until, and in connection with, and after, the apostolic council.

Second, in the postapostolic period, after the year 70, Jewish Christianity established itself. This means that not until the time of the council did the majority of Jewish Christians form a theologically conscious, profiled, and determining minority in a church which was numerically dominated by Gentiles. This implies further that Jewish Christians did not become Gentile Christians. Nor did there come into existence a kind of *tertium genus*, that is, some kind of "neither Jew nor Greek." On the contrary, the Jewish Christians looked upon themselves as the very center of the church, and with this understanding the Jewish Christian minorities continued to live in the church and survived the catastrophe of the year A.D. 70, as the non-Christian Jews survived the tragedy, although in a different way.

2

We start with some considerations of the time from A.D. 30 to 70. First, the apostolic council did not take place until about A.D. 48. This fact calls for some reflections. It is astonishing that the meeting did not take place earlier, because at that time Christians who were Gentiles by birth had lived as members of Christian congregations for at least 15 years. And there is not the slightest evidence of any protest against this, not from the mother church in Jerusalem, nor from other Jewish Christian churches in Palestine. And the apostolic decree, as Luke refers to it,[15] signifies a more restrictive policy towards Gentiles, a turning away from a more liberal attitude, insofar as the Gentiles more than before had to conform to the Jews in the church. In comparison to the insistence on circumcision from more conservative Judaists, the apostolic decree represents a milder course. But compared to the situation for Gentiles before the discussion on their status in connection with the council, the decree does represent a hardening. The Aramaic-speaking church in Jerusalem at that time was more tolerant on questions of law than during the leadership of James at a later date. We do not know for sure the attitude of the Jerusalem church towards Christian Gentiles. But it is safe to say that the church in Jerusalem tolerated the admission of Gentiles without any demand of circumcision and keeping of the torah (Acts 15:7,9,14).[16]

We may perhaps say that Jerusalem welcomed Gentiles as Gentiles in the church. We have possibly as early as Stephen's work in Jerusalem an address of the gospel to non-Jews, to Gentiles. It is a mission to Gentiles without the demand of circumcision. In this connection we find in the Stephen group a certain criticism of the law (Acts 6:11,13) which resembles the one we find in the gospel of Matthew. It is a criticism of the law within the boundaries of the law, not a criticism of the law as such.[17] What is important is that the church in Jerusalem tolerated Stephen and his mission, but for Luke, 30 or 40 years later, this is not possible insofar as he repulses any complaint against Stephen for being a critic of the law (Acts 6:8—7:53). We do not know for sure the nature of the mission of Stephen, but we are on safe ground when dealing with Antioch where from the very beginning we are faced with a mixed congregation (Gal. 2:11ff.; Acts 11:19ff.; 14–15). The church in Antioch is *the* church of the mission among Gentiles. In the congregation we find Jewish and Gentile members. This church lived for years in contact with the Jerusalem church, and there is no sign whatsoever that this was felt as abnormal or problematic.

This attitude on the part of Jerusalem is remarkable because the New Testament does not conceal that a bitter and intense fight took place for years on the question of the legitimacy of the mission to the Gentiles. It is not only Paul who witnesses to this, but even and perhaps more Luke-Acts and the synoptic gospels. But this battle—if the word is allowed—regarding mission obviously did not take place in the earliest or initial phase of the primitive church. What is the reason? It is not due to the lack of sources, and we do not find traces of an initial conflict in the church or a negative attitude to Gentiles. Nor is the reason that for years only Jews belonged to the church, because there is no doubt that the church in Antioch goes back to the oldest period. We do know that Paul was active as a missionary among Gentiles shortly after his conversion, but at that time the Gentile mission had already been started by other missionaries. And when Paul is active among Gentiles, long before the council in Jerusalem, the Jewish Christian congregations in Judea, among them Jerusalem, praise God for Paul's preaching among Gentiles (Gal. 1:23-24 compared to 1:16).

We do not know exactly how the mission among Gentiles started; it is surely not the outcome of theological reflection and discussion. The discussions on the subject did not come until years after this mission had been established. In my opinion the original mission among

Gentiles was the result of ecstatic experiences, pneumatic enthusiasm, among charismatics and Christian prophets.[18] This is evident in Acts (see the story about Cornelius, Chapters 10 and 11) and in Paul. Both Luke and Paul saw the original missionary preaching in connection with glossolalia (so Acts 2; 1 Cor. 14:21). But only years later, that is, in connection with the Pauline mission, which from the very beginning was a mission among Gentiles, did the conflict about this mission begin. The Pauline mission was nevertheless for years welcomed by the Jewish Christians in Judea.

It is a remarkable fact within the New Testament that it is not only Paul who in the years A.D. 50-60 must defend the Gentile mission—and not only his own! After the council, defense is badly needed. After the council the conflict starts. To that Paul is a witness. But even in the years between 70 and 80, Matthew and Luke are forced to make a rigorous defense of the mission among Gentiles in their writing—and this in spite of the fact that the mission at this time is established. It is still surrounded by criticism and skepticism. At the same time there is no question whatsoever about the legitimacy of the mission to the Jews. On the contrary, Luke must account for the fact that his church does not any more address the Jews, which obviously is seen as the normal aim for Christian mission.[19]

The discussion and conflict around the mission to the Gentiles, therefore, did not start in the first period of the church, but only with the events which led to the apostolic council. How is the conflict to be understood and explained? Either the Jewish Christians totally denied any mission to the Gentiles insofar as this operated with a free attitude toward the ceremonial parts of the Mosaic torah or they wanted at least to encompass it with restrictions. As I mentioned above, the apostolic decree, which perhaps more correctly should be called "the decree of James" (Acts 15:19-20: ἐγὼ κρίνω),[20] can only be seen as a tightening. It is not that the Gentiles earlier were obliged to keep the whole of the Mosaic torah which now is mitigated. On the contrary, from now on the Mosaic law, that is, those parts of it that apply to Gentiles, is imposed upon them. And this is a new situation. We have no indication that Jewish Christians demanded from Stephen, Antioch, Barnabas, or Paul a law-obedient Gentile mission. The attitude of the council according to Luke is liberal only in the claim from the activists regarding circumcision and complete keeping of the law (Acts 15:1 and 5), not in relation to the former policy of the Jewish Christians.

Acts 15 and Galatians 2 lead to the conclusion that the church of Jerusalem in connection with the council introduced a more conservative policy.[21] That the apostolic decree is a victory for Jewish Christianity is seen even by the fact that Jewish Christians as a matter of course lived according to the torah and upheld circumcision. And Acts 16:3 tells us that even Paul after the council had to circumcise one of his co-workers. I guess that the reason for the new policy from Jerusalem could be that the Jewish-Christian church could tolerate Gentiles when they were very few. In that situation they could still maintain the idea that the Jewish-Christian church belonged to the religious and ethnic fellowship of Israel. But they were confronted with a totally new situation when the Gentiles became not a few single individuals in a majority of Jews, but threatened to become the majority. We have no parallel to this situation in other Jewish groups, sects, or parties. Even if the Christian group became isolated within the Jewish people, they could still uphold the idea of being Israel, the true Israel, the kernel of Israel.[22] But is this possible when the majority of the group are Gentiles by birth? This part of the story of early Christianity has not been studied seriously up till now and we have not the occasion to deal with it here, but I think we are justified in drawing one conclusion: around the year 48 the Jewish Christians became theologically self-conscious.

Until the time of the council, Jewish Christians were a majority in the church. After that time we notice a rapid change. We do not have exact figures for those years of Jewish and Gentile Christians. But the rapid rise of churches and other Christian groups, above all in Asia Minor, Greece, and Rome, is proof of the growth of the Gentile element and the transition of the Jewish Christians into a minority. In the years A.D. 70 to 100 we have without any doubt a clear Gentile majority—that is, seen from a numerical point of view. The situation is, however, that the Jewish Christians neither allowed themselves to be forced back to a defensive position nor did they leave the church because of the rapid growth of the Gentile element. On the contrary, Jewish Christianity dominated as never before the life and thinking of most of the churches. The growth of the Gentile element and the influx of the non-Jews activate those problems which are significant for Jewish Christianity. We can refer to them by catchwords like Israel, circumcision, torah, etc. And now I come to the only attempt to give a definition of Jewish Christianity, which is a multifarious phenomenon: Jewish Christians refuse to separate Christianity from the religious, political, and cultural fate of Israel—and there is but one Israel. I am inclined to call this the common denominator which keeps Jewish Christian groups and churches and parties together. There is but one people of God, namely, Israel. The significant mark of this people of God is the circumcision of the Mosaic torah. So they stick to circumcision. The Mosaic torah is a seal and characteristic for the people of the covenant and the salvation. Therefore the law is permanently valid.

3

The important role Jewish Christianity played in the years after the council is confirmed above all by the theologian of Gentile Christianity par excellence, Paul. I have two themes here: (1) Jewish-Christian anti-Pauline propaganda and (2) Paul's theological reorientation at the end of his missionary career on the problem of "Israel."

Regarding the first theme: It is well known that a Jewish-Christian propaganda successfully invaded the Pauline missionary field and churches. It is not necessary in this context to enter into a discussion of who the adversaries of Paul actually were and how they thought theologically. It is enough to point to the fact that many Jewish Christians opposed him. This anti-Pauline movement grew gradually stronger and reached a climax in the last 10 years of Paul's active life as a missionary. Until the time of the council, or shortly before it, Paul worked seemingly undisturbed. The leading people in Jerusalem acknowledged his law-free mission among the Gentiles and accepted Barnabas and Paul as partners (Gal. 2:9-10). When Paul wrote his letter to the Galatians, this had changed (Gal. 2:11ff.). Jerusalem led by James had now adopted a harder line, and he won Peter, Barnabas, and the other Jewish Christians over to this new course (Gal. 2:11ff.). That the conflict with the leaders in Jerusalem became more intense at the end of Paul's life can be seen from Rom. 15:30ff. and is confirmed by Acts 21:17ff. According to Gal. 2:6 the leaders in Jerusalem did not demand circumcision of the Gentiles—this is so in Acts 15 as well. But at the same time Paul had to fight hard against the demand for circumcision and the willingness of the Gentiles to let themselves be circumcised. It is not necessary to know the relation between the anti-Pauline missionaries in Galatians and the leaders in Jerusalem. In any case Paul's opponents are successful, and the behavior of James, Peter, Barnabas, and the Jews in the Antiochene church clearly shows a new trend compared to what took place before the council. I would say that the behavior of the people mentioned is in harmony with an interpretation of the apostolic decree as a new and harder line. I see no possibility of denying the historicity of the decree, regardless of the circumstances under which it came into being. And as a historic phenomenon it played a decisive role in the history of the church, for example, when it came to the question of the eating of consecrated food. No one followed what Paul recommended (1 Corinthians 8–9 and Romans 14–15), but we can see that the Jewish-Christian policy gained ground.[23]

We can follow Paul's opponents above all in his last letters. Within the Christian church their letters of credit contain the same prerogatives: descent from Abraham, circumcision, a faultless Pharisaic life according to the ceremonial law (2 Cor. 11:23ff.; Phil. 3:2ff.; Galatians passim). Important is 2 Cor. 11:22ff. as it shows one distinctive trait in the portrait of Paul's opponents, namely, the combination of νόμος and πνεῦμα; they were charismatic nomists.[24] To this we will return later.

Regarding the second theme: Another outcome of the Jewish-Christian influence is that faithfulness to the inheritance from the fathers forced Paul into a reorientation and extension of his theology and thinking.[25] We found a distinctive mark of Jewish Christianity in its unwillingness to separate Christianity from the destiny of Israel. But Paul makes such a separation, that is, until the letter to the Romans. In Romans it appears that the destiny of Israel and the Jews is still an open one. It is, however, different in his former letters. In his earliest letters Paul makes a very bitter indictment of the Jews. The wrath of God has definitely fallen upon them (1 Thess. 2:14-16). The hindrances for a mission to the Gentiles—so it is said here by Paul—come from the Jews, not from Jewish Christians. Many exegetes regard the passage in question as a non-Pauline addition because it runs counter to Paul's later sayings. That it does so is obvious. But it seems more safe to regard it as a genuine Pauline saying, belonging to what we may call "the younger Paul." We have the same attitude in Paul's dealing with his adversaries in Phil. 3:2ff. In this context he labels circumcision as mutilation. All the Jewish prerogatives are now to him assets which he has written off and counted sheer loss. Circumcision and spirit are contrasts, and so are even law and spirit. Until this time Paul tried to work as a missionary even to the Jews. He wanted to "win" Jews (1 Cor. 9:20). The two groups of people in the normal Pauline churches, Jews and Gentiles, demonstrate the Pauline mission as a mission among Jews. Luke is right even in this; compare the synagogue scenes in Acts 13–18. And Paul led a life after the law based upon the principle, "for the sake of the gospel" (1 Cor. 9:23), that is, to gain individuals. But he has obviously written off Israel as a whole, as the circumcised people of God.

There is a different attitude in Romans, which a comparison between Romans and Galatians clearly proves. I think that we find the transition between the former and the latter Paul here. The situation is not that Paul gives up preaching the gospel without the law (χωρὶς νόμου). He rejects without compromise any demand for circumcision and keeping the law. But at the same time he works up in a positive way the destiny of Israel as part of his preaching of the righteousness of God. This is evident in Romans 9–11, three important chapters for understanding the history of primitive Christianity. And we should not treat these chapters only as a part of the letter to the Romans. We have no parallels to Romans 9–11 in the Pauline letters when it comes to the theological content of the chapters in question. It is impossible to deal with Romans 9–11 as a separate treatise, an excursus, a disturbing addendum, so that if we remove this part of the letter we will find the letter to the Galatians in Romans. There are in Romans 3–4 the thoughts of 9–11, although in a shorter and more thematic form.[26] This shows that the letter from the very beginning is written with an eye to Chapters 9–11 and cannot be conceived apart from these chapters.

If Paul earlier in his missionary work was occupied with individual Jews, his problem now is the whole Israel (11:15), the salvation of the people. And we should clearly see the differences between Galatians and Romans. In Romans 9–11 Paul maintains that Israel, that is, the empirical Jewish people, has not been rejected as the people of God (11:1). A minor part of this people of God is already saved and constitutes the center of the church, that is, the Jewish-Christian group (11:2-5,16-22). "The root supports you" (11:18); that is, the Jewish Christians carry the church. The rest of the people, namely, the unholy and ungodly Israel, shall be saved at the end of time, and they shall be saved as the people of God (11:25-27).

Paul has not until Romans said things like this. Only in Romans have we the saying, "to the Jew first and also to the Greek" (1:17; 2:9-10). Recall the attitude in 1 Thessalonians, where Israel had nothing but the wrath and judgment of God to expect from the future. In Galatians "there is neither Jew nor Greek" (3:28). Because Christ is the "seed of Abraham" only the persons of faith are the children of Abraham (3:16ff.). In Galatians consequently we find mention of a new "race" and a new creation (3:17ff.; 6:16), and that is because circumcision is nothing and uncircumcision is nothing (6:15). The torah is a provisional measure, an intermezzo (3:19ff.). It was given because of transgressions, to keep us prisoners in subjection to sin (3:19ff.).

In Galatians, Israel as the people of God does not seem to exist any longer.

The letter to the Romans gives a different view. The unholy, ungodly, nonrepentant Israel is forever the people of God and the children of Abraham (Chapters 9–11). The value of circumcision, and now not in a spiritualized way, is great (3:1). The Jew has an advantage (3:1; 4:1). The Jews are Abraham's posterity; he is still the father of the circumcised (4:12-16). So Paul in Romans has a very positive attitude to the Mosaic law (3:1ff.; Chapter 4 passim; 7:7ff.). In contrast to Galatians, Philippians and 2 Corinthians, there is no contradiction between law and spirit; the commandments of the law are being fulfilled by the spirit (8:4). Paul's adversaries accuse him of proclaiming a God who acts outside of the law, an accusation Paul strongly denies. As his defense in Romans, Paul repeatedly refers to traditional Jewish beliefs (3:4; 9:12,16; 11:5; etc.).

The way of thinking typical of the letter to the Romans is not in contrast to the preaching of the justification by faith in Galatians. It is more like an extension of it. The righteousness of God will in the future be manifest in the salvation of the ungodly people of God, which will be saved as the people of God. God is faithful to his own promises and words. Because the destiny of Israel, now and in the future and for ever, namely, the salvation of the people, is of vital importance, a positive attitude to Israel is necessary, a *conditio sine qua non*. The circumcision is necessary merely in order to be able to see, recognize, and know those persons belonging to the people elected for salvation. And so Paul consequently has a more positive attitude to the law in Romans than in Galatians. Circumcision and law are of the utmost importance. And Israel is actually Israel in Romans 9–11, not only symbol or example. And if Christ is the end of the law (10:4), he is certainly not the end of Israel. Rather, according to Rom. 15:8, Christ became a minister of the circumcision to maintain the truth of God, to confirm the promises to the fathers. The idea of Israel as an example of God's faithfulness to the ungodly is not only to be found in Romans 9–11. It marks the whole of the letter, and it determines parts of the paraenesis. In Romans, Paul is loyal to Jewish Christians and to Jews, in Jerusalem and in Rome. I see here the explanation of Romans 13:1-17 and Chapters 14–15 about the weak and the strong.

The letter to the Romans is understandable from the assumption that Paul either speaks to Jewish Christians or to Gentiles about Jews and Jewish Christians. I have previously maintained that the letter is an apologetic treatise to Jerusalem.[27] There is in the church of Jerusalem a growing distrust of Paul and his mission, especially after the conflict and breach between Paul and Barnabas and the fight against the most rigid Jewish Christians. Between Jerusalem and Paul there is a crisis. This can be seen from Romans 15 and Acts 21. A Pauline mission without the approval of Jerusalem does not seem possible according to Galatians 2 and Romans 15. There was, therefore, several years after the council—let us say 10 years—a church in Jerusalem with a leading and dominant position which we cannot question. And we find outside Jerusalem and in connection with the church in Jerusalem a very self-conscious Jewish Christianity. These two dominate the picture of the church as a whole, either in opposition to Paul or very skeptical of him. We do not know whether the declaration in Romans 9–11 could convince Jewish Christians that Paul was not an apostate or traitor to his people. But it is not likely when we consider the controversies about Paul in the post-Pauline period. It is so even if we take into consideration that not all parts of the later Jewish Christianity condemned Paul. The major parts, of course, reject him, but we have some witnesses who praise his law-obedient piety.

4

After the death of Paul, Jewish Christianity had a dominant place in the church and had established itself. There is now no questioning of the authority of Jerusalem. It is usually held that the period between A.D. 70 and 100 meant the total victory of Gentile Christianity.[28] I seriously question this opinion. After the death of Paul, Jewish Christians live as minorities in the churches outside Palestine. A look at the Pauline churches shows that Jews and Gentiles live together as distinct groups. They have not mingled in such a way as to become some kind of a *tertium genus*. This is so even in a late letter like Romans (see e.g. 11:13ff.; 15:7ff.). The concept of the Jewish Christians constituting the center of the church, that is the idea in Romans 11, demands that it is actually possible to distinguish between Jewish and Gentile Christians.

The general idea is that Jewish Christianity after A.D. 70 underwent a metamorphosis. They simply "disappeared" into the Gentile churches. In doctrine, ethics, and observance they lost their peculiarity and were theologically to be considered as Gentiles.

This view does not represent the truth. On the contrary, the Jewish Christian minorities constantly set the agenda of the church. We see the development of a theology that suggests that the Jewish Christians live as particular groups in many churches. Above all we find the same idea that we know from the Pauline letters. The Jewish Christians constitute the very center or the kernel of the church because they carry the promise of salvation and the history of the one and only people of God. The concept of a new people of God has not yet emerged. The idea of the minority as the church center is strengthened gradually in the years in question.

The problem of the validity of the Mosaic torah and of Israel as the elected people of God dominates the apologetic in the controversies with the synagogue. We find this, inter alia, in the gospels of Matthew, Luke, and John. And precisely in the years from 70 to 100 we find a most lively discussion of the mission among Gentiles. Long ago the Gentile mission started and only after some years, especially between A.D. 70 and 100, do we find the discussion of how this mission can be understood theologically and justified. I can only see the *Sitz im Leben* for this lively discussion in what happened to the Jewish Christians after they had to live in Gentile surroundings, separated and isolated from their own people, still claiming to be Israel. Precisely in the years from A.D. 70 to 100 the Jewish influence in the church reaches its climax. This is not only due to the influx of Jewish thoughts and ideas, but also to literary influences. We can mention here the Letter to the Hebrews, the Apocalypse of John, and the first use of Jewish pseudepigrapha as Christian documents by the means of interpolation.

We do not in these years find a uniform Jewish-Christian theology; this is something we have not had in the church until today. Rather we should talk of uniformity in praxis in a manifold array of theological ideas and conceptions—of Jewish as well as Gentile origin. What is important is that the main problems of the church were formulated by Jewish-Christian minorities and were being worked out particularly with an eye to them. Before the year A.D. 70 Jewish Christians belonged as it seems just as much to the church as to the synagogue.[29] Now they are separated more and more from their people. The synagogues exclude them, and they live in a milieu together with non-Jews, where they are minorities. But how can Gentiles and heathens become a majority in Israel? Not all Jewish Christians continued to live in the church. Some left and joined the synagogue again; others lived in isolation in the church and became Christian sects. A significant part, however, lived together with Gentile Christians. With the help of some examples I hope to show the decisive role those groups played.

Our main witness is Luke-Acts. The development in the newest exegesis of Luke-Acts has been disastrous in one respect. I am talking of the exegetical trend connected with names such as Vielhauer, Con-

zelmann, and Haenchen.[30] I do not mean disastrous from a methodological point of view. On the contrary, form and style criticism are
to be welcomed. But the outcome has been fatal to the understanding
of the history of the early church, especially when Acts is seen as a
document of Gentile Christianity, expressing the views of the established church at the end of the first century. Is there actually something
that justly may be called an established church in a Christendom that
produced such diverse writings at that time as the gospel of John, the
Pastoral Letters, the Letter of James, Hebrews, and last but not least,
the Revelation?

The idea that Luke-Acts, the two-volume work, is a product of
Gentile Christianity is in my opinion more based on the common view
that it stems from the first great era of Gentile Christianity than on
internal reasons. To uphold such an interpretation one has to neglect
the fact that the supposed Gentile-Christian author Luke presents to us
more Jewish and Jewish-Christian material than the majority of New
Testament authors do. To cling to the general idea about Luke as a
Gentile theologian one is forced to regard this material as Jewish-
Christian reminiscences, as inactive or nonworking elements within
the total Lukan concept. I would like to point to some of these elements
in order to show that they do not belong to the "outskirts," but to the
center of Lukan thought.

a) *Christology:* Jesus is the circumcised Messiah (Luke 1–2).[31] He is
   born in the bosom of the torah and Israel (Luke 1–2). From the
   beginning everything in the Jesus history happens and occurs according to the law (Luke 2:21,22,24, etc.). Jesus is the heir of the
   throne of David (Luke 1:32), and at the resurrection God placed
   him on David's throne (Acts 2:30ff.).
b) *Salvation:* The resurrection of Jesus is in itself defined as "the hope
   of Israel" (Acts 26:6f.; 24:15; 28:20).
c) *Ecclesiology:* The church in Jerusalem lived in complete obedience
   to the law of Moses. The outcome was that the church in the beginning rejected any mission to the Gentiles, but God forced Peter
   to address the Gentiles and acknowledge them (Acts 10–11). The
   apostolic decree is in itself a manifestation of the law insofar as it
   expresses what the Mosaic torah (Leviticus 17–18) demands of Gentiles, and according to this decree, which I should like to call the
   Mosaic decree, the Gentiles of the church actually conduct their
   lives (Acts 15:13-29,30,35; 16:4; 21:25).
d) *Paul:* Perhaps the most significant part of Luke-Acts when dealing
   with the question of Jewish Christianity is the portrait of Paul.[32]

This is why the Lukan Paul seems to be the Paul we can find especially in Romans 9–11. We do not know whether Paul convinced Jerusalem that he was a true Israelite, but he surely convinced Luke. Thus in Acts Paul is portrayed as *the* Jew, as the *Pharisaic* Paul, not the ex-Pharisee, because he remains a Pharisee after his conversion. You find this Paul in a number of scenes, *expressis verbis* in Acts 23:3ff. The story in 21:23ff. is not meant as an accommodation. The story emphasizes the Jewish Christian, the venerator and worshiper of the torah, that is, Paul. According to 21:21-24 Paul teaches Jews and Jewish Christians in the diaspora to circumcise their children and observe the law. He is "the teacher of Israel." This is why the promises to Israel will be fulfilled upon the people. Paul in Acts is predominantly seen as a missionary to the Jews in the diaspora, something all the synagogue scenes in the second part of Acts show.[33] "To the Jew first and also to the Greeks"—this could have been used as a slogan insofar as Paul's preaching to the Gentiles within Acts is secondary and an exemption to the rule (Acts 14 and 17), but they too shall participate in the promises to Israel. On the other hand Luke sees Paul as a gifted charismatic preacher, healer, and miracle worker.[34] His life and work are encompassed with miracles of various kinds (Acts 13:8ff.; 14:2ff.; 16:16ff.; 19:1lff.; 20:7ff.; 28:1ff.). Important is the connection of πνεῦμα and νόμος, according to Luke a characteristic feature with the early Jewish-Christian communities in general. Spirit, prophecy, and law belong together (see for example, regarding Stephen, 6:8ff.; 7; 7:51-53).

I have given a few examples of what are usually held to be Jewish-Christian remnants in Acts. In my opinion they are structure-building elements in Luke. How are they to be interpreted? Luke's explanation is very simple, perhaps too simple: The church is Israel, and it is Israel because it is "filled" with penitent and pious Jesus-believing Jews, circumcised Jews. The church is not the other or new Israel in relation to the old. The church is merely Israel, the old Israel living in the Messiah epoch of the history of the people of God. We should notice, however, that it is not the church as a whole which is called Israel, but the law-obedient Jewish Christians within the church. Those people we meet in the exordium (Luke 1–2), and we find them later in the law-observant church in Jerusalem (Acts 1–12; 15; 21). According to Luke there are two people within the one people of God, in the church, Israel and the Gentiles (Acts 15:14ff.). This is an idea which we can find even in the second and third centuries, reflected in the Syriac Didascalia, *Epistula Apostolorum*, Origen, Hippolytus, *Altercatio Simonis*, Irenaeus.[35] The Gentiles are, strictly speaking, not "people," because *the* people is Israel, whereas "the Gentiles" involve many different peoples (Acts 15:17ff.). It is obvious that Luke makes a clear distinction between the two groups in the church. The unbelieving Jews, they who do not believe in Messiah-Jesus, are not a people of God, not Israel. The promises to Israel are now given to the people and that is the church, as they have repented. And so the promises to Israel have been fulfilled to Israel. Israel as such has not been rejected, but on the contrary has been restored and rebuilt in the church (Acts 15:15ff.). It does not make sense to Luke to talk about the future of Israel in the way Paul does in Romans 9–11. This way the future of the church is the future of Israel. God's way and God's plan with history have not yet reached the goal, but the way goes via the church on to the parousia. There is but one history, the history of God with his world, and there is but one Israel. The synagogue is rejected. Any mission among Jews is no longer needed for the future, because this mission has been carried through by the apostles and by Paul. Now Israel is restored, and the time of the Gentiles has come. That the Gentiles too according to the Scriptures will participate in this salvation of the chosen people is nothing but a part of the promises to Israel (Acts 15:14ff.).

The idea behind this ecclesiology of Luke makes it important for him to emphasize that the church is leading a life strictly in accord with the torah of Moses, in which the ceremonial part is especially important. This is the reason Luke gives us a description of the church in Jerusalem and of the Jewish Christians in the diaspora, in which both appear as law-observant Jews. The law of Moses is the distinguishing mark of Israel, and because the church—consisting of believing Jews—*is* Israel, the church must keep the law. And Luke knows of many thousands of them, as can be deduced from his several reports on mass conversions (see the summing up of this in Acts 21:20). When Luke wrote Acts, the national catastrophe was approximately 20 years back. The power and vitality in Jewish Christianity is seen not least in Luke's picture of Paul. This very picture shows even the main problem for Jewish Christianity, namely, Paul. It is not decisive whether Luke himself was by birth a Jew or Gentile. What is important is that he thinks as a Christian Jew and that he is using the categories typical of Jewish Christianity. And so we have the main point: Luke conceives of the Jewish Christian element in the church as the center and kernel of the church. In his own church there was a Jewish Christian minority—this makes the two-volume work understandable even from a socio-literary point of view. This minority group has been expelled from the synagogue. But this group was all-important to the Lukan church. This is why the Jewish-Christian group carried the promises of God, and would fulfill the history of Israel. This is the Israel of God, which effects blessing and slavation to the Gentiles. When we compare this with Justin, we realize that in his church and in his time the Jewish-Christian minority was barely tolerated.[36] This is so in spite of the fact that this group even in Justin's writing is an important part of the great church. In Luke-Acts there is no mention of tolerance, but the Jewish Christians are honored. His concept is dependent upon the idea that there live two groups in the church, groups with distinctive marks, Jews and Gentiles. Nothing in Luke's work suggests that he regards the apostolic decree as obsolete; on the contrary, it is fully valid and authoritative in his milieu. It is therefore wrong to say that the Jewish Christians have now started to live as Gentiles. The truth is that the Gentiles had to pay attention to the way of life of Jewish Christians.

We will continue with the *gospel of John*. According to Rudolf Bultmann the Fourth Gospel understands the Jews as representing the world (ὁ κόσμος) in its hostility towards God.[37] I see this observation as a most important one and a clue by which the Fourth Gospel can be understood. There are, however, some critical remarks to be made on this point. First, the hypothesis needs a correcting extension; second, it is necessary to draw one forgotten conclusion from the observation.

I find it necessary to put a question to Bultmann's idea: How did this point of view, namely, that the Jews represent the God-hostile world (cosmos), come up? This leads to a further question: In what milieu and in what socio-religious context does the idea make sense? I think the answer is a very simple one. If the Jews are adversaries and foes of the church, the situation for the Johannine church is an actual conflict with the synagogue. This would further imply that in the Johannine church there is a Jewish-Christian group. It should not be forgotten that the Jews in the first century did not take interest in the Gentiles in the church. Why should they? A purely Gentile Christianity did not mean more to them than, for instance, the Mithra cult. But when it comes to the Christian Jews they took every interest, because the Christian Jews were seen as traitors and apostates.

Moreover, Bultmann sees the idea that the Jews represent the world as a purely negative stance of the author of this gospel. But Bultmann has overlooked an important fact here. The Jews in the Fourth Gospel are representatives even for the world when this world believes in or has faith in God. It is not the case that resistance and repudiation are the only characteristics of the Jews in the Fourth Gospel. Bultmann overlooks the fact that acceptance, conversion, and devotion are equally typical of the Jews who are confronted by Jesus. It has been overlooked that not only Luke in Acts, but also John refers to mass conversions among Jews. Repeatedly this gospel tells us that masses of Jews and many Jews believed in his, that is, Jesus', name (2:23; 7:31; 8:30; 10:41; 11:45; 12:11,42). This prepares for a series of sayings which sound Jewish Christian and which are too often dismissed as Jewish-Christian remnants in a Gentile-Christian gospel. But if we analyze these sayings, we soon realize that they cannot be traced back to a particular source or a specific stage of the history of the tradition or a specific stratum. The so-called Jewish-Christian sayings are found dispersed among the various supposed sources.

We have here such sayings as the idea that the coming of Jesus involved his revelation to Israel (1:31). There is no trace of the idea of a *new* Israel. Highly suggestive is the Christological idea that Jesus is "the King of Israel," which to John is not a traditional part of the passion story (see 1:49; 12:13); only John's gospel has, in the story about the triumphal entry, the expression, "the king of Israel," βασιλεύς τοῦ Ἰσραήλ (12:13).

When it comes to the significance of the death of Jesus, Caiphas unwillingly prophesies that Jesus should die for Israel (11:52). The disciple bears the honorary name, a "true Israelite"; the disciple of Jesus is *the* true Israelite (1:47). It is worth noticing that the term *Israelite* is not used as a contrast to Ἰουδαῖος, *Jew*. This can be seen, first, by the mention of the many believing Ἰουδαῖοι in this gospel, and, second, by the fact that the term Ἰουδαῖος has positive connotations in the Johannnine tradition (Rev. 2:9; 3:9; 7:1ff.). And, third, this is proved by the remarkable saying in 4:22 that salvation comes from the Jews (Ἰουδαῖοι). It should in this connection not be forgotten that the author does not take much interest in the Gentiles.[38] The salvation of Gentiles has only a shadowy life in the Fourth Gospel; they are mentioned *expressis verbis* in 12:20ff. and twice when talking about "sheep not belonging to this fold" (10:16; 11:52). This is not because John is talking of *humans* instead of *Jews*, or has any idea of "neither Jew nor Greek." John's interest is focused on the Jews inside and outside the church. The situation of the believers is the threat of being banned from the synagogue (9:22; 12:42; 16:2), which of course makes sense only when talking of Jews. Of importance for the understanding of the church and the synagogue is that it is not the church which shall be the accuser of the Jews at God's tribunal; the accuser is Moses (6:45). The gospel charges the Jews with not believing Moses (6:45ff.) and breaking the law of Moses (7:19).

To sum up so far, the supposed anti-Semitic[39] gospel of John has a double aspect when it deals with the Jews. The Jews represent the world in its hostility to God *and* the world in its faith in God. How can this be explained? The talk of Jewish-Christian remnants as passive elements in the whole of this gospel is a failure. It is impossible to distribute neatly the two opinions about the role of the Jews to different strata or stages in the story of the genesis of the Fourth Gospel. It is impossible to limit the Jewish or Jewish-Christian sayings to some primary stratum of the Fourth Gospel—in spite of the fact that the gospel of John has the most complicated literary genesis. To John, the Jews are as much the world and the children of the devil as they are the people of God and children of the truth actually "doing" the truth.

There are features in the gospel of John that show resemblance to the ones we know from Paul and Luke. There are Gentiles in John too, even if they have a shadowy existence, so to say on the outskirts of this gospel. But we find the conception of the Jewish Christians as the kernel of the church and as the true Israelites. Christ is agent for judgment. With him the judgment comes, and Israel is divided (3:18ff.; 7:43; 9:16; 10:19). The judgment decrees that two groups of human beings in the world should be separated from each other. This means according to John that something which has always been latently existent and concealed in mankind is now revealed, and has to do with the well-known separation in John between the two groups of people, groups existing already before Christ. The one consists of persons "doing" the truth and being of the truth, being of God, belonging to the sheep of the Messiah; the other group consists of those people who do evil, are from the world, are of the devil, speak lies, etc. (3:20,21; 8:23,44,47; 10:26,27; 17:6,9,14). In the decision for or against Christ, it is revealed what humans are and to which of the two groups they belong. And with the coming of Christ and the preaching of the gospel the two groups become separated from each other. Now it turns out that the nonbelieving Jews never have been the children of God, that they never have seen God or obeyed him, that they have the devil as their father and are of the devil (5:36-47; 8:30-59). A major part of Israel has never belonged to Israel, in contrast to the true Israelites. The unbelieving Jews have no right at all to the designation "Israel."

In this way the author of the gospel suggests that before Christ two groups lived together in the synagogue. After the coming of Christ this changed. Now the two groups have been parted; in other words, a synagogue and a Christian church exist separately. We recognize in these ideas the background and basis of the Johannine dualism and of the predestinarian sayings. The idea of predestination expresses the idea that the church has the innate right to the status of Israel and the pre-Christian synagogue. More correct than the term *predestination* is perhaps the word *predisposition*. Even in the time before Christ there was in the synagogue preaching about Christ. This preaching came from the witnesses to Christ, that is, Abraham, Moses, and the prophets. Together, they constituted God's testimony to or—*sit venia verbo*—sermon on his Son in the Scriptures (5:46; 8:30ff.; 12:41; etc.). Those people who have heard God's testimony and keep the law come to Christ. The Christians of today are the pious in the synagogue of yesterday. Those from the synagogue, who even in the pre-Christian times listened to God and believed in him, attach themselves to Christ (6:45). They do not constitute a new people; so Israel has not been rejected. Israel continues to live, but from now on only in Christ. That Christians are now being excluded from the synagogue (9:22; 12:22; 16:2) means nothing but their leaving the synagogue of Satan (8:30ff.; Rev. 2:9; 3:9). Then after the coming of Christ the people of God do not live any more in the synagogue, from which the people once came and where the people once lived.

Those people who "are of the truth" exist everywhere in the world. But, as I have already mentioned, John takes little interest in the Gentiles, the heathen. This has nothing to do with the idea that John is talking of humankind in general. Against this we have the classification of people into Jews and Gentiles (Greeks, 10:16; 11:52; 12:20ff.). The author knows that salvation comes from the Jews (4:22), that is, from the Jews who believe in Christ, from the Jewish Christians. The church is nothing but the coming to fruition of what even existed in the synagogue, namely, the true Israel. Through the true Israelites the other peoples will put their faith in Christ Jesus (17:20).

It is, in my opinion, experiences from the missionary work among Jews and from the Jewish agitation against Jewish Christians after A.D. 70 that are the determining factor in the writing of the gospel of John. The mystic-visionary understanding of Scriptures,[40] the idea of Israel, and the ecclesiology are very peculiar and innovative as well. But the Johannine conception has its background and basis in common with Luke and Paul. The author of the Fourth Gospel thinks and talks of

Jewish Christians as the center of the church, something that is true even in the Johannine tradition (Rev. 2:9; 3:9; 7:1ff.). This testifies to the important and continuing role the author and his church attached to the Jewish element in Christianity. The Jewish Christians make up the true Israel, which has passed the judgment and is saved.

Regarding the gospel of Matthew: This gospel is usually presented as the Jewish-Christian gospel. I have so far avoided it so as to give more of Luke and John as they supposedly are Gentile-Christian writings. It is completely out of place to talk about passive Jewish-Christian remnants in a predominantly Gentile-Christian document. That the Jewish-Christian elements are highly active and structurally dominating can be seen already from the common opinion of Matthew. It is regarded—not without protest, however,[41]—as a Jewish-Christian document by a Jewish-Christian author. In the current discussion on this theme it seems that the alternative, Jewish or Gentile Christian, leads us astray. The epilog in 28:18-20 shows clearly that we are dealing with a church which is missionary-active among Gentiles because Jesus is the lord of the nations, peoples (πάντα τὰ ἔθνη), with "all authority in heaven and on earth" given to him. The church of Matthew is a church for the nations. The church behind the gospel in which it is said "not a dot will pass from the law" (5:18), is a church for the Gentiles. But it is necessary to use a whole gospel in order to defend and explain *why* this church is missionary-active among Gentiles, even reflecting the animosity and anxiety this produces (10:5f.: "Go nowhere among the Gentiles"). It is easily seen that the church of Matthew has a Jewish-Christian element—and a dominant one too. It is significant for this gospel that engages in a struggle with the synagogue (see for example the antitheses section of the Sermon on the Mount, 5:21ff.). Even this shows that the church is a church also for Jewish Christians. We have in this gospel a clear antisynagogue sentiment *and* a preference for Jews, "for the Jews first," as well. It is a church wherein the Jews are persecuted by nonbelieving Jews (10:17ff.). This gospel shows us what happens to Jewish Christians when they live in predominantly Gentile surroundings within a church which is missionary-active among Gentiles. You must defend the mission! In any case, Jesus is the Messiah of Israel (Chapters 1–2). There is no such thing as a new Israel or a new people of God. But the synagogue is rejected, something which is evident in the passion story, above all in the Barabbas section (27:19-26). If there is nothing like a "new Israel," there surely is something that rightly may be called the old Israel, still existing, but not the people of God. God has done his utmost for the chosen people, but Israel does not exist any more as the holy people in the synagogue. Nonetheless, Jewish Christians can live with the very best conscience in "a church of the peoples" because in this church can be found the heritage of Israel, the Messiah, and the law of Moses.

How they can live in this church, how the heritage of Israel is being preserved, may be seen above all in the attitude towards the Mosaic torah. It is not possible to find anything in Matthew 5–7 that can be called a *new* torah, a Jesus torah. What we have in Matthew 5–7 is nothing but the true interpretation of the old and only Mosaic torah.[42] The law is not being spiritualized. After the mission among the Gentiles has been started and the Gentiles live as equals in the church there is still a demand that the teaching of the scribes and the Pharisees should be valid and authoritative (23:1ff.). The teachers who sit in Moses' seat are teachers for the church too. Even as hypocrites, the scribes are teachers. It is obvious that this teaching not only contains a general morality; it has to do with *all* aspects of the law. Jesus has come to fulfill the law. Not one letter, not a stroke will disappear from the law. And the true teacher in the church is the one who does not set aside even the least of the demands of the law. Sayings like these in Chapters 5 and 23, among others, explain why it is possible for Jewish Christians to exist in a predominantly Gentile-Christian church and not for one moment to give up their Jewishness. And I do think that some of our exegetical problems with the gospel of Matthew, above all focused upon what we regard as conflicts between Jewish and Gentile elements, can be traced to our failure to acknowledge a mixed church with a mixed theology, in which the Jewish Christians played a dominant part.

Also the letter to the *Hebrews* testifies to the variety of Jewish Christianity, and at the same time to the strength, power, and vitality of Jewish Christianity in the years A.D. 70-100. We have no parallel in the New Testament or in the old Christian literature to the letter to the Hebrews as far as content and structure go. When comparing this letter with, for example, Luke's and Paul's writings, we find some of the same topics and themes, e.g., the question of the law, Moses, ceremonies, the sanctuary, etc. But the way the letter to the Hebrews deals with the topics is highly original and independent. It even shows that Jewish Christianity in the last 30 years of the first century did not unreflectingly stick to traditions, but had spiritual power to reconsider and rewrite, for example, the meaning of the Old Testament ceremonial institutions after the fall of the temple.

The influence and strength of Jewish Christianity can be proved from this writing in another way as well. In the old traditions about this letter it was maintained that the letter was written to Jewish Christians. As witness to that is the address "to the Hebrews." I think that the general idea of the dying or declining Jewish Christianity after the disaster in A.D. 70 has contributed to the opinion that even the letter to the Hebrews is a document of early Gentile Christianity and written to Gentiles.

It is not decisive for the understanding of the role of Jewish Christianity if the letter is addressed to Jews or Gentiles. I would put some weight on the tradition expressed in the address, "to the Hebrews."[43] Nevertheless, regardless of the question of the intended readers, the letter is a very strong testimony to the dominant role of Jewish Christianity at the end of the first century.

Even by listing some of the main topics of the letter this becomes obvious. We have a very broad and lengthy description highly important for Christology, of the office and service of the high priest, of the priestly order, of the ritual and sacrifices in the sanctuary (7:1—9:28). Jesus died for the sons of the people and the people is Israel (3:12; 13:12). The Mosaic law is a preparation for the Christian faith, and between the old and the new order or covenant, there is an evident continuity. Jesus is more than Moses, namely, the fulfillment of Moses, because Moses is himself a witness to Christ (3:1ff.). The prescriptions, purgations, and cleansings have not lost their meaning (9:12). Jesus takes to himself the sons of Abraham (2:16). In my opinion the letter was written in order to prevent a relapse back into Judaism, the synagogue (10:25,29; 13:9-14), or perhaps even conversion to Judaism.

If the addressees are Jewish Christians or a Jewish-Christian part of a mixed church, the letter proves that it is all-important for those Christian Jews after A.D. 70 to come to terms with the Jewish traditions. It shows clearly that it is out of the question for those Christians to become Gentile Christians in doctrine and observance. Therefore the content of this letter cannot be defined as Gentile Christian.

The influence of Jewish Christianity is even more commanding if the readers are Gentiles by birth, and living in a mixed church. First, it is clear that even Gentiles take over and are influenced by Jewish Christian ideas and ways of thinking—it was not the other way around. I cannot see how the material and way of thinking in the letter can be understood except by Jews or Gentiles who have learned from Jewish Christians, and in their interpretation of Christianity are heavily dependent on them. It shows an increasing and growing Jewish-Christian influence in the third generation.

If I am right, namely, that the problem in the letter and the reason why it has been written is a tendency in the church towards conversion to Judaism, we are again confronted with two possibilities. If the readers are Jewish Christians, and we therefore have to talk about a return to Judaism and Jewish faith and life, it clearly shows that Judaism and Christianity have not been completely separated. If the readers are Gentiles by birth, and we have to talk about conversions, we are faced with the fact that Gentiles have been taught Judaism in the church by Jewish Christians. Either way this is a new testimony to the strength of Jewish Christianity especially at the end of the century.

5

I have tried by the means of some examples to demonstrate the spiritual strength and theological consciousness of Jewish Christianity even in the last decades of the first century. I could easily have given more examples, even from within the New Testament. An analysis of the Letter of James and the Revelation would surely have been rewarding.[44] In some of the canonical writings we have located evidence for the common opinion that the adoption of Jewish material took place above all in the third generation of Christians. And we can see this hypothesis confirmed by the oldest noncanonical literature like 1 Clement, Didache, Hermas, Papias, and Ignatius. The situation in the oldest postcanonical literature is different from the one we know in the New Testament. Within the churches there are active Jewish-Christian groups, but they are no longer considered to be the very center of the church (Ignatius, 1 Clement) and many warnings against Jewish-Christian preaching and practice are given.

I see no other satisfactory explanation for the adoption of Jewish material in the third and later generations than a spiritually strong and active Jewish Christianity. This can be seen even in the fact that around the turn of the century we find Jewish pseudepigrapha embodied in Christian books, e.g., Hermas, Barnabas, and 1 Clement. I even think that the reworking of Jewish pseudepigrapha by the means of interpolation started in order to solve the problems of Jewish Christianity within the church.[45]

We will have to reconsider the role of Jewish Christianity in the first century, above all in the years A.D. 70-100. Jewish Christianity, that is, the nonsectarian, "liberal," and cooperative Jewish Christianity living within the border of the church, died out gradually, but not until the second century. I cannot go into any long discussion of the reasons for the decline of Jewish Christianity, and can give nothing but some suggestions:

The number of Jews within the church gradually goes down. We get more and more pure Gentile Christian churches, and the role of Jewish Christianity as the center of the church is reduced to a certain number of born Jews with contacts to the synagogue.

Gentile Christians become theologically more and more independent of Jewish Christians. We see the development of what may be called a Gentile Christian theology and way of thinking.

Here the Old Testament and Israel do not constitute the only background (cf. the Apologists). And we see the rise of a theology in which the Old Testament becomes the book of humankind, of Christians, and not of Israel and the Jews, e.g., the Letter of Barnabas. The Old Testament is separated from Israel. Within Judaism a consolidation takes place. The sects and parties disappear, and rabbinism becomes a monopoly with its strong hold over Jews, and so Judaism is far more resistant to Christianity than before.

As a result of the consolidation of Judaism in rabbinism, we find a strengthening of Jewish "antimission" directed against the church.

A further result of the consolidation is an increasing political pressure upon the church. Christianity was not "permitted religion," *religio licita*, anymore, and it was possible to distinguish between Christianity and Judaism. They became more and more separated even from a political point of view.

After A.D. 100 we find a strengthening of Jewish nationalism which made it more difficult to live as a Jew outside the regular Jewish institutions.

Decisive for the existence of Jewish Christianity in the church was the role of the Jerusalem church as the very center. This church in Jerusalem, which existed even after A.D. 70 and until the second Jewish war,[46] gradually lost its importance as the mother church. And the Gentile-Christian congregation in Jerusalem could not replace the old church as the members were not Jews.

The problems with the relation to the institutions had as one result the rise of Jewish-Christian sects, which greatly weakened the influence of Jewish Christianity within the church.

Last but not least, anti-Semitism gained foot even in the church and made it difficult for the Jews to live there.

We usually say that history is written by the victor and for the victor. When we think of the New Testament, this is not quite true, because it is not correct to characterize the New Testament as a document of Gentile Christianity, at least not without strong reservations.

3

The Unknown Paul

1

There is no sensationalism tied to the title. I have no new sources or new methods. It is, of course, well known that we have nothing but fragments of the life and thought of Paul. And yet, Paul is far more than his letters. We know that Paul preached on his journeys, that he in person and orally, not only by his pen, guided his Christian communities. Paul used a Christian tradition in his work and teaching, but he wrote down only parts of this tradition.[1] Paul knew about the life and words of Jesus, but he does not in his letters unveil how much of the Jesus-tradition he was familiar with.[2]

The greatest part of Paul's life and work belongs to the unknown Paul. This is obvious when we consider the commonly accepted presuppositions of Pauline exegesis. The Pauline letters are so-called occasional writings. They are determined by specific situations and problems in the Christian communities and in the life of the apostle. This confines our knowledge. When we are faced with the actual questions and problems of a specific church, we do not know whether they are of a general application, that is, bear upon early Christianity in general. If a letter is determined by the polemic or apologetic attitude of the apostle, we have another problem: What about the unpolemical Paul? What about all those aspects of his preaching that nobody objected to? We have no biography, no *apologia pro vita sua*. He has not rendered any account of his theology in any letter. The letter to the Romans is no exception, even if exegetes repeatedly have tried to treat the letter as if it were such an account.[3] If the letter were his testament,[4] we would have found what we are looking for. But what we find in his writings are only parts of what Paul has written. We do not even know how much of the written Paul we possess.

We have to come to terms with the fact that we possess only fragments of Paul. Vanished almost completely is, for example, the Pauline missionary preaching. Not only do we have occasional writings from him, but even "occasional speeches." He dealt orally with questions and problems of his churches. We know for sure that the early Christian missionary preaching as part of the gospel gave reports of persons and churches who had accepted the gospel (1 Thess. 1:8; Rom. 1:8).[5] The life of a church was simply part of the gospel. And parts of the Pauline paraenesis have disappeared. Paul at times writes that any exhortation from him is needless, because the church lives as it ought (1 Thess. 4:9; Rom. 15:14).[6]

We have to come to terms with our fragments. But it is impossible to restrict our study of Paul to what his letters offer. We must advance to Paul the theologian and preacher in order to understand his thoughts and ideas in their totality. If we restrict ourselves to his letters, we would never be able to understand him. Consider, for example, 1 Thessalonians. If you read this letter isolated from the others, you will not be able to find much genuine "Paulinism" in it. One can thus readily understand why F. C. Baur denied the authenticity of the letter,[7] as he found it to be unoriginal and nondogmatic because of the absence of the idea of justification by faith and the polemic against Judaizers. 1 Thessalonians is not the letter to the Galatians—and so it is not from Paul! If we would read 1 Thessalonians as a Pauline letter we have to supplement it, that is, we will have to look for the theology in other letters. And regularly we use the letter to the Romans in order to give a supplement, forgetting the fact that Romans itself is difficult to interpret.[8] Very often we look upon the Romans as some sort of compendium or "summa" of the Pauline preaching. If we so do, we complicate the exegesis. We have, for example, in 1 Thessalonians some very harsh attacks on the Jewish people (2:14ff.). These verses tell us that the time of Israel as the people of God has come to an end. The judgment is there and it is definitive. But Paul says different things about Israel in Romans 11, and so we are forced to give another interpretation of 1 Thessalonians.[9] In the same way we deal with the letter to the Galatians. Because the letter to the Galatians is fragmentary we fill in from Romans, and so the letter to the Romans is looked upon as a completed letter to the Galatians. The result is a leveling and a harmonizing of the essential and fruitful differences among the letters in question.[10] And when we pull out the differences—those that refuse to be concealed—we explain them with the help of different situations at the time the letters were written. Accordingly the letters have the same theology, namely, that of the letter to the Romans.

What do we look for in exegesis? For Paul, of course—for the genuine Paul, the theologian, the specific theology in his letters, the special interests in his thoughts. The conditions for modern exegesis of Paul are such that we focus upon the theological aspects, which on the other hand means that historical insights from a former generation of theologians have partly disappeared, for example, A. v. Harnack, J. Weiss, and H. Windisch. But we cannot deny the influence of our exegetical fathers on dialectic theology, the Luther renaissance, Kierkegaard studies, etc. The theological exegesis of Paul is embodied in our program. Typical are the newest commentaries on the letter to the Romans from H. Schlier and E. Käsemann.[11] We can discuss the issue whether the course of exegesis of the last 60 years has been favorable for insights from the history of religions, from cultural history and sociology. It is a part of our tradition that the specific character of Pauline thought holds the center of the stage. We are looking for the application of the Pauline theology in the various situations of his letters. And in designating his letters occasional writings we have managed to conceal something, namely, the Pauline features which are not peculiar or specific and have no distinctive features apart from the average, common faith of the early Christian church. You can find these things in his letters too. But it is hard to become aware of them as they are mostly hidden as marginal notes, utterings, and references, independent of the situation that occasioned the letter. These small and insignificant elements have not engaged the exegetes; they are of less interest than the profound Pauline ideas of justification, law, and grace. We have in his letters a series of unpolemic references not occasioned by the situations at the writing down of the letters, references which lead us to the Paul behind the letters. Our exegesis of Paul, however, pursues the distinctive aspects and peculiarities, and these other references have not been given their due. They have not been gathered and systematically worked up.[12]

We have for years taken great pains to distinguish Paul from his tradition, e.g., the hymns and formulas he had at his disposal. It has been said again and again that Paul deals with his tradition in a thoroughly critical way, polemicizing and correcting. It is seldom noticed, however, that Paul himself does not say in so many words that he treats the tradition polemically. And we should not forget that the word *tradition*, in the singular, does not well suit the pre-Pauline material and the pre-Pauline history. Paul had to choose among traditions, and he lived in a church in which throughout the first century there was nothing like an "establishment." And up till now we have not been able to fit Paul into one theological formula. When we admit this, we start talking of remnants—Jewish or Jewish Christian—in his theology, for example, judgment according to our works, or the salvation of all Israel in the end, etc.[13]

The Paul who is hypercritical of the tradition in the church apparently drops every criticism when it comes to Judaism. Or, it can be maintained, Paul was not able consistently to follow through with his theology, and in this way Romans 9–11 can be denied a place in Pauline theology.[14] Another possible explanation, according to which Paul cannot go through with his theology, is accommodation. That means that Paul in his missionary practice and life could allow for theological impossibilities, e.g., a life according to the law of Moses.[15]

I will make the picture even more complicated. We do not have one "edition" of Paul in the New Testament. We have at least three. We have (1) the Paul of the Pauline letters; (2) the Paul of Acts;[16] and (3) the Paul of the Pastoral letters. How do we account for three different pictures and portraits of Paul at the same time? How is it possible that the Paul of Acts and of the Pastorals, different as they are, can come into existence at the same time? Do we in Acts find the genuine Paul or parts from him? We should not answer too quickly, for if we give an affirmative answer, we at the same time say that Paul is more than the Paul of justification by faith. That is what is at stake. It is not decisive that the Lukan portrait of Paul is not consistent with the Paul of the Pauline letters, because Paul was obviously a multifarious, complex, and tense person. Of course in Acts there is not the Paul of the letter to the Galatians, that is, where Paul is "most Pauline." We should remember that the letter to the Galatians has very few elements of tradition, when compared, for example, with the letter to the Romans.[17] But how is it with the Paul of 1 Thessalonians and Romans 9–11? If 1 Thessalonians had been an anonymously transmitted document, very few would have considered Paul as the writer on the basis of its theology.

My methodological starting point is that Paul's letters are sources containing more of Paul than we usually look for. This has to do with the character of the Pauline letters as occasional writings. In his letters we find elements that neither stem from nor are occasioned by the specific situation of the addressed congregations. Or we have to do with generally acknowledged topics, noncontroversial themes. Long ago parts of this material have been analyzed, e.g., various elements of a Christological, sacramental, or soteriological nature. It has not been denied that we have such material in the letters of Paul.[18] We should, however, avoid the word *tradition* in the singular when we deal with the first century. We have in the first century no *tradition* unless by that word we mean the process of tradition, the transmission. As seen in the actual contents, there are traditions of all kinds, different, divergent, manifold. If this is the case then tradition and redaction, tradition and theology, coincide. Methodologically it is normal that Paul accepts the tradition he uses, and we should so understand it as accepted if he is not expressly opposing it. We have to leave out of account in this connection the work done in separating the elements of tradition in Paul's letters. But I would mention as an example only this: When Paul uses tradition, e.g., the motif of ἱλαστήριον with atonement and renewal of the covenant (Rom. 3:24), this is no less Pauline than his proclamation of the justification of the ungodly apart from the law.

What can we achieve when searching after the unknown Paul? We will not learn more about the theologian Paul, but we can get a clearer picture of the historical Paul. We will thus discover the historical conditions behind the doctrine of justification and its historical limitations. And we will give a valuation of the legitimacy and value of the portrait of Paul in Acts and so perhaps be able to see Paul in a different position in the history of early Christianity from the usual one.

2

Paul is personally and as a theologian a most complex and manifold man. You find in him obvious tensions. He is, on the one hand, the suffering, weak, and persecuted apostle; on the other, the powerful and charismatic prophet.[19] But we do not find these tensions and contradictions in Paul in the New Testament outside his own letters. In Luke's Acts the charismatic element is dominating; in the pastoral letters it is the theme of suffering. Paul, who prefers to speak with his understanding (1 Cor. 14:19), is an ecstatic and speaks in tongues more than all (1 Cor. 14:18). He will know nothing but the cross of Christ (1 Cor. 2:2f.), but still maintains that miracles and signs are the marks of his preaching (1 Cor. 2:4).[20] He himself has performed miracles everywhere, and at the same time carries the messenger of Satan in his flesh (2 Cor. 12:7ff.).

These tensions are to be found in his theology also. He speaks as no one else of the justification of the ungodly, and at the same time insists on judgment according to human works. Is the latter a Jewish remnant? The contrasts within his theology regarding the law are well known.[21] He tells us that circumcision and uncircumcision avail nothing, and that Israel is definitely condemned (1 Thess. 2:14-16). On the other hand, circumcision and law are great advantages and Israel will be saved in the end (Romans 9–11).

That Paul actually is such a complex personality is confirmed by the fact that there were many different opinions on what Paul taught and preached. In this connection I have in mind not only the pastoral letters and the Lukan portrait of Paul in Acts, but even what Paul himself refers to in his letters. It is here not a matter of misunderstandings by his opponents or the falsely-drawn consequences of Pauline sayings and preaching, such as Rom. 3:8, "Why not do evil that good may come?," or Gal. 2:17, "Christ, an agent of sin." Such misconceptions we are able to explain. It is more difficult when it comes to the accusations that Paul preaches circumcision (Gal. 5:5), and at the same time is understood as one who wishes to tear down the law (Rom. 3:31; 7:7ff.). How is it possible to find Paul in Acts as the dedicated defender of law and circumcision, the true Pharisee, and at the same time in the Pastorals as the great opponent of the circumcised and of the Jews, of the Pharisaic attitude to the law and of Jewish "myths"?[22]

The old answer to the complexity of Paul in the New Testament portraits of Paul was that after his death he was adjusted theologically. I do not think this holds water. I do think that the various pictures of Paul can be traced back to himself.

The Lukan portrait of Paul is today by leading exegetes characterized as inauthentic and a distortion, but is in my opinion part of the unknown Paul from the Pauline letters. We have to be aware of the fact that the letters conceal aspects of the genuine Paul. They hide the uncontroversial Paul, what he had in common with all other Christians, especially that which connected Paul and the leaders of the church in Jerusalem.

Above all, how is it possible for Luke, writing Acts about A.D. 85, to picture Paul as the law-observant Pharisee?[23] In this tradition Paul is being re-Judaized, gradually becoming more and more Jewish, which is hard to understand when the usual idea of the history of early Christianity posits the victory of Gentile Christianity around A.D. 70. A. v.

Harnack maintained that the Lukan Paul could be recovered in the Pauline letters, especially his attitude to the Jewish faith and to Jewish Christianity.[24] This view has not met with approval. Later Ph. Vielhauer, who more than others has stressed the theological differences between Paul and Luke, has pointed out that we can actually trace the Lukan portrait of Paul back to the Pauline letters.[25] The consequences are, however, not weighty, as Paul personally and practically could adjust himself to various milieus and ways of life, that is, when no theological principles were at stake.[26] He could, e.g., live in an orthodox Jewish way.

Paul's ability to adjust admits of no doubt. But what do we achieve by that? We may be able to keep Paul's doctrine and teaching theologically "pure." And we have here to some extent an unknown Paul before us inasmuch as this aspect of Paul has not been examined thoroughly. Still we have to go further than Vielhauer and look for other solutions. Paul sometimes refers to his way of life (Phil. 3:17; 1 Cor. 4:16; 11:1), his good works, his ethical instruction of others (1 Cor. 4:10). The practice of Paul has not so far been examined. And we cannot with the help of the catchword *accommodation* neatly separate Paul's doctrine and teaching from his way of life. With Paul's background in Judaism in mind we should find the solution. There is no orthodoxy in Judaism, only orthopraxy. The important thing is life according to the law. My thesis is that Paul had far more freedom in his theology than in his life-style and practice. It is often the case that the practice reveals the theology. See, e.g., Acts 21:24: All accusations against Paul are nullified by the simple fact that he has taken upon himself a vow.[27] Further, Galatians 2: In the conflict over table fellowship in Antioch, we can read the opinion of Peter from his actions. And Rom. 2:12 suggests that from the good works of the Gentiles you can infer that the law is written on their hearts.

It is a modern way of thinking that we can separate the theology of the apostle from his acts. It is obvious that Paul lived as a pious Jew (1 Cor. 9:19-21). Paul held the law to be an intermezzo in history, "because of transgressions" (Gal. 3:19). He named Christ "the end of the law" (Rom. 10:4). But still he lived according to the same Jewish ceremonial law, and he did it not only for missionary purposes. That Paul himself understood his behavior in this way ("that I might gain the more") is not decisive, but rather how he understood and interpreted his life. From a Jewish point of view, at last one thing is clear: A person who lives according to the law professes the law, so

to say, as dogma. Faith in the law lies in the observance of the prescriptions of the law. So we can easily understand that he was accused
of preaching circumcision (Gal. 5:11). And even more: Paul teaches
the Jewish Christians to uphold circumcision and all that this included
(1 Cor. 7:18). This verse is not to be understood as if it has to do with
the removing of the marks of circumcision; the question is the way of
life of the Jewish Christians (vv. 17-18: περιπατεῖν)—to walk in the
manner that obtained at the time of God's call, that is, e.g., for the
Jewish Christian, as a circumcised Jew. And so the Jewish Christians
are bound to obey the law in toto, the ritual part included (Gal. 5:3).

We have here parts of the unknown Paul. He lived as a Jew. He
characterized himself in his pre-Christian period as one who observed
the law meticulously (Phil. 3:5), although his compatriots transgressed
it (Rom. 2:17ff.; 7:14ff.). He can even say that the Jews do not possess
the law (Rom. 8:4ff.; 9:31). But Paul adheres to the law as a Jew and
as a Christian. The unknown Paul, whose Judaism has consequences
for his theology, maintains that he remains a Jew and a Pharisee, and
that the traditions of the fathers are important to him (Rom. 9:7; 11:2;
Gal. 2:15; 2 Cor. 11:22). Paul regards himself primarily and in the
long term as a missionary to the Jews, sent to Israel in order to proclaim
salvation for the people.[28] As apostle to the Gentiles he has the salvation
of Israel in mind (1 Cor. 9:20; Rom. 11:14,17,25ff.). His concept of
mission is testified to by the many Jewish names of his fellow workers
and by the various Pauline churches that normally consist of Jew and
Gentiles.

When we talk about Pauline practice, his own way of life and his
instruction of Jewish Christians, we find parts of a portrait of Paul that
indicate that Luke possesses something of the unknown Paul.[29] In Paul's
letters we have only fragments of the unknown Paul—the law-observant, Pharisaic, Jewish-Christian Paul. This picture is partly covered
in the letters, but it is certainly a part of the genuine Paul, just as the
images of the missionary to the Gentiles and the Paul of the doctrine
of justification are genuine. If you interpret Paul solely by means of
his letters you easily lose Paul the Jew. It has, however, been preserved
in the oral tradition that lies behind the Acts of the Apostles.

But how can you harmonize the Jewish Paul with the Paul of the
letter to the Galatians? I do not want any harmonization, as this portrait
of Paul is part of the multiplicity and variety of Paul personally. Naturally he confused people and did it still more by declaring: "To the
Jews I became as a Jew. . . . To those outside the law I became as

one outside the law'' (1 Cor. 9:20-21). He is ready to serve all people; that is his intention. At the same time he lives with and without the law. He tries to "please all men in everything" (1 Cor. 10:32). But for his contemporaries and for the future the decisive thing was not Paul's own personal reasoning, but how his own time understood him. This unknown Paul, the Christian Pharisee Paul, can be theologically harmonized with only one of his letters, namely, Romans. We will return to that.

3

The letters of Paul not only conceal the Jewish-Christian Paul, but even the Paul who lived and taught in the same way as the greater part of the church did. And it is concealed because it was not disputed. What we label typically and specifically Pauline thoughts, e.g., the doctrine of justification and antinomianism, are developed in Galatians and partly in Romans. What kind of a Paul portrait would we get if we had only the other Pauline letters? We could hardly distinguish him from large groups in the church, that is, in regard to theology and Christology. And when disturbances connected with Paul arose, e.g., in the question about the inability of the law to save humans, Paul does not differ from other Christian preachers, with the exception of the most conservative Jewish Christians. This is the case when it concerns the incapability of the law. The situation is quite different—and here is the line of demarcation—when dealing with the power of the law to lead into devastation and destruction (so Galatians and Romans 7).

   We have in the Pauline conception of the law two elements: On the one hand, there is a radical denial (Galatians and, in part, Romans), on the other, a "conservative" affirmation.[30] In the latter the legitimacy of the law in the church is fully acknowledged.[31] This conservative element Paul has in common with the rest of the church. The radicalism, the denial of the law, the touch of antinomianism in which the law can demonstrate almost demonic features, is found solely in the letter to the Galatians. The other, the conservative attitude, we have in the other letters, if they at all mention the problem of the law. The problem is absent in 1 Thessalonians, Philemon, and 1 and 2 Corinthians. And Paul talks unpolemically about judgment according to works. This last theme is usually considered a Jewish-Christian remnant in Paul,[32] but this explanation in my opinion is false. We should instead see it as a common Christian element; it is obvious that you cannot harmonize the justification of the ungodly with judgment according to works. The theme of the judgment according to works could, however, have a preventive effect, namely, in contolling the radicalism of speaking of the justification of the ungodly.[33] But Paul does not mention judgment according to works when he most radically denounces the law, that is, in Galatians.

The speeches of Peter and Paul in the Acts of the Apostles, as far as their theology is concerned, are hard to distinguish.[34] They speak in the same way. The prevailing exegesis of Luke-Acts has a solution to this problem: in the speeches the speaker is not Peter and Paul, but Luke. And this is true insofar as Luke has written the speeches himself and given them his own personal color. And yet Luke is right: until some time after the apostolic council in 48 the speeches of Paul[35] and Peter did not differ remarkably. What we label as distinctively Pauline does not come out so strongly in his speeches as in his letters, especially the polemical ones. If the doctrine of justification is hardly mentioned in Acts, this is true even for 1 and 2 Thessalonians, the letters to Corinth, and the Pastoral letters. We have no right to read this doctrine into these letters or take it for granted that it is somewhere in the background of the letters.

We have no possibility of describing in detail that preaching and life which lacked what we call specifically Pauline elements. In general I would point to the need to penetrate more deeply into the subject of the unknown Paul. Besides that I will make some comments on the subject, miracles—law—Spirit. I do this because this theme is a main one even in the Lukan portrait of Paul and also it leads us to the unknown Paul. In this context I will deal first with the problem of law and Spirit and then return to the miracles.[36] Law and Spirit are main words in the Lukan portrait of Paul, and Luke gives us to a great extent the unknown Paul. We are not used to this combination, but rather to the contrast of letter and Spirit, which means law and gospel.

But there is a close connection between law and Spirit, and Luke tells us what it all is about. The church, led by the Spirit of God and filled with all the charismatic gifts, fulfills the law of Moses. We have to remember that the Spirit and spiritual experiences indicate the borderline between the church and the synagogue or, if you like, between letter and Spirit (Gal. 3:1ff.; Acts 2). And in Luke-Acts you will find that those who practice glossolalia in the mother church in Jerusalem are the true, law-observant people (Acts 2; 3; and 5). They are at home in temple and synagogue. The charismatic prophet, Stephen, is to the greatest extent law-observant (Acts 6:8-15; 7: esp. vv. 51-53, 54-60).

The Jews do not keep the law because they do not possess the Spirit of God (Acts 7:51-53). It is of course a problem that the synagogue accused the church of not adhering to the law of God, that is, denying God himself and the Holy Scriptures. The church answers that the law is not being kept by the Jews, and to this Paul consents (Romans 2; 8:7-8; 9:31; cf. 2 Cor. 11:22; Phil. 3:3; Gal. 5:23). In the introduction to Luke's gospel (Luke 1–2) we find the same phenomenon, the combination of law and Spirit. The people in the introduction adhere to the law and are filled with the Spirit, which clearly indicates to me that this is a Christian and not a Jewish part of the work (1:11,41,60,67, 80; 2:21,22,25ff.,39,42ff.). What we find in Acts is not unique to Luke, but common Christian thinking in the oldest church. Luke is occupied with the problem of the law[37] and with the accusation that the church does not take the law seriously, an accusation he energetically protests: the church lives totally according to the law because it possesses the Spirit.

This topic is broadly developed in Luke-Acts, but in Paul only sporadically to be found, although in very important contexts. We know of the antithesis, spirit-letter, but not—if the word is allowed—the addition. I would put it as follows: the antithesis is characteristic for Paul in one stage of his work, and the addition is common Christian belief, which is found also in Paul. In Galatians 3, especially 3:1ff. and Chapter 5, Spirit and law are contrasts (so also Rom. 2:29). In Gal. 5:23 life in the Spirit keeps the law in check. The law is not against the ethical charismatic. In Rom. 8:3 life in the Spirit is the true expression of what the law intended. There are in Romans statements which should be viewed as impossible. There is, e.g., the statement in Rom. 7:14 which is at the same time clear and ambiguous: The law is πνευματικός,[38] "spiritual." This is remarkable because the word πνευματικός usually signifies the charismatic, spiritual life in Christ. So Spirit and letter belong together.[39] In other contexts it is clearly said that the Christian charismatic is the true Jew with the genuine circumcision (Rom. 2:29). And what about Rom. 8:3-4? The purpose of the work of Christ is that the legitimate demands[40] of the law should be fulfilled. Rom. 8:5 tells us that the law stems from the Spirit and belongs to the Spirit; that is, the church but not the synagogue keeps the law. Rom. 8:3-4 stands out in the Pauline literature, but it is not isolated insofar as Romans 8 is a recapitulation of Chapters 1–7.[41] And we can see that for Paul the worship in ecstasy, glossolalia, enthusiasm, and fulfilling the law belong together (cf. Rom. 8:3ff.,15,26ff.).[42] It is so even for Luke and this is common Christian belief. The specific

Pauline version is that this worship with all its charismatic and spiritual elements is an expression of justification by faith. You can, so to say, hear and see justification in the worship of the church.

4

Paul almost never uses the word νόμος to describe the Christian way of life, and so the word has for him connotations different from those in other New Testament writings. It is striking that, of all his letters, in Romans he uses νόμος in a common Christian way (8:4f.). In order to get at the historical Paul we use this very letter to fill in the gaps in our knowledge. Is this justified? We have given an answer tentatively. We have the unknown Paul in fragments in Acts and in the Pastoral letters. We can trace the portrait of Paul in Acts back to the marginal notes in the Pauline letters.[43] This assertion requires a clarifying of the letter to the Romans and especially how the letter is to be understood within the history of early Christianity.

I have for some time had my doubts regarding the general and common concept of the development of early Christianity, that is, the history from Jewish-Palestinian Christianity to Hellenistic-Jewish Christianity and Gentile Christianity via Paul to the complete victory of Gentile Christianity after A.D. 70. This concept is partly based on the supposed death of Jewish Christianity after the destruction of Jerusalem and was used as a major argument against F. C. Baur. We have done Baur an injustice. His understanding posits a strong Jewish Christianity after A.D. 70. And it is not easy to explain how especially this part of Judaism was not able to survive the catastrophe. The Jewish-Christian part of Judaism must then have been more nationalistic in outline than other parts. The most recent research on Acts is inconsistent with this general concept insofar as this research emphasizes the Jewish elements in Acts.[44] And how can you account for the fact that the Jewish influence in the church reaches its climax in the third generation of Christians,[45] that is, when Jewish Christianity is dead?[46] A glance into the Pauline letters tells us about an increasing Jewish-Christian opposition against Paul after the apostolic council in the 50s and 60s. The Pauline letters, revealing the growing opposition from the Jewish Christians, tell us that Jewish Christianity became theologically active and profiled not till after the council in 48 and that the consolidation of this movement in the church took place after A.D. 70. This corresponds to what happened in Judaism with Pharisaism in that it became consolidated in rabbinism. And how is it to be explained that Paul before and until the apostolic council was accepted by the Christian Jews (Gal. 1:23)? A mission without circumcision and keeping of the law, a mission to the Gentiles, was accepted by the church before Paul, namely, the mission from the church in Antioch. We find the same picture in Acts. Paul was accepted very early (9:26ff.; 11:19ff.; 15). Later they opposed him (Acts 21:17ff.). The council did not take place until 48, but years before that and for a period of 15 years Gentiles had lived in the church without being circumcised and without observing the law. Jewish-Christian theology developed over the years, and the Jewish-Christian influence grew stronger with the years.[47] From the very beginning meals with Gentiles partaking with Jews caused no problem, but later a crisis developed and with it a stricter line from the Jews. We can see this in Gal. 2:1ff.: from the beginning Jews, among them Peter and Barnabas, took part in the common meals, but after some years they withdrew.

How does this bear upon the unknown Paul and the letter to the Romans? The accusations against Paul referred to in Acts 21: 21,28 are understandable from the context of the letter to the Galatians, but not from that of Romans. According to Acts, Paul is attacking circumcision (21:21) and in Galatians he declares that circumcision is nothing (5:2f.,6; 6:12ff.). In 1 Cor. 7:18f. he asserts that circumcision means nothing, but the Jewish Christians should not become epispasts, that is, try to remove the signs of circumcision. But in Romans there is much profit in circumcision; it is indispensable, consistent with the saying, "to the Jew first. . . . " If there were no circumcision still valid, Paul could not have written Romans 3 and 9–11.

That Paul speaks against the temple (Acts 21:28—a charge Luke clearly denies) is understandable from Galatians. There the present Jerusalem "according to the flesh" forms a contrast to the Jerusalem "which is above" (4:26). In Romans we have but one Jerusalem, and from Jerusalem the Messiah will come to deliver his people (11:26; cf. 15:19,25,26,31). That the accusations against Paul above all concern the Paul of Galatians is the case even in later Jewish Christianity. The letter to the Galatians holds a unique position within the *corpus Paulinum*, not only because of the harsh tone and the polemic, but mainly due to the radical and uncompromising theology. My conclusion is that Galatians is written as an answer to Paul's being challenged by a growing, extremely active, and strong Jewish Christianity. Therefore he is very anti-Jewish in Galatians.

But what about the letter to the Romans?[48] It is tempting to see Romans as a synthesis between Galatians and a more friendly and irenic attitude towards the Jewish Christians. But Romans is no such synthesis. We may, however, illustrate a point: the hard attacks on the Jews in 1 Thess. 2:14ff., from an earlier stage in Paul's work, have found their definitive form in Galatians. After Galatians it should be quite impossible to find any positive connection between the gospel and the old people of God, between justification by grace and the continued significance of circumcision, between the descendants of Abraham[49] and the old Israel.[50]

Then comes the turning point, and it comes with Romans. A. v. Harnack maintained that Paul did not hold fast to his original intention in his letters.[51] Such a statement seems preposterous, but it is rewarding to heed it. Harnack is partly right: Paul did not succeed in following up his intentions from Galatians in Romans—if he so wished.

In this connection we have to do above all, but not solely, with three chapters in Romans, 9–11. We have no parallel to these chapters in Paul's other letters, but the chapters may partly be explained by his way of life.

Romans 9–11 has given the exegetes heavy headaches, and many have tried to get rid of them in one way or other in labeling them an excursus, an interpolation, later additions, a relapse into Jewish-Christian thought, etc. Roman is such a wonderful and theologically clear letter apart from these three chapters!

In my opinion Paul did write Chapters 9–11, and he knew exactly what he was up to. But it has to do with a turning point in his conception of the people of God. As mentioned above, there are no parallels to Romans 9–11 in other Pauline letters. And we have in Romans in general more of Jewish traditions than in any other Pauline letter. We have more exegesis of the Old Testament.[52] The very amount of traditional material in Romans is striking; so is the Jewish influence on the church in the third generation as well as the increasing authority of the church in Jerusalem after the apostolic council. The Jewish Christians seem numerically to decline, but theologically to become more and more influential.

If this holds water, it is easy to understand the transition from Galatians to Romans, that is, theologically. Paul is being influenced by a strong Jewish Christianity and prepared for reconciliation. What he presents to the church in Rome is less "Pauline" than the letter to the Galatians. He is now more influenced by a "liberal" Jewish-Christian tradition. And this Paul, especially the Paul of Romans 9–11, makes the Lukan portrait of Paul understandable.[53]

It has to do not only with Romans 9–11, even though Israel in this context is the Israel of God and remains the Israel of God. It is the Israel that God finally will save, the Israel of the promises. Other parts of Paul provide us with material for the Lukan portrait, but Romans 9–11 is especially characteristic. In the exegesis, however, the letter to the Galatians seems to provide the criteria for the interpretation of the letter to the Romans. And so sayings in Romans not compatible with those of Galatians are labeled as *heilsgeschichtlich* (related to the history of salvation) or, it is suggested, did not succeed in implementing his original and genuine intentions.[54]

The conclusion to be drawn is that Paul in Romans with his intense struggle for the unity of the church approaches a Jewish-Christian theology insofar as he adds the fate of Israel positively to his theology. He mitigates to a great extent the very hard consequences stemming from his Christology and ecclesiology with regard to Israel, law, and church as we find them in Galatians. By this I do not mean that you can formulate the letter to the Romans as consisting of Galatians plus Romans 9–11. Romans is not simply an addition of perspectives; we realize that when we see that the theme and concern of Romans 9–11 is to be found in Romans 3 in a shorter form. And we see that the law in Romans plays even a very positive role,[55] even though it is clear to Paul that no salvation by the law is to be found—an opinion common in the early church as a whole. And in general it is not denied that there are differences between Galatians and Romans on the question of the law. The problem, however, is whether we have to do with contradictions or differences. It is noteworthy that the subject of judgment according to our deeds, which tends to disappear in Galatians, returns in Romans. We should not deny that these two letters differ on such central points as law, Israel, and circumcision. According to the letter to the Galatians, there would seem to be only one answer to the question, "What advantage has Israel?," namely, "None at all!"

The solution of the problem of Israel in Romans 11, that is, "all Israel will be saved" (11:25), is characterized as a sudden revelation coming to Paul.[56] I do not believe that such a sudden revelation came to Paul in a moment of despair while wrestling with the problems of Israel in writing his letter. But it is obvious that this solution to the problem of Israel is not to be found earlier than in his letter to the Roman church. And it is clear that the addressees did not know about it until this letter; see Rom. 11:25: οὐ γὰρ θέλω ὑμᾶς ἀγνοεῖν, "I would not that you should be ignorant. . . ." This is a formula introducing new, unknown insights and teachings (Rom. 1:13 [6:3]; 1 Cor.

10:1; 12:1; 2 Cor. 1:8; 1 Thess. 4:13). We have in Rom. 11:25 no *anamnesis*, no tradition, but something new and unheard of from Paul.[57]

One important thing is to be added: It is conspicuous that Paul, when he raises anew the problem of Israel, finds a solution that is (1) distinctive to him and (2) not destructive of his theology up to that point. The very theme and question of "Israel" we find in Luke-Acts, Matthew, John, Hebrews, and in Revelation in various forms, but we have no parallel to the Pauline solution. And the new line in Paul is completely in accord with his thoughts on the justification of the ungodly. What he says about Israel and its salvation is, so to speak, the climax in history, because this is the most radical and unconditional implementation of the justification of the sinful: God is saving his people by grace alone (Rom. 11:25ff.). The church, however, lives in the shadow of the coming judgment according to works. And in his letter, intended for the Romans and the church in Jerusalem, to which he now is going, it is important for him to say that he does not teach and maintain that God has rejected his people. Israel will be saved and so the word of God has not failed.

5

I have tried to point to a program for Pauline exegesis. We will have to look for the unknown and historical Paul. We will have to do something more than analyze the traditional material in his letters, namely, the material which is not determined by the occasion of the various letters. We will have to analyze his practice and look for the unpolemical apostle. We will have to take into consideration multiplicity and tensions in Paul. And so we will have new avenues of approach to Acts and the Pastoral letters—both of which contain parts of the unknown Paul. Luke builds on traditions about Paul and on material to be found in the marginal notes in Paul's letters. The Pastoral letters are built on what we usually hold to be genuine Paulinism.

And so the apostle to the Gentiles is a determining factor in the process of Jewish Christianity becoming theologically conscious and growing into a great power in the church throughout the first Christian century. Paul himself at the end of his activity is a witness to this increasing power. So much of our concept of early Christianity depends on Paul that the study of the unknown Paul will add substantially to our knowledge of our Christian forefathers.

4

Paul in the Acts of the Apostles: Tradition, History, Theology

The historical value of and truth in the Lukan picture of Paul is the main point in this paper. Insofar as this problem cannot be isolated from the question of the possible tradition, or rather traditions, that the author of Acts had at his disposal, I will give some attention to this question as well. And the questions of tradition and history are dependent on a third important question: What kind of a picture of Paul do we actually have in Acts? The task advertised in the heading of this essay could have been substantially lightened if we could rely on an agreement among exegetes on this point. The limit set for this essay forbids me to go into a lengthy presentation of the discussion of what the Lukan Paul actually is.[1] On the other hand it is impossible, taking the status of current study of Acts into consideration,[2] simply to drop the question. The problem is there and we will have to say something about it, even if it can be done only by the help of catchwords and superficially treated texts.[3]

First of all some few remarks on the question of tradition in general: It is in my opinion almost a gamble to base one's solution of what the Lukan Paul is on the separation between tradition and redaction. Only in the last few years no less than four monographs on the Lukan Paul have been presented to us: those of Burchard,[4] Löning,[5] Stolle,[6] and Michel.[7] The four authors, however, have not come to an agreement when dealing with the problem of the content and extent of the Lukan Paul tradition and the question of the way the author of Acts treats the supposed tradition.[8] That may be taken as a demonstration of the situation in the study of Acts today. We may and must perhaps be allowed to come to one conclusion after years of hard work on Acts: Luke, the highly gifted and skilled author and historian, recasts his possible sources and traditions—his "dossier"—on Paul so thoroughly that he gives them his own stamp.[9] That makes a sharp distinction between redaction and tradition difficult, to say the least.[10]

We should, moreover, try to avoid the word *tradition*. The term *tradition* in the singular, when not used for *Gattung* or the process of formation of tradition in general, is misleading when we are dealing with the first Christian century. There is nothing which justly can be called *tradition* in the first century. What we have are traditions, various, manifold, and many-sided. Is the word *tradition* in the singular at all useful and meaningful when talking about the Paul of Acts? Luke's problem was the incessant, ever-growing crop of sayings, rumors, gossip, apologetic, polemic, veneration, admiration, declaration of aversion, etc., from Paul's foes and friends, and from Paul himself.[11] Even a superficial look into the Pauline letters shows us what could be found of what we in a perfunctory way call "tradition." Luke had too much material on the disputed missionary Paul. He had to choose and select. If this holds water, tradition in this case becomes redaction per se. This statement is meant only as a warning. I am not out to stop the necessary work on Lukan tradition even if we ought to be skeptical as to the validity of our results.

In order to evaluate the Lukan Paul we must have an idea of the Pauline Paul first of all. When we compare the Lukan Paul with the Pauline Paul, as it is regularly done, is it actually the Pauline Paul we are dealing with? There are of course even here blind alleys. Philipp Vielhauer says in his stimulating essay on the Lukan Paul[12] that greater parts of the Lukan portrait of Paul can be found in the Pauline letters. The reason for this, according to Vielhauer, is that Paul could adapt himself practically to various conditions, so to say, in spite of his theology.[13] The older theological term for this is "accommodation." The alternative then is theology or practice. Paul could practically behave and do things which he could not do in "theology," if the word is allowed. Examples here are that he could live according to the Mosaic law—live as a Jew.

In my opinion, an understanding like Vielhauer's in this respect overlooks Paul's background in Jewish orthopraxy. By analogy to a

Jewish-rabbinical idea I am tempted to reverse Vielhauer's statement: Paul had more freedom in theology than in practice. This is an important point which we will return to below.

More about the question of the Pauline Paul: I am inclined to assert that the versatility and complexity of Paul in his character, personality, and theology at times are absent when we compare the Lukan Paul with the Pauline one. Are we really aware of the charismatic, miracle-believing, visionary, and ecstatic Paul from the first century?[14] And it must not be forgotten methodologically that Paul's letters, thanks to their specific purpose and character, keep back what Paul had in common with nearly all Christians and with the leaders in Jerusalem.

The question whether we deal with the historical Luke when analyzing the Lukan Paul has already been touched upon. Is Acts really a document of Gentile Christianity[15] (which always should be treated as a multifarious phenomenon!), expressing the views of the established church at the end of the first century?[16] And is there anything that justly may be called an established church in a Christendom capable of producing such diverse writings at that time as the gospel of John, the Pastorals, the letter of James, Hebrews, and last but not least, the Revelation?

Vielhauer is right.[17] You may actually find greater parts of Luke's picture of Paul in the Pauline letters. I think we can trace the Lukan Paul, the material connected with that Paul, back to Paul himself. I can exaggerate this point by saying that we can extract the Lukan Paul from the Pauline letters, if not in detail, yet to a great extent. But still, as we can realize, the Lukan Paul is not the Pauline Paul. It goes without saying that there are differences and not only small ones. This is our problem.

My thesis is as follows: The Lukan Paul, the picture of Paul in Acts, is a completion, a filling up of the Pauline one, so that in order to get at the historical Paul, we cannot do without Acts and Luke. By this I do not mean that we in Acts can discover how the contemporaries of Paul saw him, his successors, followers, co-workers, companions, disciples—if I am allowed, his *Wirkungsgeschichte* (historical impact). Nor do I talk about the way the next generation could tolerate and "swallow" him, whereas we in the Pauline letters find Paul as he saw himself. I mean on the contrary that Luke's picture completes partly what lies in seclusion or restrained in Paul's own letters, thanks to their specific purpose, and partly what can be found in the "outskirts" or in the margin of his former and first letters, and partly what we detect, when we realize what became of Paul in the end theologically; I am thinking of Romans 9–11.[18] We could say regarding the Lukan Paul that that which lies in the shadow in Paul's letters Luke has placed in the sun in Acts.

Now we can turn to the question of the historical value of Luke's Paul. In order to present a sketch of Luke's Paul I will confine myself to two features.[19]

The main theme is Paul the Jew, the Jewish-Christian Paul. Luke presents him as the Pharisee Paul who remains a Pharisee after his conversion and never becomes an ex-Pharisee. We find this Paul in a number of scenes, *expressis verbis* in Acts 23:6ff. The story in Acts 21:23ff. of Paul and the (Nazirite) vow, is therefore never meant as accommodation, pragmatism, or tactics, but gives us theological consistency. The vow story in Acts 21 emphasizes that Paul is a Jewish Christian, and as such is a venerator of the Mosaic torah. According to 21:22-24 the story of the vow illustrates not only what Paul personally could do, but also what he teaches Jews and Jewish Christians in the diaspora, namely, to circumcise their children and observe the law. This is not—as Luke sees it—a question of tactics or practice; it has to do with the promises to Israel which shall be given to the people if they repent. The passage in question tells us indirectly that Paul predominantly is a missionary among the Jews in the diaspora; recall the synagogue scenes in the second part of Acts (13:14ff.,44ff.; 14:1 [16:13]; 17:1ff.,10ff.,17; 18:4,19; 19:8ff.). The synagogue is above all the place for Paul's missionary work. Paul preaching to Gentiles is within the composition of Acts an exception to the rule, as is clearly to be seen in Chapters 14 and 17.[20] When preaching in the synagogue Paul demonstrates that the promises to Israel shall be fulfilled upon Israel (Acts 13:17ff., esp. vv. 17,23,26, and 32f.). That the Gentiles too according to the Scriptures shall participate in this salvation of the chosen people is nothing but part of the promises to Israel (Acts 15:15ff.; Luke 24:47; Acts 3:25; 14:47).

The second theme, when treating the picture of Luke's Paul, is Paul as a visionary, charismatic preacher, healer and miracle worker (Acts 13:8ff.; 14:2ff.; 16:16ff.; 19:11ff.; 20:7ff.; 28:1ff.). The given passages show in different ways Paul's life and work encompassed with exorcisms, healings, raisings of the dead, and other miracles of various kinds. Throughout Acts as a whole we realize how Paul's activity is guided directly from heaven, by God, by Jesus, or the Spirit with the help of visions, auditions, different ecstatic experiences, heavenly inspiration, etc.[21]

I am in this context not looking for various pieces of the Lukan picture of Paul, so to say, separately. This would not be of any great help insofar as it will take us only to hunting up the same kind of pieces in the Pauline letters. Important on the contrary is the coherence we realize in Luke's dealing with the worshiping Jewish Pharisee and the charismatic missionary Paul. Luke does not separate πνεῦμα and νόμος, charismatic life and observance of the law. This does not only apply to Paul in Acts, but is in Luke's opinion a characteristic feature within the primitive Christian communities and groups in general. Two examples must suffice: (1) The charismatic, glossolalia-practicing church in Jerusalem with Peter in the van, is a gathering of Jews maintaining and venerating the torah (Acts 2:1ff.,46; 3:1; 5:12,42; etc). We have the same combination in the exordium to Luke's gospel, the combination of Spirit, prophecy, and law (Luke 1:11,41,66,67,80; 2:21,22,25ff.,39,42ff.).[22] (2) Stephen is characterized as an adherent of the law and as a charismatic-ecstatic prophet (6:8-15; 7:51-53, 54-60).[23] Suggestive are verses 7:51-53: The nonbelieving Jews resist the Spirit, which means that they do not keep the law! In Luke's work the combination of νόμος and πνεῦμα is all-important. And Paul is within this frame portrayed as the charismatic gifted Pharisee.

We will now turn to the Pauline Paul and compare him with the Lukan one. In the debates at the turn of the century about the question of the authorship of Acts it was maintained that the author could not possibly be the companion of Paul by the name Luke;[24] this is how the Lukan Paul could have an attitude towards Jewish faith and Jewish Christians that contradicted Paul's personal and actual behavior. Adolf von Harnack in particular opposed this opinion,[25] but was not too successful, partly because the time was up for Harnack as a theologian. At the same time some of the very valuable insights of Harnack got lost. We will refrain from the question whether Paul's companion Luke is the author of Acts or not. But I do not for a moment doubt that the author of Acts knew Paul well, if not personally.[26]

My starting point in this context is that opinions differed on what Paul actually preached and taught. It is not merely that opponents of Paul inferred from his preaching and teaching anything else than Paul himself could and would do. I am here thinking of passages like Rom. 3:8, "Why not do evil that good may come?" and Gal. 2:17, "Christ, the agent of sin." Our question is how Paul could possibly be accused of preaching circumcision (Gal. 5:11) and at the same time be blamed for annulling the law, declare it as sin, etc. (Rom. 3:31; 7:7ff.; etc.).

I see this question as a parallel to our main question: how is the Lukan portrait of Paul historically possible?

The answer is in the first place simply that the Christian Paul lived as a practicing Jew. This is said clearly in the most cited passage, 1 Cor. 9:19-21. Paul lived among Jews unto the Jews as a Jew. However you interpret this in detail, it should go without saying that it has to do with the ceremonial law, because this was the sign of true Jewishness. We know how Paul makes out this particular behavior of his. The catchwords are "gain" (κερδαίνω) and "for the gospel's sake." But one more important question in our context is how Paul's behavior must be understood and perceived. Taking into consideration what orthopraxy meant to Jews it is clear that Paul is one who maintains the law of Moses in life and practice, even proclaims the law. He confesses his faith in the law simply by doing it. To Jewish Christians it was obvious and confusing(!) that Paul had a positive attitude to the torah, that is, not only to the law in a Christian interpretation, but the torah, so to say, as perceived by Jews.

At the same time it is clear that Paul repeatedly, and not only when as in 2 Corinthians 11 he "speaks as a fool," emphasizes that he himself is a Jew and not a sinner of the Gentiles (Gal. 2:15; 2 Cor. 11:27; Phil. 3:4; Rom. 11:1-5). It is not sufficient to say that he has been a Jew—he is one. Invariably he sticks to the traditions of the fathers. He is accused of preaching circumcision to the Gentiles, something he strongly denies (Gal. 5:11). We should, however, not overlook the fact that he in one particular way exhorts Jewish Christians to adhere to circumcision (see 1 Cor. 7:18). This last mentioned passage differs from the one in 1 Corinthians 9, where we find Paul's personal, and perhaps individual attitude as a missionary. 1 Corinthians 7:18 shows what he teaches others to do. The term περιπατεῖν in this context makes it clear that 1 Corinthians 7 not only gives a warning against undergoing an operation in order to remove the marks of circumcision; rather, the Jewish Christians ought to live, περιπατεῖν, the way which the circumcision of the torah prescribes. Correspondingly, we must infer from Gal. 5:3 that Paul assumed that Jewish Christians should do the whole law, which evidently means to include the various precepts.

We are now dealing with elements lying in the shadow of Paul's letters, but placed in the sun by Luke. And we are approaching the main point in the picture of the Lukan Paul, namely, the missionary to the Jews, the Paul who preaches in the synagogue insofar as this is the true place for the gospel. There is no reason to doubt that Paul

even saw himself, primarily and at long sight, as a missionary to the
Jews. In his capacity as an apostle to the Gentiles, he has the Jews in
mind.[27] 1 Cor. 9:20 tells us that he wanted to "gain" (κερδαίνω) the
Jews. Rom. 11:14 discloses how Paul wants to provoke to emulation
his people in order to save some of them. The two groups of people
in the normal, Pauline churches, Jews and Gentiles, demonstrate Pauline mission as mission among the Jews. We find many Jewish names
among his companions and assistants. He knew many Jews in the
churches personally, something which is evident from Romans 16.[28]
Yet I have not mentioned Romans 9–11 where it is beyond question
that Paul's mission among Gentiles has the salvation of Israel in view
(Rom. 11:17ff.,25ff.).[29]

I have so far refrained from explaining why Romans 9–11 in my
opinion contain the last stage in Paul's thinking, theology, and prophetic preaching. 1 Corinthians 9 and other passages tell us about Paul's
life after the law, his adhering to the traditions of the fathers, etc.,
based upon the principle, "for the sake of the gospel," that is, in order
to "gain" some. He is talking of individuals (9:19-23). In Romans it
is different. Paul has in Romans a series of sayings disclosing a very
positive attitude to the Mosaic law (3:1ff.; 4 passim; 7:7ff.; etc.).[30] The
point of view is not the salvation of individuals, of some, and he is
not using the principle, "for the sake of the gospel." Here the problem
is the whole of Israel (11:26) and the principle is "for the sake of the
Scriptures" (9:6) or "God's faithfulness and trustworthiness"
(11:1ff., 29ff., etc.). The problem concerns the promises given to the
unholy people, to Israel "after the flesh." This line of thought A. v.
Harnack denounced as breaking away from universalism, something
that created confusion and destroyed the theology of Paul.[31] Others
reject it as a lapse into *Heilsgeschichte* (salvation history), not true
theology anymore, and some designate the same chapters a separate
treatise, a long interpolation, an excursus, etc.[32] We are, however, in
Romans 9–11 confronted with that part of Paul which above all is the
basis and foundation of the Lukan Paul: the destiny of Israel, now, in
the future, and for ever; the salvation of the people; the fulfillment of
the promises to God's people—all these elements are of vital importance for Paul and his preaching especially in that critical phase of his
life and work when he wrote "The Letter to Jerusalem," as Romans
may be called.[33] In this context a positive attitude to Israel κατὰ σάρκα
is unavoidable and necessary, merely in order to be able to see, recognize, and know those persons belonging to the unholy people elected
for salvation. We have in Rom. 11:17ff., the passage about the olive

tree and the branches, a way of thinking on a par with the Lukan one about Israel as the people of God and the joining in of the Gentiles with that same people. The destiny of Israel occupies the Lukan Paul, and this very theme becomes decisive for the Pauline Paul. They have not the same solution. To Paul, Israel will be saved in the future (Romans 11); for Luke, Israel is saved now or in the past, namely, in the church. And insofar as the problem "Israel" becomes decisive for Paul in the way we see it in Romans, we have the explanation of the fact that Paul in Romans has a more positive attitude to the law than in Galatians.

I am therefore inclined to assert that what Luke writes on the subject of Paul is historically correct, even if not in detail—and we have in Luke of course not the whole of Paul. But the practicing Jew Paul, the missionary of Israel and to Israel, the theologian for whom Israel's salvation is the goal of his work—all these important Lukan views can be found in Paul's letters.

We mentioned above another feature in Acts, namely, Paul as performer of miracles, as a believer in miracles as part of the gospel, and as an ecstatic, visionary charismatic. These phenomena are nothing but illustrations of things merely mentioned by Paul himself, but of considerable importance in his life and work. The gospel, τὸ εὐα-γγέλιον, consists of word and power (δύναμις), of preaching and miracles (2 Cor. 12:12; Rom. 15:19; 1 Thess. 1:5; etc.). Luke knows that Paul is a charismatic personality, but he fails to tell us that Paul is a weak and sick charismatic—so according to Paul himself (2 Corinthians 11–12).[34] The tension in Paul, with the inseparable elements of power and weakness, Luke has not grasped.

We have no possiblity within the limitations of this essay to deal with this topic, but I will still make one point. Luke and Paul, both of them, are working with the same set of theological questions and subjects, at least partly. A regular complaint against Luke is that he is not familiar with the Pauline concept of justification of the ungodly, with the righteousness of God, with the idea of faith and law. That is evidently correct. Luke has these subjects, but only as rudiments. And Luke is not—even as others were not—capable of perceiving the Pauline doubleness, that is, heterogenous views on the law in dealing with its intention and purpose. Luke has no, or only rudimentary, thoughts about atonement. But at the same time Luke deals thoroughly with the question of the torah, as this is a serious part of his theology.[35] He is eager to demonstrate that the charismatic, spiritual church maintains, lives after, and fulfills the law of Moses, ethically and ceremonially.

Obviously the Christian churches had to stand up on this point against serious complaints from the synagogue. Luke's answer to this is that especially those who are led by the Spirit are the ones who in work and life maintain the law as opposed to the synagogue that is without the Spirit.

This particular problem is Paul's problem too. He too is eager to show the positive connection between πνεῦμα and νόμος. Rom. 7:14 tells us that the law is πνευματικός; Rom. 8:4 that the law is being fulfilled in those whose conduct is directed by the Spirit. The error of the synagogue is that the Jews cannot be subject to the law of God and therefore are not able to please God and obey him (Rom. 8:7-8; 9:31). We have the same idea in Gal. 5:23; 2 Cor. 11:22; and Phil. 3:3. Luke gives us a lengthy and broad narrative description of the pious, law-upholding church, whereas Paul has brief and compact statements; the object is the same for both, and certainly so if the whole letter to the Romans is included.

I am not asserting that Luke is, so to say, copying and writing down Paul "himself," his theology, doing this mechanically and dependently. Luke is independent and very much so. He is an excellent historian. He is not able (or willing!) to talk about justification by faith as Paul does. This is, however, not the whole of Paul, not the historical Paul. So far we ought to grant that what our fathers, e.g., A.v. Harnack, said was right, namely, that Paul did not fully and to the end stick to his intentions[36]—if he so wanted! Paul is interpreter of the Scriptures; he is a prophet and not a systematic theologian. The very character of his letters is an obstacle to forcing him into a system. And not only so. Paul himself, as a charismatic, gifted exegete and prophet, as interpreter of the God who acts in history and today, makes this impossible. In his letters, what we can call the Jewish Paul lies in the shadow, and we exegetes have not focused that part of Paul. Luke has done it, and so his impression of Paul is indispensable, that is, if we want to get at the historical Paul—in his letters and outside them. He was certainly more multifaceted than we are inclined to think.

5

The Signs of an Apostle: Paul's Miracles

Translated by Roy A. Harrisville

1

The Paul of the epistles wages war with the word alone. He carries out his task through sufferings and temptations. In Acts, this Paul emerges as miracle worker, a magician.

So said Bruno Bauer in 1850,[1] and for many exegetes his opinion still appears the appropriate one. In the New Testament we encounter the suffering proclaimer of the Pauline epistles as well as the triumphal, mighty miracle doer of Acts, and "never the twain shall meet." Yet the debate concerning the historical and theological value of the portrait of Paul in Acts continues.[2] For a time, it seemed to have reached its end point, chiefly through the investigations and impulses of Philip Vielhauer in his essay, "Zum 'Paulinismus' der Apostelgeschichte."[3] We are greatly indebted to Vielhauer. Nevertheless, there is a series of unanswered questions, and not only respecting details. It actually appears as though the question of the Lukan Paul is of greater moment today than was long assumed. This is also true of the question regarding the significance of miracle in Luke's description of Paul.[4]

At first glance, this question seems the least suitable where a solution to the problem of the Lukan Paul is concerned.[5] On the one hand, Bauer's above-cited statement appears, *mutatis mutandis*, to have become almost a *communis opinio* of the leading exegetes. On the other, not much can be done with miracle stories in general from a purely historical perspective. Still more, on precisely this topic of miracle, it is necessarily very difficult to find any links at all between Luke and Paul. Now, in my opinion, this is also connected with the fact that we are working with an imperfect portrait of Paul, in which, among other things, we neglect to give any place in our methodology for the Pauline letters as occasional writings, which for this reason *per definition* do not say everything there is to say. That means that in this instance the Paul of the epistles was quite clearly not only a man of the word, but also a man of miracle. This is too often forgotten or overlooked, and when this occurs we encounter difficulties. This can be clearly demonstrated in the case of E. Haenchen. He is of the opinion that Paul was the suffering proclaimer of the word and not a mighty miracle worker.[6] But of course he is also aware that Paul may occasionally speak of his miraculous deeds.[7] How can the two strains be united? Actually, not at all, or only in such fashion that the alleged miracles of Paul were so insignificant and so little out of the ordinary that his opponents denied him the capacity to perform miracles.[8]

This explanation is not exactly satisfactory, though Haenchen here makes appeal to the work of E. Käsemann on 2 Corinthians 10–12,[9] describing it as "irrefutable."[10] It is certain that despite the opinion of his opponents, Paul actually claims the signs of an apostle; it is certain also that he maintains these signs have been universally and publicly known; and finally, that these signs are not at all less extraordinary than those of other apostles (2 Cor. 12:11-12).[11] This already approximates the Lukan Paul. But when Luke describes Paul as the mighty miracle worker—which he actually does—do we not ignore the fact that even for Luke Paul is the persecuted and suffering missionary? Does Luke extract himself from this dilemma by means of miracle? Among others there is the following explanation of Luke's portrait of Paul: Luke could only see Paul with the eyes of his own time, for which reason he could only describe Paul according to the requirements of primitive, Christian pneumatic existence.[12] Does the explanation suffice? Is it otherwise for Paul? Did not even Paul regard himself with the eyes of his time? Further, how, from this perspective, is the author of the Pastoral letters to be understood? For—in contrast to Luke—he does not describe Paul as a miracle worker. Is he thus less bound by his time than Luke? Perhaps the author had a tradition concerning Paul which said nothing of miracle stories. If we reckon with this probability we encounter difficulties with Paul's own statements regarding miracle.

In his day, A. v. Harnack wanted to demonstrate the proximity between the Pauline and Lukan Paul.[13] He tried to exhibit the various elements of Luke's description of Paul in the Pauline letters. From a purely methodological point of view, this attempt was not satisfactory. But it may not serve to excuse the fact that many of Harnack's valuable insights have been forgotten. Nonetheless, in his studies on our problem, still worth reading to this moment, Harnack did not investigate the problem of miracle. This is true also of Philip Vielhauer's observations respecting the rediscovery of Luke's portrait of Paul in the Pauline letters.[14] And most recent studies on the question do not work in particular with the problem of miracle, though it is mentioned in passing.[15]

Here, then, are unanswered questions, particularly when we keep to the observation that Luke is aware of Paul the suffering apostle, and that Paul is aware of Paul the apostle mighty in wonders.[16] For this reason we intend to pursue the question of miracle in the Lukan Paul, chiefly to investigate the significance of miracle, and thus also to put the historical question by what right Luke regards Paul as the great miracle worker. To be able to shed further light on this topic, we must also treat the theological and historical significance of the few statements on miracles in the Pauline letters.

2

Luke does not base his description of Paul upon the apostle's miracles. Rather, what underlies his portrait are the narrative of Paul's call and his speeches, of which there are ten, and to which we add the speech fragments. We may omit the miracle stories without noting any perceptible change in theological content. What Luke intends to say about Paul in a theological way he says chiefly by means of speeches, while as such the segments dealing with miracles express very little that is characteristic or Lukan concerning Paul. By themselves or read in isolation, the miracle narratives and summaries offer nothing that we may describe as peculiarly Lukan. Luke obviously does not intend to express what is most important to him where Paul is concerned by aid of miracles. And if the speeches of Acts are Luke's "free" compositions, they indicate that Luke did not use them to express a theology of miracle linked to Paul. For in Paul's speeches the element of miracle is totally lacking.

On the whole, when viewed quantitatively, the miracles assume a remarkably modest place in relation to the other material. Luke is able to narrate seven of Paul's miracles (13:4-12; 14:8-10; 16:16-18; 19:13-20; 20:7-12; 28:1-6; and 28:7-8). As we see, they involve very brief narratives of two to ten verses. In addition, the miracles are so narrowly fitted into the narrative context that they have no weight of their own. Briefer still than the narratives, most consisting only of one verse, are the four summaries,[17] in two of which Paul is already mentioned together with Barnabas—in 14:3 and 15:12 (in these two, Paul and Barnabas); also 19:11-12 and 28:9. Perhaps 14:27; 15:4; and 21:19 also belong here, but this cannot be determined with certainty. When we examine the miracle material in relation to the speech material, it is insubstantial. Also, Acts is not an occasional writing in which the greatest part and often the most important is not written down. The picture is altered somewhat when we compare Paul's miraculous deeds in Acts with those of other persons. In this respect Luke is able to say much more about Paul than about the other apostles and missionaries. Of the eleven miracle narratives related in Acts, seven have to do with Paul. The same is true of the cumulative reports. There are eight in all, in addition to 2:43; 5:12; 6:8; and 8:4-7, which were mentioned above, and of these eight four have to do with Paul. Thus the portrait of the miracle worker, the mighty miracle worker, cannot at all be contested, even if one wished to do so. But despite this fact, for Luke Paul is not primarily a man of miracles.

We realize the truth of the latter statement when we investigate those portions in Luke's description of Paul in which he does not tell of miracles. What is striking here is that miracle motifs and allusions to miracles are totally absent from the speech material. This is especially clear when we investigate the narratives of Paul's call and his farewell speech. The farewell speech is rather fixed as to genre. In this speech also (20:17-35),[18] just as in the farewell speeches elsewhere, we find a review of the life of the one who is dying or departing (20:18-21). In a review of his entire life and activity in Asia, Paul speaks first of his sufferings (v. 18), thereafter of his preaching and doctrine (v. 20), and finally of the content of his preaching—conversion and faith in the Lord Jesus Christ (v. 21). But in this survey nothing is said of miracles. The picture is the same when we observe the stories of his call and conversion. To this type of story also belongs a preview of the future and the task of the one called. This is also the case with Luke in Acts 9:15-16; 22:15, 18-21; and 26:16-18. But we do note here the same topics as in Paul's farewell speech—proclamation, sufferings, and persecutions, referred to in 9:15; 22:15; 26:16–28:16; and 22:18 (26:19ff.). The motif of miracle is lacking. We encounter precisely the same thing in those signal chapters regarding Paul's trial in 22–28.[19] And these chapters are of course in general characterized by persecution and sufferings. From the perspective of structure alone, it appears as if Luke were not especially concerned to work the elements of miracle into his composition.

In the description of other miracle workers in Acts, the situation appears to be quite different, that is, in respect of composition. Peter is portrayed chiefly as a miracle worker. This aspect is more strongly emphasized with regard to Peter than to Paul. We lack any clear description of miracles in the "overture" to Paul's activity. On the other hand, we find that Peter's first public speech, his Pentecost sermon, already begins with a prophetic reference to future miracles and signs (2:17-19).[20] Directly following the speech, the apostles' many miraculous deeds are mentioned (2:43). The first missionary activity after Pentecost begins with a miracle (3:1ff.). The situation is similar in regard to other miracle workers. The beginning of Stephen's activity is characterized by miracles (6:8). Philip's mission to Samaria also begins with a miraculous event (8:4-7). When Peter begins his missionary work outside Jerusalem, from the very outset there is a welter of miracles (9:32ff., 36ff.). Particularly in his introductions to the narrative sections, it appears that Luke gives special place to miracles, and in the context this yields a strong effect. In the section on Paul in Acts, and following his call in 9:1-19, there are reports of Paul's initial missionary activity in 9:19ff. and of his preaching in Jerusalem in 9:28-29, but only in 13:8ff. do we encounter a miracle—the punishment of Elymas—which is also given strongly local coloration and is clearly without universal significance. From the standpoint of composition, the Pauline element is quite clumsily set into the context, that is, in connection with Luke's report concerning Peter. If Luke freely shaped the speech material dealing with Paul or with the narrative of his call, he did not find it necessary to report Paul's miraculous activity here as well. If the material already existed in fixed form as a tradition about Paul, Luke undertook no essential changes, as though it were beyond dispute that Paul actually performed miracles. It is impossible that Luke could omit miracles in his portrait of Paul. He emphasizes that all the important persons in Acts perform miracles—Peter in 3:1-10; (5:1-10); 9:32-35; and in 9:36-43; the twelve apostles in 2:43 and 5:12-16; Stephen in 6:8; Philip in 8:4-7; Barnabas in 14:3 and in 15:12; and, of course, Paul. The portrait of Stephen and Barnabas is typical. Luke is not aware of miracle reports concerning these two, but records their activity in this regard by means of summaries in 6:8; 14:3; and 15:12. There is only one exception to the rule that all the heroes in Acts were also miracle workers—James, the brother of the Lord. This clearly coheres with the fact that James is the uncontested and patent authority for Luke, for his community and his readers. Accordingly, it is superfluous to describe James by way of miracles in order to heighten his authority.[21] But from the viewpoint of composition, it is certain that Luke does not set forth his portrait of Paul in such fashion that the miracle narratives are its chief characteristic. For Luke, Paul's attitude toward Israel and the Law, consequently also toward "conservative" Christianity from Jerusalem is liable to attack.[22] Luke is concerned about this, and in this connection intends to allay suspicion, not, however, by means of miracles. But quite obviously Paul performs miracles, which is never doubted by his opponents. Here we might venture the assertion that in the brief hints contained in his epistles, even Paul assigns more significance to miracle or to his own miracles than does Luke in his portrait of Paul. But of this more later.[23]

As mentioned, Luke has only seven very brief miracle narratives dealing with Paul, for which we have no precise parallels in the miracle reports regarding other miracle workers in Acts.[24] If it is often difficult to separate the speeches of Peter and Paul in Acts with respect to their content,[25] this is not true of the miracle reports. The reason for this is that Luke did not himself invent these stories. Where Luke did not have a great number of miracle narratives, he made use of summaries, all of which clearly bear the mark of his style. The question is how these summaries determine the description, and above all, whether they are illegitimate from an historical perspective. It should be obvious that the summaries add force to the impress of the miraculous which Luke gives to his portrait. But they do so not by filling a gap in the Pauline tradition, that is, by means of miracles which the tradition lacked. For Luke, of course, has his stories about Paul, and it does not appear to be his intention to increase their mere number, as though quantity had been decisive. Naturally, the cumulative reports also increase their number, as if automatically. But this occurs in order to state that proclamation and miracles in essence belong together. In the cumulative reports contained in 14:3 and 15:12, Luke speaks of miracles that have occurred wherever Barnabas and Paul have been at work. In 14:3 the topic is the length of activity in Iconium. Previously, Luke reported only a miracle by Paul within a specific locale, in 13:8-10. Thus 14:3 refers to more than mere local miracles or local miracles in isolation. Acts 15:12 is even more important. This passage narrates miraculous activity during the whole of Paul's and Barnabas' activity up to the apostolic council—miracles and signs occurred, no doubt often and regularly. To this point in his description Luke has offered only two brief miracle narratives concerning Paul, in 13:8-12 and 14:8-10. He knows nothing at all of a miracle report regarding Barnabas. In the third cumulative report in 19:11-12, we encounter a mixture of cumulative report and miracle narrative. But the verses clearly imply that the two-year activity in Ephesus was also marked by miracles and that many miracles, even many extraordinary miracles, occurred. Here too we see that Luke had no miracle narrative for this period. Finally, in 28:9, and in conjunction with a very brief narrative in 28:8, we encounter a cumulative report of healings of the inhabitants of Malta. We also meet a few other passages where miracles are not named directly or expressly, utterances shaped in such fashion that in all probability they too refer to miracles. This is the case in 14:27; 15:4; and 21:19. The form of the summaries is quite stereotyped and consistent in tone, as the following indicates:

2:43: τέρατα καὶ σημεῖα διὰ τῶν ἀποστόλων ἐγίνετο
5:12: διὰ δὲ τῶν χειρῶν τῶν ἀποστόλων ἐγίνετο σημεῖα καὶ
τέρατα
6:8: Στέφανος . . . ἐποίει τέρατα καὶ σημεῖα . . .
8:6: . . . τὰ σημεῖα ἃ ἐποίει . . .
14:3: διδόντι σημεῖα καὶ τέρατα γίνεσθαι διὰ τῶν χειρῶν αὐτῶν
15:12: ἐποίησεν ὁ θεὸς σημεῖα καὶ τέρατα . . . δι' αὐτῶν
19:11: δυνάμεις . . . ὁ θεὸς ἐποίει διὰ τῶν χειρῶν Παύλου
28:9: καὶ οἱ λοιποὶ . . . ἐθεραπεύοντο
Cf. also 4:30: ἐν τῷ τὴν χεῖρά σου ἐκτείνειν σε εἰς ἴασιν καὶ
σημεῖα καὶ τέρατα γίνεσθαι διὰ τοῦ ὀνόματος τοῦ
ἁγίου παιδός σου Ἰησοῦ.

In the main, the summary is formulated as follows: God does signs and wonders through them, or signs and wonders occurred through them, or the like.

The first type is employed by Paul. If we include under this type the passages in 14:27; 15:4; and 21:19, the inference seems to be clear—these three missionary reports also deal with miracles which occurred through Paul. And the resulting portrait is that wherever Paul appeared and preached, many wonders and signs took place. This being the case, we hardly notice that nothing at all is said of these signs and wonders in the stories of Paul's call or in his speeches. This does not mean that Luke intends to alter his portrait in these narratives and speeches by means of miracles. In the speeches as they now stand, what is liable to attack in Paul is removed, and the miracle stories about Paul are not open to dispute, not contested. They also do not serve to remove what is liable to attack.

It is important to Luke that miracles occur everywhere, not so as to accent Paul's miraculous activity as such, but in order to say something about his preaching. Luke is aware of miracle narratives attached only to the mission stations at Cyprus, Lystra, Philippi, Ephesus, Troas, and Malta. In the first cumulative reports, especially in 14:3 and 15:12, Luke gives the impression that not only Paul's previous, but also his future, activity is marked by miracles. The latter is confirmed by other cumulative reports, by 19:11-20, and quite particularly, by 21:19.

But with what right has Luke shaped this portrait of the miraculous? Is it for the reason that he could see Paul only with the eyes of his time? Or, for the reason that the Pauline tradition handed down to him also—*sit venia verbo*—told of Paul's miracles? The observation that the stories of Paul's call and his speeches do not tell of miracles should actually confirm the thesis regarding Luke's creative and poetic activity. In that event, we would encounter in such portions of Acts a tradition similar to that of the Pastoral Letters, to the extent miracles are lacking. Despite that, I am of another opinion, that is, that the Lukan tradition concerning Paul contained reports of miracles. The narratives of Paul's miracles are not stereotypical and are distinct from the other miracle stories in Acts. Compared with the cumulative reports, the absence of Lukan influence suggests that Luke appropriated the narratives and did not rework them to any great extent. I would like to proceed further: Paul himself gives the impression that his entire activity was accompanied by miracles.[26] If this is true, we have before us the conditions for Luke's portrait. To this we will return later.

This leads us to the theological motifs and elements in the miracle narratives, for which a comparison with the Pauline letters serves as background throughout. But first of all we must say something regarding the problem of miracle and suffering in Luke. Present-day exegesis often gives the impression that in Luke's portrait of Paul the features of suffering all but disappear, since Paul, the man of miracles, is always able miraculously to save himself from afflictions and peril, for example, through a miraculous deliverance from imprisonment (16:25ff.; cf. the story of his deliverance in 5:17ff.)[27] Two things cannot be ignored here. First, such miraculous deliverance, or, more properly, such possibility for deliverance, occurs only once in Paul's case, in 16:26-40. Second, the possible rescue is not the all-important thing, for Paul remains in prison until his release (16:35ff.), and the story is calculated to serve the proclamation (16:30ff.). Paul is released, not in miraculous fashion, but for political reasons—because he is a Roman citizen (16:37ff.). It may be that 14:19-20 refers to a miraculous rescue. The same is certainly true of 28:2ff., where Paul survives a serpent's bite. At the most, these are exceptions which report a threat to Paul's life. On the other hand, Luke emphasizes that Paul's sojourn throughout was one of suffering. This is true of the apostles, but quite especially of Paul. The fact that Paul is threatened, persecuted, and mistreated runs like a red thread through the report. But suffering remains suffering and is in no way lessened or muted by miracles. Miraculous rescue does not occur; rather, the miracle is the proclamation which cannot be hindered. When Paul is threatened and persecuted, not rescue but rather flight occurs (9:23f.,25; 13:50f.; 14:5-6,19,20; 22:18; etc.). The way toward the kingdom of God is through much tribulation (14:22). In addition, Paul's sufferings are described in most concrete fashion, and in contrast to what is said of the tribulations of the other apostles and missionaries. Luke speaks of assassination attempts against Paul (9:29; 23:12ff.); of persecution, torture, and stoning (14:5-6; 14:19-20; 16:16ff.,22ff.; 20:23; 23:12ff.). In all the chapters dealing with his trials before authorities, the apostle's sufferings are clearly indicated but miracles are out of the question, with the exception of the miracle of the continuing proclamation. In addition, the fact that in Acts Luke uses the word πάσχω only of Jesus and Paul (1:3; 3:18; 17:3; and 9:16) makes clear that for Luke Paul is the suffering figure par excellence.

It is especially in the farewell address at Miletus (20:17-38) that Luke indicates how Paul's life and work as a whole should be understood. In this survey, Paul describes his life as one of suffering (20:19). Mention is made here not only of the suffering caused him by others, but also of his inner life, the state of his soul, his life in tears and humiliation. Even regarding the final phase of his activity Paul is aware that tribulations and imprisonment, not miracles, shall be his fate (20:23). With the exception of the allusion in 20:19, 31, Luke is certainly not aware of this weak and sickly figure from the Pauline letters.[28] But for Luke as well, Paul is truly the suffering servant of the Lord more than others. Paul must endure his sufferings and is by no means rescued through miracles.

To summarize: In Acts, the great miracle worker Paul remains a suffering figure. Luke does not use the miracle to rescue the persecuted and threatened missionary. The result is a complex portrait of Paul, missionary of suffering and mighty in miracle. By this means also Luke distances himself from usual descriptions of the divine man who is either rescued from his distresses or is able to save himself. The biographical element is essential to the question of the relation between miracle and sufferings. At issue is what Paul personally experienced. And in Acts Paul is not a type or paradigm, but a solitary figure. This can be seen with special clarity in the chapters dealing with his trials. The miracle is not calculated to rescue Paul, but to exhibit the proclamation as an irresistible force.

This is the underlying motif in Luke's theology of miracle, and, of course, is true not only of Paul's preaching. What is at stake, therefore, is the connection between word and miracle. The proclamation is truly instituted, willed by God and gaining mastery over the world, as is also indicated by the charismatic, miraculous deeds accompanying the proclamation. This leaves no doubt that for Luke the primacy is given the proclamation. A chief concern in Acts is that word and miracle cannot be separated.

The narrative of the miracles against Elymas at Cyprus in 13:4-12, as most of the other Pauline miracle narratives, has been worked into the context of the narrative without interruption, and cannot be loosed from it. We should note that Elymas is a Jew (v. 6), and he is clearly introduced as a miracle worker and charismatic, a μάγος and ψευδοπροφήτης. The retributive miracle is thus calculated to remove a hindrance to the proclamation (τὸν λόγον τοῦ θεοῦ, v. 7f.).When this hindrance no longer exists, the hearers come to faith (v. 12). The connection between miracle and word is so intimate that the miracle is a part of the διδαχὴ τοῦ κυρίου ("the teaching of the Lord," v. 12). The overwhelming divine power which belongs to the proclamation is made manifest through the miracle. Verse 12 appears to indicate that the miracle is an integral part of the proclamation, though this cannot be demonstrated with certainty. Whatever the case, the indissoluble connection between word and miracle is clear.

This connection is also confirmed by other utterances concerning miracles. It is stated expressly in the cumulative report of 14:3. Against the resistance of the unbelieving Jews, God himself confirms (μαρτυροῦντι) his word—διδόντι σημεῖα καὶ τέρατα γίνεσθαι διὰ τῶν χειρῶν αὐτῶν ("granting signs and wonders to be done by their hands").

In the prayer of 4:25-31, παρρησία ("boldness") for preaching God's word comes through his permitting healings, miracles, and signs to occur through Jesus (4:29-30).

In the passages cited the connection between miracle and word is directly stated. In other contexts we find proclamation and miracle mentioned side by side without direct, logical connection. The healing of the lame man at Lystra (14:8-10)—a narrative also very deftly worked into the narrative context—is described in conjunction with the proclamation (14:7). In this passage, the narrative does not serve to point up the connection between miracle and word, but creates a point of departure for a misunderstanding of the missionaries' identity (14:11-18). At the same time, however, there is also a correction of false impressions by means of the preaching (vv. 15ff.). Here the primacy of the word is evident, since the miracle can lead to misunderstandings. Yet, here too the connection between miracle and word is clear, though indirect. But it is joined to that important Lukan motif: The miracle easily leads to misunderstandings when isolated from the proclamation (14:11-18). This also means that Luke can apparently conceive a proclamation without miracles, but no miracles without proclamation (on the motif of misunderstanding cf. also 28:6).

In 16:16-18 also we encounter the connection between miracle and word, without its being directly, logically stated.[29] Persecution comes through the miracle of exorcism and from this again emerges proclamation and conversion. So also in 19:13-20, in the "inverted" narrative of the demons at Ephesus, where the demons win out. Through what takes place here, the word of God "grows" (19:20).[30] In Luke's most independent miracle narrative, that is, the narrative most easily detachable from its context—the raising of the dead at Troas in 20:7-12—miracle and word also appear side by side (20:7). Acts 2:43; 6:6-8; 19:10; and 21:19 also express the indirect connection between miracle and word.

We also encounter statements about miracles—though only a few—that appear as if "isolated." No relation to proclamation can be seen; only miracles are reported. Acts 15:12 sums up the entire missionary activity of Barnabas and Paul in miraculous deeds. It may be that in context, verse 12 is supposed to confirm the preaching of Peter (15:7ff.) which is naturally also that of Paul.[31] And so here too we may have a clear connection. But the situation is different in 28:1-6; 28:7-9; and 15:4. Nevertheless, Luke's composition as a whole allows no separation of miracle and word.

By way of summary we can say that for Luke Paul's miracles comprise a secondary part of his preaching and teaching, for the miracles demonstrate the irresistible nature of God's word. Add to this the fact that through miracles Paul is characterized as authorized preacher and missionary. The signs of an apostle accompany him.

One characteristic of Luke's conception of Paul is that Paul is described as a charismatic. This is evident from the miracle stories, though in these the miracle worker is regularly perceived as a passive instrument of God's activity, as is most often given formulation in the cumulative reports—God does signs and wonders through them. Other features in his portrait of Paul make clear Luke's insight into the charismatic aspect: In his activity, Paul is accompanied by the Spirit (9:17; 13:2,4,9; 16:6,7,18; 19:1,21; 20:22,23; and 21:11); visions and auditions determine his actions (16:9-10; 18:9; 23:11; and 27:23). It is indirectly stated that he speaks in tongues (19:6). In addition, Paul survives the bites of serpents, is miraculously rescued in peril at sea, and is himself totally filled with divine power (19:11-12; 27:23ff.; and 28:3ff.).

This leads to the next element in our interpretation of Paul's miracles. The miracles are worked and determined by the Spirit of God. Here, in other words, we have an obvious link to the description of the Spirit's outpouring in 2:1ff. This outpouring is manifest, among other things, in signs and wonders (2:17ff.; cf. especially v. 19). What Peter states here in prophetic fashion takes place immediately afterward through the apostles (2:43). We encounter this connection between Spirit and miracles in a special way with regard to Christ himself: through the gift of the Spirit he had the capacity for miracle, of course in such fashion that God was with him and acted through him (10:38). The same is true also of Stephen.

The same is clearly true also of Paul. Because he is endowed with the Spirit he is able to perform miracles. This is already implied in Acts' description of the significance of the Spirit in general, but is seldom directly stated in the miracle narratives. It can be clearly seen in 13:9ff., thus in the narrative of Elymas' punishment by miracle. Paul can see through as well as punish Elymas in a miraculous way, because he himself, Paul, is filled with the Holy Spirit (πλησθεὶς πνεύματος ἁγίου, 13:9). And in the Western text of 16:18 we find that Paul drives out the spirits because he acts τῷ πνεύματι ("by the Spirit").

It is the conviction of primitive Christianity that the synagogue does not possess the Spirit. The church as the true people of God is manifest also in the gift of the Spirit.[32] The Spirit is given the people of God (2:17ff.), and because Israel—that is, unbelieving Israel, the synagogue—does not have the Spirit it does not belong to the people of God. The history of the impenitent people of God with the Spirit is the history of resistance (7:51; cf. 28:25). And because the synagogue does not possess the Spirit it is also not capable of performing true miracles. This feature is given special emphasis in Acts' description of Paul's miracles, and can be seen more particularly by what we may term inverted miracle stories, that is, stories in which the alleged miracle worker fails completely. This feature is especially clear in the unique story of the unsuccessful exorcists in 19:13-20. Wandering Jewish exorcists are the subject here (19:13). They are not insignificant or unimportant miracle workers, an aspect stressed by the remark that they are sons of the high priest, Sceva. The inferiority of the synagogue is manifest first of all in the fact that the Jewish exorcists must use the hated names of Jesus and Paul (19:13). But their miracle working totally miscarries. The demon is not driven out, but shows itself to be superior; it flies at them and expels them from the place, bruised and banished. The Jews are incapable of performing miracles, that is, they no longer have divine authority.

From the viewpoint of the fixing of motif, we encounter a similar story in the report of Elymas' punishment through miracle in 13:6-12. This Elymas, a Jew, is regarded as a miracle worker and prophet (v. 6), and attempts to frustrate faith in Jesus (v. 8). But his alleged miraculous power is completely unmasked. He fails with Paul, and is himself struck blind by Paul's miraculous power (vv. 11-12). For Luke, Elymas is representative of a Jewish attitude, that is, of giving hindrance to faith, a strain running like a red thread through Acts. Obviously, Luke is aware that miracles can also take place outside the church. But if so, Luke regards them as magic and witchcraft, as is the case with Simon Magus (8:9ff.). Simon is also a failure, as is manifest from his inability to do what is decisive—he cannot give the Spirit (8:4ff.). Consequently, he too is not a genuine miracle worker.

Luke thus sets forth the frailty of the synagogue by making clear that it cannot perform any miracles, but also that the Jews fail totally when they attempt to do so. For this reason we encounter those peculiar, "inverted" miracle stories such as in 19:13ff. There is absolutely no parallel to these stories in the New Testament. Apart from this type, Acts deals with "ordinary" miracles, especially with healings and exorcisms (14:8-10; 16:16-18; 19:11-12; 28:7-8,9), and in only one instance with a raising from the dead (20:7ff.). Often, miracles are mentioned without a closer definition of their type (14:3; 15:12; etc.). In comparison with the gospel of Luke, the miracles are not exaggerated, perhaps with the exception of 19:11-12.[33] When the species of miracle is not given more precise definition, as is the case in the cumulative reports, this is consistent with the chief motif of miracle as the accompanying sign that legitimizes the proclamation.

3

We turn now to Paul. Our intention is not to give a thorough and independent portrayal of Paul's theology of miracle,[34] but rather to put the question, With what historical right has Luke described Paul as a miracle worker? The question can be most simply answered by investigating how Paul understood the "signs of an apostle" (τὰ σημεῖα τοῦ ἀποστόλου).

Here, however, we must first be reminded that the Pauline letters—in contrast to Acts!—are occasional writings. As such they obviously conceal parts of Paul's preaching and activity, since it was not necessary to treat such in a letter. Above all, the letters do not take up a series of issues, since neither for Paul nor his communities were they in dispute, controversial, or liable to attack. Most of Paul's preaching, teaching, and paraenesis was uttered merely orally. Of course, from a purely methodological and historical point of view, we may not forget that Paul could also at times appear irenic and without polemic. It is clear that he is conscious of being in agreement with the other apostles and missionaries (1 Cor. 15:11).

Miracles, that is, miracles which on his own admission Paul performed, belong to those things about which he was forced to write very little. No doubt Paul was conscious of having performed miracles (cf., e.g., Rom. 15:19 and 2 Cor. 12:12). Our question, rather, is how Paul's few utterances regarding his miracles are to be understood.

The fact in itself is worth noting that among New Testament authors only Paul describes his miracles as the "signs of the apostle" (2 Cor. 12:12). It is clear from 2 Cor. 12:12 that this phrase denotes miraculous and only miraculous deeds. Whether it is accidental that only Paul uses this phrase cannot be determined.[35] In Paul and in Acts we encounter the terms which are usual with Paul for miracles— σημεῖα and τέρατα ("signs" and "wonders") at times connected with δυνάμεις ("mighty works"; 2 Cor. 12:12; Rom. 15:19; Acts 2:19,22,43; 4:30; 5:12; 6:8; 7:36; 14:3; and 15:12). We meet them elsewhere in the New Testament only in Heb. 2:4. One would expect to find the designation "signs of an apostle" in Luke as well, but it does not appear. We may argue as to whether or not it is present in substance, since signs and wonders occur not only through the apostles, that is, "apostles" in the Lukan sense of the Twelve.

Paul assigns to miracle a certain and not inconsiderable role when he describes it as "the sign of an apostle." Just the name makes clear that Paul lays claim to miracles, since he asserts that he is an apostle, and understands himself as such. To dispute his miracles naturally also means to attack his apostolate, a feature that can be seen with special clarity in 2 Corinthians 10–12. As mentioned above, on this point it is often stated that Paul's miracles were so little conspicuous that his enemies denied that he was capable of them,[36] or that the "signs of an apostle" are not at all miracles in the usual sense of the term, but rather "the miracle of the word," hence the proclamation.[37] Or, it is said, the "signs of an apostle" can actually be construed as sufferings, that is, the divine miraculous power paradoxically appears as weakness.[38]

In this regard we must emphasize first of all that nowhere is it stated—by Paul or his opponents—that his miracles were less extraordinary than those of the other apostles. The suspicion under which Paul's enemies held him must therefore have another basis. Second, only with difficulty, if at all, can we conceive of a hidden, miraculous power camouflaged beneath sufferings, when it is precisely such power, concretized in σημεῖα and τέρατα ("signs" and "wonders"), which is to appear publicly and clearly.

I wish to assert here that miracles assume a quite central role in Paul's preaching, almost to greater degree than in Acts, where he is not at all portrayed as an apostle. Purely on the surface, this assertion does not make clear what, among other things, is involved in the fact that Paul—for easily explainable reasons—never records a miracle narrative. On the other hand, there are a few, though not many, hints and remarks in which he comes to speak of his own miraculous activity (as if only in passing) as self-evident (cf. Rom. 15:19; 2 Cor. 12:12; 1 Thess. 1:5; 1 Cor. 2:4; and Gal. 3:1-5). Though Paul seldom and only on occasion speaks of his miraculous activity, he still states clearly that miracles occur *wherever* he preaches the gospel. This is in itself self-evident, because miraculous deeds were a part of his proclamation of the gospel, and for Paul, proclamation is inconceivable apart from deeds of power.

We turn first to that "wherever." It is quite clearly expressed in Rom. 15:18-19. Here Paul summarizes his missionary preaching among the Gentiles (15:15-21). He will speak only of what Christ wrought through him by λόγος καὶ ἔργον ("word and deed," v. 18).

The ἔργον ("deed") is explained in more detail by the δύναμις ("power") given utterance in the σημεῖα and τέρατα ("signs" and "wonders"), and which in turn is interpreted as a δύναμις πνεύματος ("power of the Spirit"). This activity in "word and deed" is further interpreted as the εὐαγγέλιον τοῦ Χριστοῦ ("gospel of Christ"), and is carried out from Jerusalem to Illyricum—thus wherever Paul preached. This can scarcely be construed other than as proclamation, which is regularly accompanied by miraculous deeds. In this context, therefore, Paul gives us a survey of his activity.

Paul's regular and everywhere-occurring miraculous activity[39] is naturally also evident from the term, "signs of an apostle," in 2 Corinthians 12:12. If miracles are a mark of the apostle, Paul cannot with emphasis describe himself as an apostle without indirectly hinting at his regular miraculous activity. Can the founding of a Pauline community by an apostle be conceived apart from miraculous deeds? In 2 Cor. 12:12, Paul refers to his miracles with respect to the Corinthians—ἐν ὑμῖν ("among you"). The same is true here of his comparison with the "superlative" apostles (12:11).[40] In the context it is clearly stated that Paul's miraculous deeds can be compared with those of the other apostles. Those of Paul are just as well known as those of the others. Such would be impossible if Paul were forced to cite totally different miracles. We will return to the question why, despite this fact, the Corinthians do not believe him. Paul readily notes his initial preaching among individual congregations, with the remark that this preaching was confirmed by miracles (cf. 1 Thess. 1:5; 1 Cor. 2:4; and Gal. 3:1-5).[41] The passages should suffice to maintain that in his own opinion Paul everywhere demonstrated the signs of an apostle.[42]

It was intimated above that Paul reckons with a connection between miracle and word. We may express this even more vigorously: Paul not only regarded miracles as the "signs of an apostle" but defines the gospel as consisting in part of miraculous deeds. This can be most clearly seen in 1 Thess. 1:5. In the section on thanksgiving (1:2—2:13[16]) where he chiefly reviews the period of the congregation's beginning and founding, Paul speaks of how the message of salvation came to the Thessalonians. In this context it is stated that the gospel came to them not only in word, ἐν λόγῳ μόνον , but also in δύναμις and πνεῦμα ἅγιον ("power" and "the Holy Spirit"). The gospel is thus more than word. In this struggle (1:3,6; 2:1ff.), the Thessalonians must be strengthened, and in this struggle, δύναμις ("power"), among other things, is decisive. In this context the δύναμις is linked to the word and yet is not itself word. It is scarcely to be construed here other than is usual, that is, as miraculous power (cf. 2 Thess. 2:9; cf. also 1 Thess. 2:13). This interpretation is also confirmed by a comparison with Rom. 15:18-19. In this passage also the gospel is λόγος καὶ ἔργον ("word and deed"), the latter clearly marked as miraculous power or deeds. The two utterances clearly appear to stand in parallel.

Paul thus links miracle and proclamation more intimately than is usually done in the New Testament. This can also be seen in 1 Cor. 2:4.[43] Here Paul writes of his first visit to Corinth and in this connection comes to speak of his λόγος ("word" or "speech") and κήρυγμα ("message" or "proclamation," 2:4a). Paul's word and kerygma are defined by a demonstration of Spirit and power (πνεῦμα and δύναμις). And the initial preaching on behalf of the Galatians is characterized in such fashion that through the preaching the Spirit came upon the Galatians and by this means God worked miracles (ἐνεργῶν δυνάμεις) (3:2 and 5). It is further emphasized here that the Spirit's miraculous power is totally absent from the synagogue (3:2,5). This is clear from the contrast between νόμος ("law") and ἀκοὴ πίστεως ("hearing with faith").

For Paul as well the theme of miracle belongs to pneumatology. Paul can trace his miracles, which thus comprise part of his preaching of the gospel, to the Holy Spirit. Or, it is stated that the Spirit also belongs to the miracles. This latter aspect is clearly evident from the fact that where Paul mentions his miraculous deeds he also speaks of the Holy Spirit. According to Rom. 15:19, Christ is at work through Paul, that is, by the power of signs and wonders, and by the power of the Spirit. The relationship between the two is not explained. In 1 Thess. 1:5, the πνεῦμα ἅγιον (Holy Spirit) is named together with δύναμις ("power") and πληροφορία ("full conviction"). In 1 Cor. 2:4, the word of the apostle is manifest in πνεῦμα ("Spirit") and δύναμις ("power"). In Gal. 3:1-5, πνεῦμα and δύναμις ("Spirit" and "power") are mentioned side by side. Paul does not trouble to combine Spirit and miracles in theological fashion. If we search for such a combination, the table of charisms in 1 Cor. 12:4ff. is instructive—the gifts of grace, among them miraculous deeds, derive from the Spirit.

Among Paul's references to miracles known in public, done everywhere among the congregations, and—so we should assume—also acknowledged by them, 2 Corinthians 10–12 appears to be the exception. That is, when in these chapters Paul debates his opponents, he also appeals to his miracles, to the signs of an apostle (2 Cor. 12:11-12). He does not distinguish himself here from the other apostles. In spite of this, we have the impression that his opponents deny he is able to work miracles (cf., e.g., 2 Cor. 10:1, 10; 11:5).[44] How then can Paul appeal to his miraculous activity without reckoning on miracles of another sort, but which he clearly does not do here?[45] In this connection we should not forget that in that period many people appeared with miraculous claims, but were not on that account regarded as apostles. And the New Testament is well aware of miracle workers outside the community. In my opinion, the explanation in Paul's case lies in the peculiar circumstance that he is an ailing miracle worker, an ailing miraculous healer,[46] and the miracle worker cannot remove this ailment (2 Cor. 12:7ff.). His own illness testifies against his miraculous activity. It is in 2 Corinthians 10–12 that he speaks of the relation between suffering and miracle, weakness and strength. Paul's problem is not that he has no miraculous acts at his disposal or that he lacks visions or the prerogatives of another charismatic sort, for Paul is a typical charismatic.[47] The problem lies in convincing the Corinthians of the fact that it is also and precisely his weakness which belongs to the true life and mark of an apostle. Concretely, this means that the divine miraculous power is expressed in the weakness of the ailing apostle (2 Cor. 12:8).

We will drop the subject here and briefly summarize. Miraculous deeds are the "signs of the apostle." By his miracles, among other things, Paul proves to be a legitimate apostle. These acts are actually a part of his gospel, inextricably joined to his proclamation of the message. There is seldom mention of miracles in Paul, because they were not a regular object of intrachurchly debates. Just as word and miracle belong together, so also do miracle and Spirit. The miracles are a part of the spiritual life of the community, a life of which the synagogue is unaware.

4

Now we are able to make some reply to the question as to what Paul's utterances regarding miracle yield for an evaluation of his miracles in Acts.

If Acts gives the impression that Paul's life and activity were surrounded by miracles, such agrees with Paul's own claims. And this is true despite the fact that, in comparison with the quantity of miracles in Acts, Paul does not say very much about his miracles.

Further, there is also agreement in the fact that miracle and word belong together, though on this point Paul proceeds beyond Luke and defines the miracles actually as part of the gospel. Without miracle the gospel is not gospel but merely word, or rather, words.

Only Paul speaks of the "signs of an apostle," and for the reason that Luke holds another position than Paul's respecting the limitation of apostleship over against the Twelve. But the essence of the matter is there: In Acts the leaders of the church are also identified by miracles—with the exception of James, who manages as if without legitimation.

Further, the connection of miracle and Spirit is common to Luke and Paul. By this means also the miracles as utterances of the Spirit appear as the boundary between church and synagogue.

But the decisive difference between Luke and Paul lies in Paul's portrait of the ailing miracle worker. Certainly, Luke speaks often and much of Paul's sufferings. His miracles are not portrayed as rescue from peril. Yet, unlike Paul, Luke makes no connection at all between power and illness (δύναμις and ἀσθένεια), in order to express the paradox in Paul's understanding of miracle. At any rate, in general the two are at considerable distance from each other theologically.

What is historically correct in the details of Luke's portrait of Paul cannot be determined, at least not with the aid of the problem of miracle. On the other hand, the total portrait of a Paul who is able to work miracles, thus the signal role of miracle in Paul's activity in general is not to be doubted—at least not when we ask how Paul himself understood miracles in his activity.

6

Sons of the Prophets:
The Holy Spirit in the Acts of the
Apostles

1

In Acts the Holy Spirit is understood as the Spirit of prophecy; this
has often been noted.[1] In his survey on the literature on Acts from
1970-1975 F. Bovon[2] mentions this conception as something upon
which exegetes agree. That may be correct. It is, however, not often
indicated precisely what Luke means by the "Spirit of prophecy." And
if we would label Lukan theology of the Spirit as the Spirit of prophecy,
we must use the words *prophecy* and *prophetic* in a far more extensive
manner than usual. In some cases it has nothing whatever to do with
prophetic Spirit, as in Luke 1:35. A brief survey of the use of the
expression, *the Holy Spirit* (τὸ πνεῦμα ἅγιον), in Acts suffices to
show this:

- The Spirit gives glossolalia and prophecy (Acts 2:4,17f.; 11:28;
  19:5; 21:11).
- The Spirit enables persons to speak foreign languages (Acts 2:6ff.).
- The Spirit works miracles (Acts 2:17f.; 4:30; 13:9).
- The Spirit gives wisdom (σοφία) (Acts 6:3,5,10).
- The Spirit gives visions and auditions (Acts 8:29; 10:19; 11:12).
- The Spirit has inspired the authors of the Scriptures (Acts 1:16;
  4:25; 7:51-52; 28:25).
- The Spirit inspires prayer (4:24,31; 10:46; 19:6).

- The Spirit makes people speak openly and boldly (μετὰ παρρησία) (Acts 3:8, 13; 4:29, 31).
- The Spirit "creates" the Son of God, the Messiah (Luke 1:35; Acts 10:38).
- The Spirit gives consolation (Acts 9:31).
- The Spirit guides the missionary work of the church (Acts 8:29,39; 10:19; 11:12; 13:2,4,9; 16:6-7).
- The Spirit "ordains" the leaders of the church (Acts 20:28).
- The Spirit gives ordinances (Acts 15:28).
- The Spirit "sees through" people and punishes liars (Acts 5:5, 9).
- The Spirit gives guidance on the way of suffering (Acts 19:6; 20:22,23; 21:4,11).
- The Spirit is the means for selecting apostles (Acts 1:2).
- The Spirit is outpoured through the exalted Christ (Acts 2:33).
- The Spirit is connected with preaching (Acts 1:8; 4:8,31; 5:32; 10:44; 11:15).
- The Spirit is given at Baptism (Acts 1:5; 2:38; 10:47; 11:16).
- The Spirit is given with the laying on of hands (Acts 8:17-19; 19:6).

Even a superficial glance reveals the wide range of functions and activities ascribed to the Spirit. Does the concept of the Spirit of prophecy actually cover the whole range?

It goes without saying that prophecy is a main theme in Acts. At the same time it is clear that the activity of the divine Spirit is "the essential theme,"[3] or at least one essential theme, in the Lukan writings.

My thesis is that the Spirit in Acts confirms and supports prophecy, that is, the prophecy in the Holy Scriptures, which contains the gospel verbatim. God "testifies" by the Holy Spirit to the church that it is God's Israel and "the sons of the prophets" (Acts 3:25).[4] Further the Spirit testifies to the Gentiles who are included in God's people. The people of the spirit keep the law, whereas the other Jews oppose the Spirit and therefore are in conflict with the Scriptures and the law. The Spirit serves for Luke to secure the identity of the church. Only so can the wide range of activities of the Spirit be seen as a unity.

2

The Spirit belongs to Israel and is part of the history of the people of God. The Spirit has not appeared for the first time with Jesus, the gospel, or the church. The Spirit has always been there. In this respect

Luke differs from Paul. There is no idea about the "letter or the Spirit," γράμμα or πνεῦμα. But there is a Spirit (πνεῦμα) that always has been connected with the letter (the γράμμα).[5]

In most of the sayings about the Spirit in Acts we have the idea of Israel as the people of the Spirit. The main point for Luke is that the Spirit is an essential part of the Israel of the end-time, that is, the church.[6] And so the restoration and reconstitution of Israel is seen as the work of the Spirit.

This is very clear in Acts 1:1—2:42. The main themes in the proem (1:1-8) are the kingdom (1:3,6), the Spirit (1:4,5,8), and the witness to the ends of the earth (1:8). The restoration of the kingdom is its restoration to Israel (1:6).[7] We have no right to push aside the saying in 1:6 as some sort of nationalistic misunderstanding. This is frequently done without any justification in the text,[8] but from preconceived notions about the history of the early church and Luke's role in it. It is never denied in Acts that the kingdom is the kingdom for Israel. Only so are the repeatedly mentioned promises to Israel in the whole section of Acts 1–15 understandable (1:15-26;[9] 2:22,30,36,39; 3:35-26; 4:10; 5:31; 7 [passim]; 10:36,42; 13:26,32-33; 15:16-17). Moreover, the outcome of the mission to Jerusalem and the diaspora in the first part of Acts is the "rebuilding of the fallen house of David" (15:16).[10] The answer to the apostles' question about restoring the kingdom to Israel is that the Spirit will come upon them and they will be witnesses from Jerusalem and to "the end of the earth" (1:8). This is nothing but a part of the restoration. The "witness" of 1:8 is first and foremost a witness to Israel (2:14,22,36,39; 3:13,25; 4:8,10; 5:12ff.,29ff.; 7; 9:15,20,28; 10:36,42; 11:19,13,16ff.; 14:1ff.; 16:12ff.; 17:1ff.; 18:4ff., 24ff.; Chapters 22–28). So far nothing is said about the relation between the kingdom and the Spirit apart from the witness of the apostles as part of the restoration of the kingdom.[11]

The kingdom to Israel as a main theme in the sayings about the Spirit is seen in another "preparatory" part of Acts, namely, the restoration of the leadership of the people (Acts 1:15-26).[12] The very number 12 in this context has to do with the idea of the "twelve on Israel's thrones," the new leaders of Israel.[13] Luke has no idea of any new Israel, but he certainly sees the leaders of the people replaced after the old ones have failed, not least by opposing the Spirit of God (Acts 7:51-53). This restoration is part of the work of the Spirit (Acts 1:16). The locus of 1:15-26 tells us that the restoration of the leadership of Israel is one precondition for the outpouring of the Spirit. More is suggested in 1:16 than the idea that the words in the Scriptures stem from the Spirit. It is emphasized that the Spirit speaks in the Scriptures through David, who himself is understood as a prophet (2:30).

The outpouring of the Spirit in Acts 2 presupposes the same idea about the Spirit and Israel.[14] The first recipients of the Spirit are all Jews, above all, the twelve apostles (2:4,14). The audience consists only of Jews (2:5,14b,22). And the Spirit is offered to the people of the Spirit, namely, Israel.[15] To this people belongs the promise, the ἐπαγγελία (2:38,39), and this ἐπαγγελία is nothing but the Spirit (Acts 1:4,8; Luke 24:49).[16]

In the Christology of Acts 2 the theme is carried further. The exaltation of Jesus means his enthronement, namely, on the throne of David (Acts 2:30-33), and so the prophecy of Luke 1–2, especially 1:32-33, is being fulfilled.[17] The messiahship of Jesus as the Messiah of the Spirit is determined by his being anointed (χρίειν) by God with the divine Spirit, and this has happened for the children of Israel (Acts 10:36,38). In Acts 2:33 the exalted Messiah, now sitting on the throne of David, receives and pours out the Spirit, no longer offered as a gift to Israel (Acts 2:39).

The idea of the Spirit as the distinguishing mark of Israel as the people of God permeates the whole of Acts. Peter preaches in the speech of Acts 4:8ff., filled with the Spirit (v. 8), to Israel (vv. 5-6,8,10). Stephen is characterized by an irresistible Spirit and wisdom (πνεῦμα and σοφία; 6:5,10; 7:55). It is therefore absurd to accuse Stephen of speaking against Israel, that is, against the law, temple, and Moses (6:11,13,14; 7:51-53). The Spirit is for Luke especially connected with the temple (Luke 1–2), the law (Luke 1–2; Acts 7:53), and Moses who is prophet and miracle worker.[18] The Spirit is bestowed upon the Samaritans (8:14-17), and this is done via Jerusalem and the twelve apostles. Jerusalem is not the center of the church, but of Israel.[19]

The combination Spirit-Israel is seen also in the notion that the Spirit always has been active in the history of Israel and that the Gentiles receive the Spirit as something which is the property of Israel. So the Spirit links the Gentiles with Israel and enables them to share the promises to the people of God.

The Spirit has always been there in the history of Israel.[20] This is implied already in the relation of the Spirit to God as the "Father's promise" (Luke 24:49; Acts 1:4; 2:33) and by relating the Spirit to the prophecy of Joel 3:1-2 (Acts 2:17ff.). But it is asserted *expressis verbis* in Acts 7:51 where Luke sees the history of God's people as a history of resistance and opposition to the Spirit. The difference between the time of Israel before and after Jesus is not the difference between a time with and without the Spirit, but between different attitudes. It is not only now, in the resistance and renouncing of the apostolic preaching, that Israel denies the Spirit. It has always been so in the history of the people (οἱ πατέρες ὑμῶν, Acts 7:52). The whole history of Israel as surveyed in 7:2-50 is a history of the conflict between the Spirit and the people.[21] It is not decisive that Luke in Acts 7:2-50 does not mention the Spirit, apart from Moses as miracle worker and prophet (7:36-37). The question of the provenance of the material in Acts 7 cannot be treated here; but this is not necessary for our purpose as Luke tells us how he would have us understand the history in the speech. The fathers resisted the Spirit by killing the prophets (7:52). Now the prophets are not the main figures in the story of Acts 7:2-50, apart from the most important one, Moses (7:17-41). His lawgiving[22] is mentioned only in passing (7:38), whereas he is seen above all as the great prophet in Israel (7:36ff.; cf. 3:22). And the prophet's role in history was to proclaim the coming of "the Righteous One" (7:52b). After what is said in Acts 1:1—2:38, it goes without saying that the coming of "the Righteous One," the Messiah, means the restoration of the kingdom to Israel (1:6). And this again means that the Spirit is linked with the promises (ἐπαγγελίαι, Acts 1:4; 2:33,36,38; Luke 24:49). The Spirit is the promise (ἐπαγγελία), as it means the restoring energy of God in rebuilding Israel.

The Spirit acting in the history of Israel (7:51-52) is the power which has called the Holy Scriptures into being.[23] Only three times does Luke mention the Spirit as the one who speaks in the Scriptures (Acts 1:16; 4:25; 28:25). The idea is sufficiently clear: God's words in the Scriptures are the words of the Spirit. The Spirit spoke through David (προεῖπεν, 1:16); the Spirit spoke through Isaiah (ἐλάλησεν, 28:25); and the other way around, David spoke through the Spirit (4:25). In any case the Spirit formulates words.[24] Thus when the people have the Scriptures, they have the Spirit among them.[25] And the words of the Spirit in the Scriptures are first and foremost prophetic sayings, for example, the prophet David's words about Judas and thus about the Twelve on Israel's thrones (1:16; cf. 2:30);[26] the prophet David's words about the opposition from Israel as well as from the Gentiles (Acts 4:25-27); and finally the words of the prophet Isaiah about the hardening of the fathers, that is, Israel (Acts 28:26-27). The words of the Spirit in the Scriptures are much more than that, namely, they are the gospel. The Scriptures are the only place where the gospel is written. We will return to that later.

Israel's disobedience to the Spirit is the disobedience to the Scriptures. Even if they have the Scriptures read to them every Sabbath in the synagogue and so have the prophets and the Spirit talking to them, they are unable to recognize the words of the prophets (Acts 13:27). It is not a question of various interpretations caused by the ambiguity of the Scriptures. To Luke the Scriptures are unambiguous. You can find the whole Christian message, the gospel, verbatim in the Scriptures (Luke 24:45-47; Acts 3:18ff.; 13:29; 26:22-23; 28:22; etc.). Luke has a very rationalistic way of interpreting the Scriptures. There is no secret. You need no enlightenment in order to find what the Scriptures say about the Messiah-Jesus. And the church adds nothing to what has already been written by Moses and the prophets (Acts 26:27; 28:23). There is nothing like a veil upon the Scriptures or on the hearts of the readers so that they cannot understand them, as we read in 2 Cor. 3:12-18. Here are no hidden mysteries that only the Spirit can reveal (so in 1 Cor. 2:6ff.). The Scriptures speak openly and clearly, and what the readers now need is simply the information that Jesus is the Messiah[27] whose story is written in detail in the Scriptures. We see this in Luke 24:27,44: the problem for the readers is simply to see Jesus as the one referred to by well-known words in the Scriptures; the Scriptures are "about me" (περὶ ἐμοῦ, 24:44); or "about himself" (περὶ ἑαυτοῦ, 24:27). If they know about this "me," the Scriptures are open for them (Luke 24:45). The idea is the same in Acts 13:27: because the people of Jerusalem did "not know" Jesus, but rather misjudged him (τοῦτον ἀγνοήσαντες), that is, they did not understand that he was the one the Scriptures were all about, and so they fulfilled the words of the voices of the prophets by condemning him.[28]

The Spirit has been active in the history of Israel. It is not possible for Luke to talk about a time in the history of Israel when they have been without prophets. They can listen to the gospel of the Messiah, his death and resurrection, on the Sabbaths in the synagogue (Acts 13:27). The idea of an age without prophets is unknown to Luke.[29] The Spirit is linked with Israel and the prophets and so to the Messiah of Israel.[30] The Messiah-Jesus is not the first and only one who is led by the Spirit. We have in the proem to Luke's gospel (Chapters 1–2) a group of people acting as prophets and introducing the coming Messiah of Israel immediately before and after his advent,[31] namely, Elizabeth (1:41-45), Mary (1:47-55), Zechariah (1:67-80), Simeon (2:25-32), and Anna (2:36-38).[32] Only Anna is called "prophetess" (2:36), but the prophetic tone is unmistakable even with the others. Elizabeth and Zechariah are filled with the Holy Spirit (1:47,67), and the words of the last are labeled "prophetic" (1:67). But far more than all these, the Baptist is a prophet.[33] His father prophesies about him as the prophet of the Most High (1:67,76; cf. 7:26 and 20:6).[34]

G. W. H. Lampe may be right in saying that Luke 1–2 is characterized by the outburst of the prophetic Spirit;[35] he stresses that the setting of Jesus' birth and childhood is "the renewed activity in Israel of the long dormant energy of the Spirit."[36] Luke says nothing about this. It is not a new thing in relation to the Scriptures, the time of Israel, that the Spirit bursts out in intervals. Whether or not for Luke the Spirit is dormant is not said. It is important to stress the connection between prophecy and the coming Messiah-Jesus. And the main idea in the proem is that the coming of the Messiah means the restoration of the Israel of God and the fulfilling of the promises (Luke 1:16-17, 27, 32-33, 51-55, 68-79; 2:10-11, 25-32, 38).[37] Luke does not create any contrast between this new time and a supposed time within the history of Israel without any prophetic Spirit; rather, he sees the continuity between the prophets in Luke 1–2 and Israel, that is, the prophets of old.[38] Luke 1–2 is, so to say, "the missing link" between classical prophecy on the one hand, and the prophet Jesus and the prophets of the church on the other. The prophets of Luke 1–2 now proclaim the coming of the Messiah. The idea is not that they prophesy the Messiah, because that is not necessary and has been done by "all the prophets" (Acts 3:24). Luke does not want to add anything to the Scriptures. The new thing at this stage of prophecy is to tell who the Messiah is, to identify him. This child of Mary, this Jesus, is the Messiah of Israel. Whether Luke places the prophets of Luke 1–2 in the old or the new covenant is not important. It is highly improbable that Luke had any idea of the old and new covenant.[39] He knows about one history of God's people, and now an important new phase of this history has come.

If the Spirit has been a part of the history of Israel, first and foremost through the classical prophets,[40] and if a new wave of prophets showed up in order to introduce the Messiah-Jesus, what is then the difference between what is reported in Acts 2 and the former activity of the Spirit? At least it is clear that the story in Acts 2 does not introduce anything new and unheard of in the history of the people. The use of the Scriptures (Joel 2:28f.) to identify and explain the phenomenon at Pentecost in Jerusalem (Acts 2:17ff.) testifies to this. It is not necessary for Luke to introduce the Spirit. But it is necessary to identify the experiences of the apostles as the work of the Spirit. For the most part the answer to our question is a quantitative one. Before Jesus and the outpouring

of Acts 2, the Spirit was given only to some few prophets and sporadically.[41] Now the Spirit is given to all members of the church. "In
the church everyone is a prophet."[42] This notion is above all based on
Acts 2:17-18: In the last days the Lord will pour out his Spirit "upon
all flesh" (πάσαν σάρκα); young men and old shall take part in the
outpouring and they shall prophesy (καὶ προφητεύσουσιν).

This answer is scarcely satisfying and not based on evidence in Luke-
Acts, but on the dogma of the period without prophets in Israel. Luke
does not say anything about the frequency of the Spirit's activity before
Jesus. Acts 7:51-53 would more easily be understood to mean that the
Spirit had spoken frequently to the people. The prophets have been
there from the time of Samuel (Acts 3:24), even from the time of
Moses (3:22ff.). Opposition to the prophets involves more than those
we usually call prophets. As already mentioned, Moses is among the
great prophets (7:36ff.; 3:22ff.), David is a great prophet (2:30), and
so is Samuel (2:24). Acts 3:21 talks about the prophets being in Israel
"from eternity" (ἀπ᾽ αἰῶνος; cf. Acts 15:18). The "Scripture within
the Scriptures" is prophecy. And if Luke in using Joel 2:28ff.[43] took
the context into consideration, he would have found nothing there to
indicate that the eschatological outpouring of the Spirit would involve
everyone whereas in the former days it involved only a few. We probably get this impression from the fact that for Luke the old prophets
were above all those of the Scriptures, as well as from the quotation
of Joel 2:28-29 in Acts 2:17, overlooking that Luke is out to identify
and legitimate what happened on Pentecost, not to quantify spiritual
experiences. Nowhere in Acts do we find that all people of the church
are characterized as prophets or guided by the Spirit of prophecy. Acts
19:3ff. cannot be used as an example, because this is an extraordinary
situation from Luke's point of view. When prophets act in the church
they are explicitly characterized as prophets and as a special group in
the church (11:27-28; 13:1; 15:32; 21:9,10). The 12 apostles are prophets and guided by the Spirit (Acts 2:4ff., 14ff.; 3:8ff.). So too are
Barnabas and Paul and some other leading figures (13:1; 15:32; 11:24).
The seven "Hellenists," above all Stephen, are marked as men guided
by the prophetic Spirit (6:3,5,8,10; 7:55). That the brother of the Lord,
James, is the only one among the leading men in Acts not mentioned
as filled with the Spirit may be accidental and have to do with Luke's
traditions and sources. The church does not control the Spirit.[44] The
Spirit is not there constantly in the church and not at the church's
disposal. It is a gift (δωρεά; Acts 2:38; 8:20; 10:45; 17:7) coming
down from heaven; *ubi et quando visum est deo.*[45]

Thus the idea is not that the Spirit is now continuously bestowed on every person in the church whereas earlier only few had the gift of the Spirit, and very sporadically. This is only partly true; the actual idea is different and to be found first of all in Acts 7:51. The explanation of the disobedience of the people in the course of history told in Acts 7:2-50 is that they opposed the Spirit (ἀντιπίπτετε), namely, the Spirit of prophecy, preventing the outpouring of the Spirit. This is clear from Acts 7:55 combined with 5:32: The Spirit is given to those who ''obey him'' (πειθαρχοῦσιν αὐτῷ). In the context this αὐτῷ can mean God or the Spirit, but this is not important. In either case the idea of obedience in Acts 7:52-53 has to do with the prophecy, which is the word of God through the Spirit (see, e.g., Acts 4:25). Jesus himself is to Luke first of all the Prophet-Messiah,[46] and if you do not listen to him, you are no longer a part of Israel (Acts 3:22ff.)[47] To Luke the church is the true Israel insofar as Christians obey the Spirit. This true Israel no longer opposes the Spirit as Israel has done in the past (7:51). And if there is any opposition to the Spirit within the church, the persons in question will surely die, something that is clear from the story of Ananias and Sapphira (Acts 5:1-11).

Besides the idea of the obedient people, the difference is given with the coming of the Messiah-Jesus. So the task of the Spirit is partly a new one. The whole function of the prophetic Spirit in the time before the coming of the Messiah is according to Luke to testify that the Messiah would come to save, restore, and rebuild the people of God, and that this would happen through the death, resurrection, and exaltation of Messiah. It was important to Luke to show that this is the very idea of prophecy in the Scriptures; therefore he is eager to assert that all the prophets have spoken about the coming of a suffering and exalted Messiah (Luke 24:25-27,44; Acts 3:18ff., 24; 10:43; 24:14; 26:22). And this prophecy is, so to say, the Alpha and Omega of Scriptures. It is the true word of God from eternity (3:21; cf. 15:17-18). The first step in Luke's understanding of the history of prophecy is the word about the coming Messiah. The next is what may be called the last prophets before Christ, who at the point of his coming proclaim him as the promised Messiah (Luke 1–2). The third is what we have after Easter and Pentecost; the prophecy through the Spirit testifies that Messiah has come, and that the crucified, resurrected, and exalted Jesus is this promised Messiah.

Luke shows that the prophecies in the Scriptures could not in themselves ''identify'' Jesus as the promised Messiah. This is said in the interpretation of Ps. 15:8-11 in Acts 2:29ff. Luke must by interpretation

convince his readers that only Jesus and not David himself is the resurrected Messiah. And Peter, filled with the Holy Spirit, can tell the
inhabitants of Jerusalem at the conclusion of his sermon on Pentecost,
"Let all the house of Israel therefore know assuredly that God has
made him both Lord and Christ, this Jesus whom you crucified" (Acts
2:36). And Luke tells us that the exalted Jesus himself pours out the
Spirit (Acts 2:33). This is not in order to create an identification of
Jesus and the Spirit, or to make the Spirit a substitute for the absent,
heavenly Lord.[48] The Spirit of prophecy after the resurrection has the
task of identifying Jesus as the Messiah of the Scriptures and the promised prophet of the Scriptures. The idea is very clear in the summary
of Paul's preaching in Acts 17:2-3. Paul preaches on the Sabbath in
the synagogues and his message is taken from the Scriptures (17:2).
He "opens" the Scriptures, telling about the Messiah, his suffering,
death, and resurrection (17:3a) and asserting "that this Jesus, whom
I proclaim unto you, is the Christ" (καὶ ὅτι οὗτός ἐστιν ὁ χριστὸς
Ἰησους ὃν ἐγὼ καταγγέλλω ὑμῖν;17:3b). The idea determines the
speeches of Peter and Paul in Acts, which from the very beginning of
Acts (Chapter 2) are seen as inspired by the prophetic Spirit (e.g.,
2:22ff., 29ff.), with the conclusion in 2:36, where Jesus is identified:
The Lord and Messiah (κύριος καὶ χριστός) is "this Jesus whom you
crucified" (τοῦτον τὸν Ἰησοῦν ὃν ὑμεῖς ἐσταυρώσατε). The healing
miracles, which from the beginning of Acts are seen as the work of
the Spirit (2:17f.,19; 4:30), even testify to Jesus being the Messiah
(2:22; 10:38). So we have in Chapter 3 the death and resurrection of
the Messiah associated with the healing of the lame (3:12-16). The
idea is that miracles clearly testify to Jesus as the Messiah of the
prophecies. In the speech in Acts 3 the scriptural prophecies play a
major role (3:18,21,22,24,25). That the miracles can be seen as a
testimony, so to say, a word of confirmation, is clear (14:3). Peter is
filled with the Spirit when he testifies that the crucified and resurrected
Jesus is the one who miraculously cured the lame (4:8-10). Again death
and resurrection are associated with a miracle. When Stephen after his
survey of the history of Israel again is filled with the Spirit (7:55-56),
he can look into heaven and see Jesus there as the Son of man. What
Jesus had prophesied before his death (Luke 22:69) Stephen now by
the help of the Spirit can attest.

The main thing is that the Spirit is an inherent part of the history of
the people of God, of Israel. This is seen even in the rare sayings about
the outpouring of the Spirit on the Gentiles. It is significant that nearly
all the sayings about the Spirit in Acts are found in Chapters 1–15,

that is, in the part of Acts where we above all have depicted the initial mission of the church and the life of the church until the apostolic council in Jerusalem. Here we find 45 instances out of a total of 57 in Acts.[49] The last part of Acts has only a few sayings, most of them dealing with Paul and his last journey to Jerusalem (Acts 16:6-7; 19:2,6,21; 20:22,23,28: 21:4,11; 28:25). And even in Acts 1–15 the sayings about the Spirit and the Gentiles are very few. From the first part of Acts you get a clear impression of the charismatic, Spirit-filled life of the church in Jerusalem. When it comes to Gentiles, we have but one scene which tells us about the outpouring of the Spirit upon non-Jews (10:44f.,47; 11:15; and 15:8 all deal with the same event). The Samaritans are according to Luke not Gentiles.[50] The Spirit's activity in the church of Antioch (13:2) concerns a mixed congregation, above all active in the mission to Jews in the diaspora (Acts 13–14). Acts 19:6 perhaps refers to Gentiles, but more likely to Jews, former disciples of the Baptist. So Luke is restrictive when it comes to the Spirit and the Gentiles.

There is of course nothing in the life of the Gentiles or the Gentile nations that can be compared with prophecy in the history of Israel.[51] So when Luke deals with history, he always means the history of Israel with prophecy as the dominant theme. The Gentiles do not have the Holy Scriptures. When Luke touches upon the history of the Gentiles, it is only in passing (Acts 14:16-17; 17:26-27). The Gentiles have no previous history of any interest to Luke apart from the fact that their history shows traces of the Creator, who of course is the God of Israel. When it comes to the future the situation is different. The mission to the Gentiles is not an invention of the church or the apostles, but solely the responsibility of the Spirit. The Spirit is responsible for the missionary efforts of the church in Antioch (Acts 13:2ff.). The Spirit directs the geographical route for the missionaries (16:6-7). But above all, the important step of undertaking missionary work among Gentiles is totally determined by the Spirit, which can be seen from the story about Cornelius in Acts 10–11 and in its echo in Acts 15:9-10,14.

That God forces a reluctant Peter into missionary effort among Gentiles is convincingly demonstrated by M. Dibelius.[52] In this context we have no less than six sayings about the outpouring of the Spirit on Gentiles (10:44, 45, 47; 11:15, 16; 15:8). It is striking that Luke stresses this as a miracle. It is unprecedented that non-Jews receive the gift which belongs solely to Israel. This is emphasized in four of the six sayings:

10:45: Those "of the circumcision" present in the house of Cornelius marvel (ἐξέστησαν) that the gift of the Spirit is poured out even on Gentiles (ὅτι καὶ ἐπὶ τὰ ἔθνη ἡ δωρεὰ τοῦ ἁγίου πνεύματος ἐκκέχυται).

10:47: The church cannot deny the Baptism of Gentiles as "they have received the same gift as we," that is, the Jews, "those of the circumcision," *in casu*, the whole Jewish Christian church.

11:15: Peter reports that the Spirit came upon the Gentiles "as even upon us in the beginning" (ὥσπερ καὶ ἐφ᾽ ἡμᾶς ἐν ἀρχῇ), referring to Acts 2 and the outpouring upon Israel, the Jews in Jerusalem. In 11:17 the gift to the Gentiles is called "the same gift as given to us."

15:8-9: God testified for the Gentiles in giving them the Spirit "as he gave to us" (καθὼς καὶ ἡμῖν). Further God did not differentiate "between them and us by cleansing their hearts."[53]

The last sentence shows us that the Gentiles are unclean, that is in relation to Jews.[54] And the idea about ritual purity separating Jews from Gentiles is dominant in Acts 10–11 (to which 15:7ff. refers; 10:-14,15,28,34f.; 11:3,8,9).[55]

All the sayings about the outpouring of the Spirit on the Gentiles show the same thing. It is a miracle that God has given the Spirit even to people outside Israel. The gift of the Spirit is the sign that even Gentiles shall be saved (11:18; 15:8). The Spirit does not create a new Israel, something like a *tertium genus*, but God's work through the Spirit has the outcome that even Gentiles become members of the people of God, Israel.

When Luke in various ways emphasizes the connection between Israel and the Spirit and shows that the Spirit always has been a part of the history of Israel, he demonstrates the continuity between the church and Israel. Where the Spirit is, there you find the people of God.

3

Acts 3:25 names the Jews in Jerusalem "the sons of the prophets."[56] In Acts 7:52 the Jews in Jerusalem are the sons of those "fathers" who murdered the prophets. According to 7:52 the inhabitants of Jerusalem have already rejected the preaching of the apostles, and so they are merely sons of the murderers of the prophets. They have themselves killed the Prophet, Jesus (7:52). The idea of the Jews being murderers of the prophets is elsewhere known to New Testament writers (Matt. 5:12; 23:30f.; Heb. 11:33-38; James 5:10; cf. Luke 11:47,49; 13:34). But only Luke sees the Jews as "the sons of the prophets."

The sons of those who murdered are characterized as sons because they have themselves murdered (7:52b). The idea of "the sons of the prophets" is not that the Jews, in this case the believing Jews in the church, are themselves prophets. As mentioned above, we do not often in Acts find prophets and prophetic sayings apart from the prophets in the Scriptures. To be the sons of the prophets means that they are heirs of the promises, the salvation, foretold by the prophets in the Scriptures (3:24,25b; cf. 13:32).[57]

This brings us to the problem of the relation between the prophets in the Scriptures and the prophets and prophecies in the church. In other words, what does the "spirit of prophecy" actually mean? Both scriptural prophecy and the one in the church stem from the same Spirit.

When Luke in Acts uses the term "prophet," he means the prophets in the Scriptures and Christ as the promised prophet (3:22f.; 7:38). The prophets in the church are mentioned only in 11:27; 13:1; 15:32; and 21:9f. So to Luke the prophets are above all the "classical" ones.

The gospel is for Luke already present in the Scriptures, that is, in the prophetic writings which verbatim give the content of the Christian message, namely, the suffering, death, resurrection, and exaltation of the Messiah. You can find the gospel, so to say in detail, in the Scriptures (Luke 24:25-27,44-47; Acts 3:17ff.,25ff.; 4:24-26; 7 (passim); 8:32-35; 10:43; 13:27,34ff.; 17:2-3; 23:14; 26:22; 28:23). We have the kerygma—if the word is allowed—without any reference to the Spirit and the prophets only in Acts 4:10 and 5:59ff. The kerygma not only corresponds with the Scriptures, but also its content is derived and drawn from the Scriptures. So Luke finds everything about Jesus in the prophets—not only the general idea of the Messiah, his death and resurrection, but even details of his story (cf. Luke 18:31-34; Acts 4:24-26). Therefore he underlines the "everything" (τὰ πάντα) in the Jesus story as already written down (Luke 18:31; 24:47). Paul himself does not say anything apart from what "the prophets and Moses" already have said and which is written down (Acts 26:22). Even the part of the passion story which deals with Judas is to be found in the Scriptures (Acts 1:16-20). So too are the outcomes of the Jesus event, namely, the forgiveness of sins (Acts 10:43), the preaching to all the nations beginning in Jerusalem (Luke 24:47), and the outpouring of the Spirit (Acts 2:17ff.). Obviously the Scriptures, and that is for Luke the prophets in the broadest sense of the word, contain everything that the church preaches. This is confirmed by the saying about the benevolent Jews in Beroea (17:11). After they have heard the gospel they turn to the Scriptures in order to find and confirm the gospel there (ἀνακρίνοντες τὰς γραφὰς εἰ ἔχοι ταῦτα οὕτως).[58] The gospel is already there in the synagogue, in the reading from the Scriptures (Luke 4:16ff.; Acts 13:15,27). The problem for the reader is not what the text says, but to identify the persons mentioned, that is, first of all Christ. Even the apostles and the missionaries are mentioned in the Scriptures (Acts 1:16ff.; 13:47), but above all Christ.

This question of identification obtains even for the public appearance of Jesus himself. Jesus declares his messianic status by reading the Scriptures in the synagogue (Luke 4:16ff.)—Isa. 61:1-2, about the Spirit of the Lord. And Jesus declares that he has the messianic Spirit (Luke 4:21);[59] the whole question in the context is the identity of the Messiah (4:22ff.). What is said in Isaiah is, so to say, the gospel of Jesus word for word.

Additionally, the Ethiopian eunuch can read and understand what Isa. 53:7-8 is all about; the content is clear. But the problem is the identity of the person mentioned by the prophet (Acts 8:32-35). When Paul speaks to Herod Agrippa, the problem is whether the king believes the prophets or not (Acts 26:27): what Paul has said is already there in the Scriptures. The "opening" of the Scriptures (Luke 24:32,45; Acts 17:3) is simply the identification of the Messiah, or of Jesus as the Messiah.[60] And this identification is stressed in the stories about Paul's call. The main question he directs to the person appearing to him from heaven is, "Who are you, Lord?" (9:6; 22:8; 26:15).

If the whole gospel and its content is found already in the Scriptures, what is the function of the Scriptures in this connection? This is the problem of the relation between the Spirit and the preaching, the λόγος τοῦ θεοῦ.

Obviously, the Spirit does not give the church the words of the gospel, because these words are there already. What is said about the assistance of the Spirit to persecuted Christians in Luke 12:12, that the Spirit will teach the disciples in time of persecution (τὸ γὰρ ἅγιον πνεῦμα διδάξει ὑμᾶς ἐν αὐτῇ τῇ ὥρα ἃ εἰπεῖν) means that the Spirit will supply them with the right words.[61] But as the words of the preaching already are present in the Scriptures, the idea is different when it comes to preaching.

The connection between the Spirit and preaching, or prophecy, has often been emphasized,[62] but it is not clear how this connection is understood by Luke. When Fr. Bovon in his survey of the exegesis of Acts takes it as common opinion that the Spirit is tied to prophecy,[63] we have to ask why there are 34 sayings about prophecy in Acts, but no mention of the Spirit in them. To be sure, prophecy in the Scriptures is the work of the Spirit, as we see in Acts 1:20; 4:25; and 28:25, but there the idea is that the Spirit once spoke to and through the prophets.

Luke introduces preaching 46 times with terms like "testimony," "testify," "bear witness" (μάρτυς, μαρτυρεῖν). But we find in these cases the Spirit mentioned only in Acts 1:8 and 5:32. No explanation is here given of how the connection is to be conceived. The word "proclaim" (κηρύσσειν) is never tied to πνεῦμα. Sixty times Luke uses "the word" (ὁ λόγος) to refer to preaching, but only in four of these does he mention the Spirit. Finally, Luke uses the term ῥῆμα for preaching six times, but connects it with the Spirit only once.

We thus discover the somewhat amazing fact that the Spirit in Acts is only connected with the preaching of the gospel. That the Spirit is a part of the preaching is found only in the following cases:

Acts 1:8: The apostles shall receive power (δύναμις) when the Holy Spirit comes over them, and shall be witnesses.

2:4: The apostles were filled with the Spirit and spoke in tongues.

4:8: Peter was filled with the Holy Spirit and preached.

4:31: The church in Jerusalem was filled with the Spirit and preached the word of God boldly (μετὰ παρρησίας).

5:32: The apostles and the Spirit are witnesses.

In all these cases the Spirit precedes the preaching in some way or other. It is the other way around, however, in 10:44 (cf. 11:15); when Peter preached, the Spirit fell upon those "who heard the word."

Only in these few instances is there a direct, *expressis verbis*, connection between the Spirit and the preaching of the gospel, but it is not said how the role of the Spirit is understood. It is perhaps clear from the negative point of view: the different words in the content of the preaching do not come from the Spirit, but are derived from the Scriptures. On the other hand we have the role of the Spirit tied to (1) the idea of preaching "with boldness" (μετὰ παρρησίας) and (2) the miracles and wonders that testify to prophecy in the Scriptures and identify Jesus as the Messiah of the Scriptures.

The preaching is done "with boldness" when the Spirit inspires the apostles (Acts 4:13; cf. v. 8; 4:29,31; 14:3). This παρρησία, "freedom of speech," in Acts has to do only with preaching (2:29; 4:13, 29, 31; 9:27, 28; 13:46; 14:3; 18:26; 26:26; 28:31). The παρρησία concerns situations when the apostles are threatened, persecuted, in court, prisoners, that is, in dangerous situations. Regularly the παρρησία confronts a hostile audience or publicity. Preaching with "boldness" with one exception addresses Jews (2:29; 4:13, 29, 30; 9:27, 28; 13:46; 14:3; 18:26; 19:8, 26). The exception is Acts 28:31, where Paul obviously addresses Gentiles (28:28).

The connection between Spirit and the word of God does not concern the content. The words of the gospel do not come from the Spirit, but the way they are spoken is given by the Spirit. When Peter addresses the Sanhedrin, he is filled with the Spirit (Acts 4:8). The Sanhedrin experiences the Spirit, namely as the παρρησία, coming from men who are ἀγράμματοι καὶ ἰδιῶται ("uneducated and common"; 4:13), perhaps meaning "without any knowledge of the Scriptures." It is obviously more than a question of personal qualifications. The Spirit gives the gospel not in secret, not within a congregation, but publicly, openly. The speaking with "boldness" never refers to anything in the church apart from its public life.[64]

This manner of speaking serves to demonstrate the proclamation as the word of God.[65] The "boldness" is the gift of the Spirit, and this is further developed by the means of miracles and wonders. The connection of Spirit and word is given in the miracles accompanying the preaching.[66] And this too has to do with the παρρησία. In the prayer of Acts 4:24-30 the congregation asks God to enable them to speak the word of God with παρρησία while God causes healings and signs and miracles to happen through the name of Jesus (v. 30). And so in 4:31 they are filled with the Holy Spirit and speak the word of God with παρρησία. The wonders accompanying the παρρησία are the work of the Spirit, which show the word to be the word of God. The same idea is expressed in 4:33: The apostles witnessed[67] the resurrection of Jesus with "great power" (δυνάμει μεγάλη). In Acts 8:6 Philip's preaching is confirmed by the miracles he performs (on Philip being guided by the Spirit see Acts 6:3, 5; 8:29, 39 [21:9]). Acts 14:3 shows that God witnesses or testifies to his word by miracles and signs (παρρησιαζόμενοι ἐπὶ τῷ κυρίῳ τῷ μαρτυροῦντι ἐπὶ τῷ λόγῳ τῆς χάριτος αὐτοῦ, διδόντι σημεῖα καὶ τέρατα γίνεσθαι). The word μαρτυρεῖν is regularly used about the preaching, but in this context the miracles in themselves are the testimony. When the apostles "and the Holy Spirit" (καὶ τὸ πνεῦμα τὸ ἅγιον) are "witnesses" (μάρτυρες) about the death, resurrection, and forgiveness of sins, Acts 5:32, it means that the apostles' testimony is accompanied by παρρησία,

4:8, 13 and by the miracle told in 3:1-10. Acts 5:32 gives us the con-
cluding words of the persecution scene which starts with the wonder
in 3:1-8. The word is powerful because the miracles happen (thus even
Acts 13:12 and 19:10-11).

Even the speaking in tongues, the glossolalia, is to Luke an attendant
circumstance, accompanying prophecy. When the Holy Spirit fills the
apostles or others they start speaking in tongues, something directly
to be derived from the operation of the Spirit (2:4 [11]; 10:46; 19:6).
Speaking in tongues is mentioned very rarely in Acts. Speaking in
tongues and prophecy are kept together. The outpouring of the Spirit
in 19:6 means ἐλάλουν τε γλώσσαις καὶ ἐπροφήτευον ("they spoke
in tongues and prophesied"). The interpretation of the outpouring of
the Spirit is the speaking in tongues (2:4, 17a, 18b; the last passage
is important as the phrase "and they shall prophesy" [καὶ
προφητεύσουσιν] is a Lukan addition to the text from Joel 2:28ff.)
Speaking in tongues and prophecy are not identical phenomena for
Luke.[68] In Acts 19:6 they are mentioned side by side. Speaking in
tongues as well as prophecy come from the Spirit; the prophecy introduced in Acts 2:17-18 is not speaking in tongues, but the understandable
languages which the listeners from various parts of the world can hear
from the apostles (2:11); even the speech of Peter (2:14-36) is prophecy.
The miraculous and incredible thing is not the content of what the
apostles speak, but that they are able to speak the foreign languages
(2:6, 11). This is what accompanies the prophecy. It is not the words
used, but the way the missionaries speak that is here important in
interpreting what the gift of the Spirit is. This corresponds to the speech
in 2:14-36, as this among other things gives a very "rationalistic,"
understandable interpretation of the Scriptures (2:25-36). The outpouring of the Spirit is manifested in ecstatic glossolalia in the form
of praise to God (2:11; 10:46). So prophecy is not identical with speaking in tongues, but glossolalia accompanies prophecy, or rather,
preaching.

Because the gospel is to be found within the prophetic writings, the
word of God does not come from the Spirit. The Spirit manifests itself
in παρρησία, miracles, and ecstatic speaking in connection with
preaching.

Luke still knows that the Spirit utters words. But the spoken words
of the Spirit are never the gospel or the word of God. It is the word
of God only when it comes from the Spirit as the one speaking in the
Scriptures (Acts 1:16; 4:25; 28:25).

Apart from these instances the words uttered by the Spirit are of a different kind, not words of the gospel in the specific sense, but all sorts of words and commands affecting the life of the church, from "commonplaces" to prophecy of a coming starvation, "words for the moment." This is clear from the following survey:

8:29: The Spirit commands Philip: "Go up and join this chariot," that is, of the Ethiopian eunuch. In 8:26 the orders are given to Philip by an angel; so it is not only the Spirit that is important but also the command from heaven.

10:19f.: The Spirit tells Peter to follow the delegates from Cornelius; indirect speech (parallel, 11:12).

11:28: The prophet Agabus signifies by the Spirit (δὶα τοῦ πνεύματος) the coming great famine; indirect speech.

13:2: The Spirit orders the church in Antioch to "set apart for me Barnabas and Saul for the work to which I have called them."[69]

15:28: The Spirit and the church in Jerusalem have given the regulations in the apostolic decree.

20:23: The Spirit witnesses that imprisonments and afflictions await Paul; indirect speech.

21:4: Disciples in Tyre say through the Spirit that Paul should not go up to Jerusalem; indirect speech.

21:11: Agabus refers to the Spirit ("Thus says the Holy Spirit") and relates in exact words what is going to happen to Paul in Jerusalem.

23:9: The Pharisees hold it possible that the words uttered by Paul, probably the ones in v. 6, derive from "a spirit" (πνεῦμα) or an angel.

There are in Acts several occurrences of similar words and commands, but they differ from the ones above with respect to the source of the words (angels: 5:19; 8:26; 10:3,22; 11:7f.; 27:23f.; kyrios: 9:9,10f.; 18:9; 22:19; 23:11; voice (from heaven): 10:13ff.; 11:7ff.; 22:7ff.; cf. also 11:13; 16:9; 22:13).

Prophecy in the church differs greatly from that in the Scriptures. The whole truth is already written down and Luke does not want anything to compete with it. The Spirit does not repeat or "copy" the words of the prophets in the Scriptures. The Spirit is not the interpreter of the Scriptures as it does not divulge the truth in the Scriptures. It does not give "spiritual" words or new insights, and it says nothing about the future activity of Christ, for example, his coming and judgment. The prophetic words of the church are with one exception (11:28) words to or about the apostles and missionaries of the church and their activity or fate. It is remarkable that the words about the assistance of the Spirit during persecutions and trials, which Luke mentions twice in his gospel (12:11-12 and 21:12-15), play no role whatever in Acts 22–28 where we have the broad and lengthy description of the legal process against Paul. These chapters dominate the picture of Paul in Acts. This "assistance" is there in other cases (Peter: Acts 4:8; Stephen: 6:10). But for Paul, Luke emphasizes his faithfulness to the Scriptures and the Jewish law (21:20ff.; 22:3ff.; 23:1,6; 24:14ff.; 26:4f.,22,27; 28:23).

The closest approximation in Acts to the idea of prophecy in the Scriptures is the words about the famine in 11:28. Prophecies about the future of the gospel, however, are not given as revelations to the prophets in the church, but rather as prophecies from the Scriptures. The speech of Peter in Acts 2 is dominated by the notion of fulfilled prophecy, that is, prophecy from the Scriptures (2:16ff.), but even so, not everything in the prophet's words are fulfilled (2:18-19). The same is the case in Acts 3. The coming of the Messiah-Prophet fulfills prophecy (3:21,22,24); but something remains (3:20,21). The prophecies are partly fulfilled. What is going to happen in the future can be found in the Scriptures. This idea we have in the prayer in Acts 4:23ff. (see vv. 25-28, 29-30) and also in Acts 13:16ff., where the Jesus event is fulfilled prophecy even though something remains for the future. And this future is not revealed by the prophets in the church or by Paul, but by quotations from the Scriptures (13:41). The resurrection of Jesus is in itself fulfilled prophecy (Acts 2:25ff.), and the coming resurrection is even prophesied "in the law and the prophets" (22:14-16, cf. 26:6-8).

And so what we may call the "gospel" or "kerygmatic" prophecies always come from Scriptures and not from the prophets in the church. This confirms again that the true prophecy and the source of prophecy for Luke is the Scriptures. That the Scriptures for Luke are spoken words, oral speech, does not alter this. In some cases we should expect sayings to be labeled "prophecies," like Paul's words in his farewell speech (Acts 20:18-31), where he depicts the dangerous future of the church, the heresies, etc. (20:29-30). But this view of the future is introduced by the singular "I know" (οἶδα, 20:29).

The main idea is clear. For the most part, the Spirit is the Spirit of prophecy as it testifies in various ways to the words of the Scriptures. And these words are infallible, whereas Paul can refuse to obey the words of the Spirit when they come to him from prophets in the church (21:4).[70]

Still the Spirit-prophecies of the church serve to demonstrate that the church is the people of God. That these prophecies do not characterize the Spirit, but tell us about the *unde*, the "whence" of the church, is clear from the fact that it is not only the Spirit that utters prophetic words or commands from heaven. They come from the Lord, angels, voices from heaven, etc. The same command may stem from an angel or the Spirit in the same context (8:26,29). The personal character of the Spirit,[71] which is clear in some of the prophetic words, e.g., the Spirit talking as an "I" (13:2), should not lead us to speculate about the Spirit being conceived as an angel (cf. 23:8)! The fact that the Spirit speaks, utters words, is not enough to characterize the Spirit as person or personal, because the words are sometimes uttered by prophets in the church, and their "ego" is naturally "possessed" by the Spirit when they speak to the church. And when the Lord, that is Jesus, speaks to Paul in Paul's call (Acts 9:5; 22:28 and 26:14), this does not mean that Jesus is seen as an angel or as identical with the Spirit.

To Luke the idea is very simple. The church does not lead and guide itself; God does, through Jesus, the Spirit, voices, visions, etc. This is probably the reason why the Spirit very seldom is given or comes by the means of human instruments, an office in the church, or apostles; we have this only in 8:15ff.; 9:17; 10:44 (parallel 11:15); and 19:6. As a rule the Spirit acts and speaks directly from heaven (1:5ff.; 2:4ff.,33,38; 4:8,31; 5:32; 6:3,5,10; 8:29,39; 9:31; 10:19; 11:24,28; 13:2ff.,9,52; 15:28; 16:6,7; 19:21; 20:22f.,28; 21:4,11). In some of these cases it may be that the words come through prophets in the church, but that is very seldom expressly stated. It may be correct to say that "the Spirit is given only when the Twelve are present or a member or a delegate of the Twelve is on the scene," but then the idea is that of the people of God, not of an intermediary office.[72]

Moreover, these prophecies separate the church from the synagogue or the rest of the people. Such prophecies do not occur outside of the church. Other prophets, Jewish ones, are mentioned in Acts. Luke then calls them false prophets or magicians; so Bar-Jesus (13:6), probably the same person as the magician, Elymas (13:8). Such a prophet has not the Spirit, as can be seen from his failure (13:11). Simon Magus in Acts 8 is a Jew[73] and performs miracles (8:9-11). He is then converted and baptized (8:13), but his false "nature," his lack of the Spirit, is demonstrated (8:18-24). The seven Jewish exorcists in Acts 19:13-17 do not have the Spirit, as is demonstrated by their being overcome by an evil spirit. Visions and prophetic words are nowhere described as occurring in the synagogue, because its members do not obey the prophet Jesus, and so have not the Spirit of prophecy and will be expelled from the people (3:22-23). Members of the church, by contrast, are the true ''sons of the prophets''[74] and the ''sons of the covenant'' given to Abraham (3:25). This again makes it obvious why prophecy first and foremost is the prophecy in the Scriptures. Prophecy in the church only confirms the Christians as the sons of the prophets, namely, those of the Scriptures. Prophecy is for Luke the expression of continuity in the history of Israel. The law cannot in the same way serve this purpose for the simple reason that the church consists not only of Jews but also of Gentiles. They have the same Spirit as the Jews (10:44,45,47; 11:15,16; 15:8). But they keep the law of Moses only partly, that is, those aspects contained in the apostolic decree (15:20,28; 21:25). The prophets and prophecy are ''from eternity'' (3:21), but the law came into history at Sinai (7:38).

4

In Paul's preaching the contrast between ''letter and Spirit'' (γράμμα and πνεῦμα) is constitutive (Rom. 2:29; 7:6; 2 Cor. 3:6ff.; Gal. 3:2-4; Phil. 3:3). Paul ties the Spirit exclusively to Christ and the gospel. He never uses the Spirit in dealing with the Scriptures or the prophets of old.[75] The Spirit came to the world at a certain time in history, namely, with Christ (Gal. 4:16). Paul never speaks of the Spirit as a phenomenon before Christ, with the exception of Gal. 4:29 about Isaac as born ''after the Spirit''; this has to do with the promises (ἐπαγγελίαι) which to Paul are the same as the gospel (Rom. 4:14ff.; Gal. 3:9,14,18,21ff.; 4:23).

When we turn to Luke we are in a different world. For several years there has been a discussion about the meaning of the festival of Pentecost in the first Christian century.[76] When did the festival of Pentecost come to commemorate the giving of the law at Sinai? As far as I can see, this might well have been the case long before Luke wrote.[77] We do not know for certain. Some scholars want to see the description of the outpouring of the Spirit on Pentecost (Acts 2) as a contrast to or correlative of the giving of the law at Sinai.[78] There is no reference to the law in Acts 2, and certainly nothing about a new law. There is nothing in Luke-Acts depicting the gospel as a contrast to the law or a replacement of the law. Some exegetes have tried to understand the apostolic decree as such a replacement,[79] but that is impossible.

On the other hand, Luke is fully aware of Pentecost as a Jewish festival, and he does not write the story from an etiological point of view to demonstrate the origin of some sort of a Christian festival at Pentecost. Acts 20:16 tells us that Paul hastened his journey to Jerusalem because he wanted to be at Jerusalem on the day of Pentecost. This is more than providing chronological information. Pentecost here is of course the Jewish festival.[80] And Paul goes to Jerusalem in order to take part in Jewish ceremonies. He wants to worship in Jerusalem, to make sacrifices in the temple, to be purified in the temple, and to perform another important part of the requirements of the law, namely, to give alms to his people (Acts 24:11, 12, 17f.). Sacrifices and alms-giving Luke knows as important elements in the law of Moses.[81] Paul in Acts lists these intentions to accomplish the requirements of the law as his sole motivation for going up to Jerusalem. After his years of missionary works he goes to Jerusalem to do according to the law. At least this shows that Paul does not act against the law and that there is no contrast between the preaching of the gospel and the requirements of the law.

Luke combines Pentecost and law, but we have no right to say that he regarded Pentecost as the feast for the giving of the law at Sinai. Whether there is any connection between the Jewish legends about the law given in 70 languages at Sinai and the miracle of the different languages in Acts 2 we are not able to say.

But it is clear that the outpouring of the Spirit is combined with a Jewish festival and also that Paul's last journey to Jerusalem has to do with Pentecost and his performing the requirements of the law. The Spirit is mentioned in its bearing upon Paul and his work in some few scenes (9:17; 13:2-4,9; 16:6-7; 19:7ff.,21; 20:22-23; 21:4,11; 28:25). Five of these sayings deal with Paul's last journey to Jerusalem (19:2; 20:22-23; 21:4,11). The journey to Jerusalem to fulfill the law is also "arranged" by the Spirit. Paul is ordered to Jerusalem and at the same time told what is going to happen to him there, viz., prison and persecution. That the Jews attack this man of the Spirit whose journey was motivated by his desire to act according to the law shows that they fight against the law and the Spirit (cf. 7:51-53). Luke, however, sees no contradiction between the Spirit and the law of Moses. He positions the outpouring of the Spirit on a Jewish festival regardless of how this feast is interpreted, and so it is clear even here that the Spirit is an occurrence within the history of Israel.

Luke's point of view is that the Spirit leads to obedience to the law of Moses; in the church this obedience has been made possible, and because the church has the Spirit and obeys the law, this church is Israel. But the unfaithful part of the people opposes the Spirit and does not keep the law (7:51-53). There are for Luke no tensions within the Scriptures, as we see them in Paul's thinking. To Luke the law (νόμος) contains prophecy as well as commandments.[82]

From the very beginning of his work Luke shows the harmony between Spirit and law (Luke 1–2). The coming of the Messiah of Israel is proclaimed by an outburst of the Holy Spirit, expressed in prophecy, and centers on the identity and task of the Messiah (1:4ff.,46ff., 59,67ff.; 2:25-32, 36ff.). At the same time the law-observant people perform for this Messiah who is created by the Spirit (2:21, 22,23,24,27,37,39, 41ff.) what is required by the law. Israel, with its center in the temple of Jerusalem is the setting for the Messiah (1:16,32,33,54,55,68-79,80; 2:10,11,22,25,32,34,41ff.).[83]

With the help of Luke 1–2 we are able to understand the otherwise obscure words, Spirit and law, or rather obscure parallelism between them, in Acts 7:51-53.[84] The verses are the conclusion of Stephen's speech in 7:1-50, and serve at the same time as a commentary to the speech. We are here told that the Jews present and listening to Stephen, as well as their fathers, always have resisted the Spirit (7:51). They have done it by killing "the Righteous One," Jesus, as their fathers killed the prophets (7:52). So the prophets "represented" the Spirit as Jesus now does. Moreover, the present Jews are characterized in 7:53 as "You who received the law as delivered by angels and did not keep it." What is the relation between 7:51-52 and 7:53? Is the law here simply added to the Spirit without any inner connection? The Jews have opposed the Spirit, and also have not kept the law. Are these two different charges?

Luke always sees Spirit and law together; both characterize Israel as the people of God and of salvation. There is in Luke-Acts no theological explanation given for the relation between Spirit and law. It is enough for Luke to show that they belong together. The church has Spirit and law; the synagogue has only the law—but they do not keep it (7:53; 15:21). Moses is in Acts 7 what he is throughout Acts: the charismatic prophet, miracle worker, and the one who gave the law (7:36-37 and 7:38; 3:22; 6:11,14; 13:49; etc.).[85] The disobedience of Israel in Acts 7 is placed in the context in such a way that it has to do both with the prophet Moses and with the giver of the law (7:39 compared with 7:36-38). If one asks about the central thrust of the law

according to Acts, the answer in Acts 7 is simple: it is the struggle
against idolatry. There is a clear connection between the speech's "corpus" and the charge brought forward in 7:53. The law is for Luke
above all the first commandment about the one and only God of Israel.[86]
When they do not obey Moses, that is, the law from Sinai, they turn
to other gods (7:40ff.). So it is clear why Luke accuses them of being
"uncircumcised in heart" (7:51), as they "in their hearts . . . turned
to Egypt" (7:39). They are uncircumcised, that is, they act as Gentiles,
an expression found elsewhere in Acts (e.g., 4:27-28). Circumcision
is the sign of Israel as the people of God (Luke 2:21; Acts 7:8; 15:1,5;
21:21; etc.).

The notion about the law to Luke is that the law reveals Israel to
be the people of God—and that explains his underlining the ritual side
of the law. When the Jews reject the Spirit and the law they are no
longer Israel and God's people.

Stephen is accused of speaking against the law and of saying that
Jesus would alter the law of Moses (Acts 6:11,13-14). At the same
time, Stephen is a charismatic prophet (6:3,4,8,10; 7:55). It seems as
if Spirit and the law are in conflict for the Jews; probably Luke knows
about the Jews complaining against the church and the charismatics
for neglecting or breaking with the law. Stephen rejects the accusations
by demonstrating that the characteristic thing about Moses was that he
was prophet *and* giver of the law (7:35ff.). Not Stephen, but the Jews
are in conflict with God and the law (7:51-53). They have not the Spirit
and so they do not keep the law.

It is thus significant that they who have the Spirit at the same time
keep the law.[87] This was not so only at the dawn of the coming of
Messiah (Luke 1–2); it was so in the life of the Messiah-Jesus himself.
Already Acts 6:13-14 shows that Luke regards Jesus as one who kept
the law (the witnesses in 6:13 are "false"), something which in turn
determines his presentation of Jesus in the gospel.[88] The Christians
have obviously no problems in keeping the law. The whole church in
Jerusalem, guided by the Spirit (1:8; 2:4,17ff.,38; 4:8,31; 5:3ff.;
6:3ff.), at the same time lives according to the law. This is said in a
very typical way (Acts 11:3) and we cannot dismiss this saying by
thinking that these objections come only from one party in the church
(11:2). Peter responds on behalf of the whole church (11:4ff.). And
the expression "those of the circumcision" is used of the church in
Jerusalem (10:45). According to Acts 10–11 it is unthinkable for Peter
to do anything against the law (10:14,28; 11:8). When Peter enters
the house of Cornelius, he is not acting against the law because God

has declared the Gentiles to be clean; God has himself purified them (10:15,28; 11:8). The last word about the whole Jewish-Christian church, first of all the one in Jerusalem, asserts that they are "all zealous of the law" (21:21). We have the same situation with Paul. He is the prophetic charismatic, who has always kept the law and keeps it now, performing even more than the law requires (16:3; 18:18; 21:20-26; 22:3; 23:1-5; 24:11f.,14,17,18; 26:5; 28:17). All charges against Paul for breaking the law (21:21,28; 28:18) are shown to be false. His last journey to Jerusalem he accomplishes in order to fulfill the law (24:11-12,17-18). It is clear from the charges in 21:21,28; and 28:17 that the law Paul obeys is the law that demonstrates that Israel is God's people.

It seems not to be a problem for the church to keep the law. All charges against the church for acting against the law are false (6:13; 21:24). There is no truth to reports about Paul telling Jews to give up the law, as he himself is a practicing Jew who keeps the law, as the church does: ἀλλὰ στοιχεῖς καὶ αὐτὸς φυλάσσων τὸν νόμον ("but that you yourself live in observance of the law"; 21:24).

On the other side there are examples that show that even the high priest does not keep the law (23:3). This is said generally about all unbelieving Jews (Acts 7:53). The picture is clear: those who oppose the Spirit do not keep the law, but those who have received and obey the Spirit do. The Gentiles do not even have the law and so they do not keep it; this is clear from Acts 10–11 and 15. Luke does not offer this as a theological explanation, but simply as what he regards to be empirical facts.

What is said about the Jews who oppose the Spirit in 7:53 recurs in another form in 15:11. The idea here is that "the fathers and we" (in this case, the Christians and their Jewish forefathers) were not able to bear the yoke, that is, the law. In 7:53 we have to do with willful transgressions; in 15:10 with the contention that the burden was too heavy. We have before us two different traditions about the meaning and understanding of the law. And we have two different situations: charges against the Jews (Acts 7), and the controversy about the Gentiles' obligations to the law of Moses (Acts 15). We cannot here deal with the question about Luke's traditions and sources, but simply try to discover how he understands these two points of view.

Nothing from Luke 1–2 onwards seems to indicate that the Christians are unable to keep the law. Common to Acts 7:53 and Acts 15:10 is that the law has not been kept in the history of the people. Common also is the question about idolatry. When the people turned away from

Moses and the law (7:35-38) they turned to idolatry; they worshiped and sacrificed to idols (7:39-43; ἀνήγαγον θυσίαν τῷ εἰδώλῳ, 7:41). In 15:19-20,28-29 and 21:25 we are again faced with the question of the idols (ἀλισγημάτων τῶν εἰδώλων, εἰδωλόθυτον); in both cases we have to do with the First Commandment. The other point of view has to do with the very number of commandments. What is laid upon the believing Gentiles is nothing but the "necessary things," the "essentials" (τούτων τῶν ἐπάναγκες, 15:28). We have here a distinction within the law between necessary and not necessary, at least for the Gentiles. When it comes to the Jews in the church, in Acts they keep not only the essentials, but the law as a whole. That the law for Luke does not give salvation is clear, and this is emphasized even in Acts 15 (v. 11). But there is a difference now compared to the time before the coming of the Messiah. The Christians keep the law, whereas the Jews did not (7:53), not even "the essentials." After the outpouring of the Spirit disobedience to the law is no longer the question; the church consists of people "zealous of the law" (Acts 21:21) and of Gentiles keeping "the essentials."

Even when Luke deals with the Gentiles he combines law, Spirit, and Israel.[89] The gift of the Spirit is given to the Gentiles (10:44-46; 11:15; 15:8) and the case is similar with regard to the law, because the apostolic decree is part of the law—not the whole amount of commandments, but "the essentials" (15:28). And so the Gentiles obey the law, whereas the Jews in the wilderness did not (7:39ff.). The relation between the decree and the law is clear; the decree is never mentioned unless the law is the subject (Acts 15:1,5,10,20,28,29; 16:4; 21:20-25). And the Holy Spirit is the authority behind the decree (15:28). The Spirit gives the Gentiles ceremonial commandments and regulations. In this case the Spirit is the authority behind "the essentials" of the law. The idea that the apostolic decree was a substitute for the law completely breaks down in face of Luke's argument in Acts 21:20ff. In this context the problem is again the law (21:20,21,24). Verse 25 with the decree seems completely out of place here, with the story continuing in verse 26. It is understandable only if the question is the church's relation to the law. Paul himself keeps the law (21:20b,21-24). What about the Gentiles and Paul's churches? They too keep the law, that is, the necessary part found in the decree.

For the people of the Spirit the law is no longer a burden. The believing Jews, among them Paul, keep the entire law; the Gentiles part of it. There is harmony between Spirit and law.

7

The Center of
Scripture in Luke

Translated by Roy A. Harrisville

Can we actually speak of a center of Scripture in Luke,[1] and thus of
a critical core that determines the understanding of the whole? Luke's
intention is clearly expressed behind Paul's words in Acts 24:14: "[I
believe] everything laid down by the law or written in the prophets."[2]
Though in its various forms the term "everything" (πᾶς) is a favorite
of Luke, a term by which he often accents his claim to "complete-
ness,"[3] with the result that it becomes almost idiomatic, we still cannot
ignore the fact that he actually intends to omit nothing that the Scripture
offers.[4] We see this not only in the word πᾶς ("everything"), but in
Luke's use of the Old Testament as a whole. In Luke, at least in
theory—if there is such a thing as theory in Luke—there is no midpoint.
It would be more proper to say that everything is Scripture, everything
is important, everything is binding,[5] and everything is God's[6] or the
Spirit's word. Luke is the fundamentalist—*sit venia verbo*—in the New
Testament. It is impossible for him to regard Scripture in such consciously "critical" fashion as does Paul, for example, in Galatians 3
or Romans 10. Paul obviously does not believe everything written. For
example, he does not believe that the man who practices the righteousness which is based on the law shall live by it, though that stands
written (Rom. 10:5).

Yet, though Luke believes everything, and though he is the theologian of Scripture par excellence, for him Scripture does in fact have

a center. If we do not recognize this, his conception of Scripture can be understood only with difficulty.

In the New Testament, we have no parallel to Luke's use of Scripture in Acts. This is already evident in part from the standpoint of form. We note three different usages: First, there are direct quotations, as we find them everywhere, but especially in the first half of Acts. Second, there are the summary references, where all that the Scripture says is referred to in summary fashion (Acts 3:18,24; 10:43; 17:3; 18:28; 24:14; 26:23; and Luke 24:26,46).[7] Third, there are the many recitals of narrative and indirect quotations[8] in the two historical presentations, or resumes, of Acts 7 and 13:17-25.[9]

To the first form we of course have numerous parallels; to the second only a very few.[10] The second at least indicates that Luke is prepared to regard Scripture as a totality. For he not only speaks of what one or a few of the prophets say, but is concerned with all the prophets (3:18,24; 10:43).[11] In the New Testament, only Luke speaks of "all the prophets," and by this he understands all the Scriptures of the Old Testament—Moses, the prophets, the Psalms or "the writings."[12] The mere fact that Luke offers this summary of scripture content is important for our understanding of the "center of Scripture." For here too Luke represents something special among New Testament authors.[13]

The attempt to express in summary form what Scripture says does not mean that Luke extracts an ideology from the Scriptures, and in so doing ignores other statements of the text. He simply does not speak of *the* Scripture, but singly, of "the Scriptures" (αἱ γραφαί, 17:2; 18:28). This has nothing to do with the fact that Luke would have had no term such as "Scripture" to express the collection of the various writings. This too may be left undetermined. Luke—again, the only one in the New Testament—strives to show where in the Old Testament the authors used by him are to be found. He is not only aware of quoting from "the book of Psalms" (Acts 1:20; cf. Luke 20:42-43), an expression which occurs in the New Testament only in Luke.[14] He is also aware and states that what is quoted is found in the second Psalm (Acts 13:33), or that it appears "in another place" (13:55). He can speak of "the prophets" in general (3:18,24; 7:42; 10:43; 13:41; 15:15; 28:23), or of "the prophet" (7:49). But he also names various prophets by name, thus Joel in 2:17 and Isaiah in 28:26. He is interested in the identity of the author of an utterance in Scripture. This is especially true of David (1:16; 2:25,34; 4:25), but also of Moses (3:22; 7:37).

We need not decide here which and how many of Luke's quotations and interpretations he has drawn from the tradition; in my opinion, these are very few.[15] But it is clear that his formal references, quotations, and references to authors do not derive from the tradition. How else shall we explain the lack of parallels? In any event, this fact gives evidence of an entirely independent study of Scripture, by which Luke deduces his understanding of Scripture from studies of the individual (I would prefer to say, of all) writings—the Law, the Pentateuch, by no means excepted.[16] He does not treat the Scripture *en bloc*. And he does not write for a milieu in which one spoke of Scripture in general or lived by collections of testimonies which actually contained only Christological proof-texts. Further, the peculiar forms of quotation make clear that Luke is also concerned to indicate the human agency of the Word of God.

For Luke, Scripture is above all an oral, spoken word. This is clear from his forms of quotation. The Scripture is not privately studied or read in the community, but read aloud and publicly interpreted. Naturally, in Acts Luke can introduce his quotations and references with the formula, "it is written" (1:20; 7:42; 13:33; 15:15). But this often does not happen. On the other hand, Luke refers 22 times to what has been spoken, said, commanded, preached, etc.[17] He actually speaks— again, the only one in the New Testament—of "the mouth" (στόμα) of the prophets (3:18,21; 4:25; 13:27); of the voice (φωνή) of the prophets. The situation is different in the gospel where—due to dependence upon the tradition—Luke makes almost exclusive use of the expression γέγραπται, "it is written." For good reason, the Word of God in Scripture is for Luke a word which has been and shall be spoken, since the word is always a prophetic word, a word also heard weekly in the synagogue—except that members of the synagogue do not hear or accept it (13:27; 15:21; cf. 2 Cor. 3:12-18). The only parallel to this approach in the New Testament is the Epistle to the Hebrews. In Hebrews there are 23 quotations from the Old Testament. A quotation is never introduced with an "it is written" or the like.[18] The reference is always to what is "said" in Scripture (εἶπεν, λέγει etc.). And the one who speaks in the Scripture is God (Heb. 1:5ff.; 2:6,12; 4:3ff.; 5:5; etc.); in exceptional cases the Spirit[19] (3:7,10,15), or David (4:7).[20] These exceptions indicate that for Hebrews it is decisive that God speaks in Scripture, a concept also determinative for Luke in Acts. But above all God speaks through the prophets then and today, that is, in the church.

It is easy to state where Luke locates the center of Scripture: in its prophetic aspect. This is true of the prophetic as phenomenon as well as of its content. And Luke finds the prophetic not only in the so-called prophetic writings, but in all the writings of Scripture, in the writings of Moses as well as in the Psalms and the prophets.

In this connection, the summary scriptural references are especially instructive. They recapitulate what Scripture says (3:18,24; 10:43; 17:3; 18:28; 24:14; and 26:22ff., and in addition, Luke 24:26,46). In three of these summaries, "the Scriptures" are referred to (17:3; 18:28; and Luke 24:46). The remainder, by their more detailed definition of "the Scriptures," indicate that the term implies the prophetic element: Acts 3:18,24; 10:43; 24:14; 26:23; and Luke 24:25-27. In these passages, reference is made to the prophets.[21] Several times "the law" or "Moses" is added (26:22 and Luke 24:27); in Luke 24:44 also "the Psalms." But it is clear that for Luke the prophetic element is also present in the "law," in "Moses," and in "the Psalms."[22] The content of all these writings is everywhere the same—the suffering and the glory of Christ.[23]

The peculiar significance of the prophetic for Luke is also expressed in his statement that the prophets are present "from of old."[24] God speaks through the prophets who are from eternity (3:21). Luke can speak in this fashion only of the prophets in Scripture. This phrase is not to be construed as referring to time, but to that quite peculiar authority of the prophetic words, for the very reason that they are quite especially the words of God (on this concept, cf. the γνωστὰ ἀπ᾽ αἰῶνος ["known from of old"] appended in Acts 15:18 to the utterance of God in Amos 9:11f.). The prophetic word is from all eternity, because it is God's Word. Acts 15:7 and 21 are also similar to Acts 3:21: "In the early days" God chose Peter as missionary to the Gentiles, and "from early generations" Moses is preached in the synagogue. This gives expression to a peculiar authority, though for Luke the prophetic antedates the law. In this way Luke, and he alone in the New Testament, characterizes these "eternal" prophets as "holy" (Acts 3:21; cf. also Luke 1:70). Luke uses such designations to express in his own way what Paul describes in more apt theological fashion as the superiority of the promises over the law, as he does, for example, in Galatians 3.

Luke is not concerned with individual prophets. He cites only a very few of the writing prophets in the strictest sense of the word, that is, Joel, Amos, Isaiah, and Habakkuk. But he is definitely not concerned with a selection, with "testimonies," but speaks emphatically of "all the prophets'' (3:18,24; 10:43; Luke 24:27), or generally of "the prophets'' (3:21; 7:42,52; 13:27,40; 15:15; 26:22,27). At issue is the prophetic per se, the center of Scripture, that which in the genuine sense may be described as the Word of God.

David, father of the Messiah, is the prophet par excellence, the central figure in Scripture. For Luke, David stands where Moses stands for the rabbis. And where Luke is concerned, this is not at all to be evaluated as tradition. Rather, he reworks the tradition in quite independent fashion. David is especially important as the ancestor of Israel, as *the* patriarch, for only he is given this title in Luke.[25]

First of all, David is himself a writing prophet,[26] because he is recognized as author of the Psalms, which for this very reason are described as prophetic writings. That David is the prophetic author of the Psalms is stated indirectly in 1:16,[27] and directly in 2:25,34; 4:25;[28] as well as in Luke 20:42-44. It is also directly emphasized that David is a prophet (Acts 2:30).

Second, David is the one through whom the Spirit speaks. Three times Luke writes that the Spirit is the one who speaks in Scripture, and in two of these passages David is the subject: 1:16 and 4:25.[29] The latter passage also implies that the speech of the Spirit is that of God, for God speaks through the Spirit and thus also through David. Scripture as words of the prophets throughout history is simply the word of the Spirit.

This also explains the fact that despite the stress on the outpouring of the Spirit after Christ's exaltation (Acts 2:1ff.), the Spirit has always been present in the history of God's people, and did not first appear with Christ. In the course of Israel's history, the Jews have always resisted the Holy Spirit (7:51). Rather than listening to the words of the prophets, they have persecuted them (7:52). Still more, they have killed those who preached beforehand of the coming Messiah (7:53). Those who preached thus are simply the prophets. This is indicated especially in the summary statements (3:18,24; 10:43; 17:3; 18:28; 26:22ff.). In the context of Stephen's speech the discussion turns on the prophet Moses (7:20-40). Though not killed by his people, he was nonetheless disavowed (7:25,40). And, he was continually repudiated by the fact that the Jews did not keep the law (7:53)—also to be construed as an attitude resisting the Spirit.

When the Spirit was poured out on Pentecost, nothing radically new was added to the history of God's people. The Spirit was always present for the people, namely, as Scripture and as prophetic word in Scripture. What is new is that the Spirit no longer or not only speaks to the people through individual prophets,[30] but that now all within God's people become prophets. Through the outpouring of the Spirit Israel becomes the people of the Spirit (cf. 2:17-18, where the prophetic element in the Spirit's outpouring is accented,[31] particularly by the addition of the καὶ προφητεύσουσιν ["and shall prophesy"] in v. 18). What we encounter in the Christian community, also described as "sons of the prophets" (3:25), is a portion of the people which does not resist but rather receives the Spirit. The Spirit in Israel's history is for Luke the Spirit of prophecy and thus also of Scripture, as is evident from 7:51-53, but is made explicit in 1:16; 4:25; and 28:25.

Today, this Spirit is present in the community. Today there are also prophets (2:17; 13:1ff.; 21:10; etc.), but this does not apply to the synagogue. Of course, this does not mean that the Spirit is not present in the synagogue. The Scripture is of course read there (13:27). For Christians, the synagogue is also the house of Scripture.[32] When Christians appear in the synagogue and interpret the Scriptures, the Spirit is obviously also present, though many resist him. In the community, however, the Spirit is present in the Scripture as well as in the believers (Acts 4:25 and 31).[33]

Third, David is not only the prophet, but father of the Messiah, and as such the king of Israel (13:22; Luke 1:32). As such he plays a great role in Luke's interpretation of Scripture, and indeed, in a certain "negative" respect as well. Individual utterances of Scripture do not apply to David, and David himself is witness to this. The polemic-negative interpretation of Scripture used by Luke in this connection is also unique to the New Testament.

We turn first of all to Peter's speech in Acts 2:14-35. Ps. 16:8-11 is cited in 2:25-28 and interpreted in 2:29-31. David's death and grave are referred to in verse 29. "To this day" his tomb is to be found in Jerusalem (v. 29), indicating that David is not the risen Messiah. David cannot at all be the subject, since he already saw corruption (διαφθορά) and the *topos* of Messiah's resurrection deals precisely with corruption. This is what the Scripture says (vv. 27 and 31). Luke counters the notion that David is or will be the subject in this Psalm, and does so with quite rational and illuminating arguments, not with esoteric mysteries of scripture exposition.[34] The scripture words apply only to Christ, and to this David as prophet is the first witness.[35] For naturally, in this Psalm, David is speaking as a prophet (v. 30). He is not speaking of himself, but of his Son (vv. 30-31). David is here the prophetic king whose posterity in the resurrection is portrayed as the Messiah of Israel—and the resurrection is interpreted as the enthronement of this charismatic Messiah! Once more Luke emphasizes that these events do not have to do with David (v. 34). David did not ascend to heaven. Thus the text used, Ps. 110:1, does not deal with David at all, but with Christ. For this reason, David did not pour out the Spirit. Though David is the prophet par excellence, he is surpassed here by his Son. The hearers can see and hear for themselves that Israel's Messiah is presently active through the Spirit. Jesus' exaltation is confirmed by David himself, the embodiment of the people of God. The conclusion to the speech (v. 34) sets forth what is at issue for Luke: Jesus is the charismatic Messiah of Israel, the true descendant of David, the prophet-king. In a unique way, Israel's traditions are connected here with the charismatic experiences of primitive Christianity. For Luke, David is the central figure in Scripture and therefore also in history. The Scripture contains the authoritative words of David which consequently contain the truth of the Christian proclamation.

Paul's first speech in Acts 13:16-41 also indicates the special importance of David for Luke's understanding of Scripture. This speech of Paul has programmatic significance for Luke. It not only contains a survey of Israel's history (13:17-25), but also no less than four scripture quotations (vv. 33,34, and 35).[36] The latter in itself is striking, since there are scarcely any scripture quotations in Paul's speeches elsewhere in Acts. We meet them only in Chapter 13 and in 28:25-28. In general, Luke is content to state that everything Paul said agrees with Scripture, the "law and the prophets" (24:14; 26:22). Luke thus intends to show that Paul, whom he regards as a charismatic,[37] chiefly appears as interpreter of Scripture. Historical survey (13:17-25) and kerygma (13:26-31) are so interwoven that the kerygma is understood as a link in the history of Israel (cf. v. 23 with 26 and 27).

David's decisive role is expressed in a threefold way. First of all, Israel's history is narrated in such fashion that it is oriented to David as its culmination (v. 22). David is the elect one "after God's heart" (v. 22),[38] of whose posterity God has brought to Israel a Savior (v. 23). Second, the contemporary hearers, the Israel of today, are given the sure promises or words of David (v. 34). Third, there is the negative proof from Scripture in verses 35-37: David saw corruption (v. 36). Thus in Ps. 16:10, quoted in verse 35, the reference is to Jesus, not David. In isolation, Luke's exposition of Psalm 16 in verses 35-37 is unintelligible, but takes on clarity with the aid of Acts 2:25ff. Luke clearly assumes that the reader is already aware of the interpretation in Chapter 2. In this context the author of Psalm 16 is God (cf. the preambles to the scriptural quotations in vv. 32, 34, and 36).[39] Luke maintains that David "saw corruption." But it is added that David served God "in his own generation" (ἰδίᾳ γενεᾷ ὑπηρετήσας τῇ τοῦ θεοῦ βουλῇ, v. 36). There is thus a clear historical dimension to Luke's exposition of Scripture: David no longer serves God. He once did so; now his significance lies in his scriptural words,[40] in his promises which have already been fulfilled (13:37-39). The story of David and consequently of Israel is misunderstood when it is not interpreted as culminating in Jesus. And for Luke this culmination can be demonstrated not only with the aid of individual words of Scripture quoted, but also by means of historical survey combined with the kerygma.

For Luke, the prophetic is an essential mark of the messianic, and he intends it to be construed as scripture prophecy. For this very reason David is of such importance to him that he may in fact be described as the center of Scripture, since in David the prophetic and the messianic conjoin. Because the prophetic element is also united to Scripture here, it is all but inconceivable that the Jews did not recognize Jesus and acknowledge him: he is actually proclaimed through the reading of the prophets on the Sabbath (Acts 13:27). According to Luke's conception, the dwellers in Jerusalem and the leaders of the Jews have not understood the utterances of the prophets (13:27), though these are continually read aloud. Luke does not offer another explanation; he does not appeal to any theory of hardening, or to a uniquely enlightened, charismatic reading of Scriptures. In Acts 2 and 13 he argues in entirely "rational" fashion: if one knows the Scriptures and David's history, one should clearly understand Jesus' messianic significance.[41] That it is precisely in the synagogue and through the recitation and interpretation of Scripture on the Sabbath that Jesus' true significance is proclaimed—as in Acts 13:16-41—is also shown by the fact that some in Israel have understood the salvation in Jesus.

The negative-polemic use of Scripture in Acts 2 and 13 indicates what is at stake when Scriptures are not understood, that is, the messiahship of Jesus and the salvation of Israel. The Scriptures are in themselves clear, and there is no special exegesis. Luke finds no special mysteries in the wording; there is no "spiritual," mystical understanding, but only the literal. Nevertheless, Luke often states that the Scriptures must be opened[42] (Acts 17:3; Luke 24:32,45; cf. also Acts 8:31 and 35). Luke alone offers the concept of "opening" in conjunction with his scripture exposition. It appears as early as in Luke 24: The disciples do not understand or believe the Scriptures; Jesus himself must interpret them (διερμηνεύειν, vv. 25-27). The subject is that which is written of Jesus himself (τὰ περὶ ἑαυτοῦ, v. 27). Thus,

Jesus "opened" the Scriptures (διανοίγω). The expression is a bit different in Luke 24:45: He opened their minds (νοῦς) to understand the Scriptures. Again, he is subject, or that which is written of him (περί ἐμοῦ). We meet the same concept in Acts: the Ethiopian chamberlain cannot understand the Scriptures, that is, apart from instruction (8:31). The portion of Scripture to be explained is Isa. 53:7f., in Acts 8:32-33. But this portion is not even interpreted by Philip. For Luke it is also superfluous, for the only important question is, "About whom does the prophet say this, about himself or about someone else?" (8:34).[43] For this reason Luke can content himself with letting Philip preach about Jesus (v. 35), obviously with the aid of the Scriptures.

The question of the chamberlain in 8:34 is the central question in Luke's scripture exposition, as is clear also from Acts 2:25ff. and 13:34ff.: Does David write about himself or about someone else? Only as one allows the Scripture in the relevant passages to speak of Jesus, does an opening of Scriptures occur. The only instruction needed is simply this application to Jesus. The Scriptures speak clearly and unproblematically.[44] For this reason also there appears that emphatic "about me" in Luke 24, which does not mean that Scriptures speak of the Messiah, for that is obvious. The intention is rather to state that when combined with the Scriptures, the story of Jesus provides the opening.

It is often the case with Luke that an "external" event opens the Scriptures. In Acts 13:46-47, for example, we encounter a striking, double argument for the Gentile mission: (1) Because the Jews do not accept the message, Paul now turns to the Gentiles.[45] (2) It has been commanded in the Scriptures to preach on behalf of the Gentiles. These two reasons are actually only one. Because the Jews now reject the gospel, the time for Scripture has come—it summons to go to the Gentiles. We meet the same thought in Acts 15:15ff. James could understand the Gentile mission on the basis of the missionaries' experiences. But these experiences make clear how Scripture is to be understood. In this instance, the Scripture is Amos 9:11f. The missionary experiences open the Scripture. The external events "agree with" (συμφωνεῖν) the Scripture. Consequently, the scriptural is unequivocal and clear.

Acts 8 is not concerned with the suffering as such, which is not offensive or alien to the Jews, but rather with the one to whom the sufferings actually apply, in casu, the prophet himself or Jesus. Now, as is often inferred from Luke 24, Luke has no particular theory according to which Jesus himself must open the Scriptures if they are to be understood at all. Jesus is merely the first to interpret the Scriptures with reference to himself. This "opening" is done subsequently by others, as is described in Acts—indirectly by the interpretation of Scripture, thus, for example, in the Petrine speeches of Acts 2 and 3; and directly, for example, by Philip (8:35), or by Paul (17:3).

The significance of the prophetic as the center of Scripture is also expressed in Luke's portrait of Moses. For Luke, Moses is obviously the lawgiver. But he is above all a prophet or, if you will, a prophet of Christ.

The explanation of Deut. 18:15-20 in Acts 3:22-23 and 7:37 is particularly instructive here. Peter's speech in 3:12-26 illustrates how important the prophetic is for Luke. In the context of 3:17-26, it is stated that all the prophets have the sufferings of the Messiah as their actual theme (v. 18).

All the prophets, from Samuel and those who come afterwards, have proclaimed these days, the days of Christ (v. 24).

God has spoken through the prophets "from of old" (v. 21).

The Jews are the sons of the prophets (v. 25).

The latter idea is peculiar to Luke, insofar as it is precisely the prophetic which is set forth as Israel's chief characteristic. Indeed, in primitive Christianity the Jews are represented as murderers of the prophets or as sons of their murderers (Matt. 23:31; Luke 6:23; and Acts 7:52). But in Acts they are the sons of the prophets, which again throws light on the charismatic, primitive community. Luke is also original regarding what is essential for us in this connection: Moses himself is a prophet who also preached beforehand of Jesus as the coming prophet (3:22). Everyone who does not hearken to this prophet, Jesus, will be destroyed from the people (3:23). In this passage, use is made of Deut. 18:15-20, which also occurs in the New Testament only in Luke. In 3:22 Moses is plainly portrayed as a prophet.[46] He clearly belongs to the prophets named in verses 18 and 21. This means that Moses is the prophet ἀπ' αἰῶνος ("from of old," v. 21), so that all others take after him.[47]

The charismatic-prophetic quality in Moses is further detailed in Acts 7. In verse 37, Deut. 18:15 is quoted once more. But what is added here is that Moses is portrayed as a miracle worker (7:36). He performed "wonders and signs" in Egypt (τέρατα καὶ σημεῖα). Here, Moses' performance of miracles and his prophetic activity are also combined with the giving of the law (7:28), so that Moses represents that very combination of Spirit and law which is decisive for Luke's description of the primitive community.[48] In the context, the law is subordinated to the charismatic, and in the following verses (39ff.) it is expounded in such fashion that the intention of the law is construed as confession of God as God and in turning away from idols. When the law is not observed, idolatry results.[49]

The preaching of the prophet Moses and of the other prophets has exactly the same content. This is expressed more specifically in 26:22-23. Paul merely preached what the prophets and Moses predicted would come to pass—the death and resurrection of the Messiah, and, in addition, the mission. The entire Christian message can be found in Moses, so that he is to be understood as a witness to Christ. "The prophets and Moses" in this passage is not an expression for Scripture in general, as if Luke were actually speaking only of the sum of Scripture. Rather—just as he also has interest in the various writings—he is obviously thinking of specific passages in the Mosaic writings, without citing them. The exception is the text in Deut. 18:15-20, which in the context of Acts 7 and the Moses-sequence there (7:20-40), is also to be understood as a text on suffering.

Lastly, Luke comes to speak of Moses in Acts 28. In the final encounter between Jews and Christians in Acts, Paul attempts to convince the Jews about Jesus "from the law of Moses and from the prophets" (28:23).

Thus for Luke, Moses is primarily a prophet and witness to Christ. For this reason there was also a preaching of Christ in the synagogue, since Moses was recited aloud there. Now Luke is obviously aware that Moses is also a lawgiver or mediator. But in that case he speaks of the νόμος Μωυσέως ("law of Moses"); faith frees from everything from which one could not be freed by the law of Moses, νόμῳ Μωυσέως (13:38-39). This is scarcely more than a reminiscence of Pauline preaching. For Luke, Acts 15:1,20-21 is more important. The apostolic decree is a summary of the law, as is expressed of Gentiles living among Jews. When Moses is preached in the synagogue (15:21), obviously the law is in view. Acts 15:5 also belongs in this context. Further difficulties among Christians in connection with the law as code are referred to in Acts 6:11,13,14; 18:13,14; 21:20,24,28; 22:3; 23:4,29; and 25:8. All these passages indicate that for Luke the law is important as ritual law.[50] In the Gospel of Luke, the law is referred to both as ritual law (e.g., in 2:22-24,29; 5:15) and as moral law (in 10:26f.).

Moses, therefore, appears here both as prophet as well as giver of the law. "The law" is a prophetic word, and it is a ritual and moral code. For Luke, the struggles over the law are not merely an echo from the former time of the church.[51] Such indicates that for Luke Scripture actually has a center. This center is constructed in such fashion that Moses the lawgiver is subordinated to Moses the prophet. The prophetic words are spoken by God "from of old,"[52] while the law was added at a definite, later point in time (7:38,53). Luke has no theology of the law as does, say, Paul. And, there is no reference to the law's being without validity; at least, it applies to Israel without restriction. Nevertheless, the law remains inferior, that is, in relation to the prophetic element in the Scripture, and to which also Moses belongs. If the prophetic words are God's very own words, the *ipsissima vox*, the law appears through the disposition of angels (7:53).[53] Thus though Luke does not recognize the alternative, law or faith, but rather views both as one, the prophetic as the authentic in Scripture cannot be overlooked.

The Scripture is Israel's Scripture; it belongs to Israel. This point of view is so obvious to Luke that it is needless to explain it. He gives it repeated expression. But what Luke must set forth explicitly is that the church is Israel, and that the church precisely as Israel has title to the Scripture. For, according to Luke, without the Scripture there is no people of God.

The history that Scripture describes is that of Israel, and only that. The history of the Gentile nations is not a history of salvation, and for Luke a history of mankind does not exist. For this reason Scripture also does not furnish a history of the individual, but only of Israel, and a history of Gentiles insofar as they have had something to do with Israel.

This can be seen from the historical resumes in Acts 7:2-52 and 13:17-25. Israel's history is introduced without any explanation, and precisely because it is Israel's history and consequently also the history of the church. This can best be seen in the survey in 13:17-25, where everything climaxes in the promise of a Savior for Israel (v. 23). The kerygma is now a portion of this history, that is, the story of how the word of salvation was, as it were, vigorously rejected by Jerusalem and thus also fulfilled (vv. 26-31). The Jews—*in casu* those in the Diaspora—are the children of salvation, heirs of the history of Israel. The words of Scripture thus apply to them (cf. 13:32-44, and particularly v. 33). The entire speech is addressed to Israelites (13:16), and for Luke Israelites are Israelites in every sense of the term. "Israel" is not used as a name for the church of Jews and Gentiles; and in the Lukan writings Gentiles are never described by this term.

From time to time the addressees of Scripture are designated "the fathers."[54] The Scripture was not, or at least not merely, written "with reference to us." The word of the impenitent people's hardening in Isa. 6:1f., the last word from Scripture in Acts 28:25-27, is applied by Paul to the Jews at Rome. The word is spoken "by the Holy Spirit . . . through Isaiah the prophet," πρὸς τοὺς πατέρας ("to [your] fathers," v. 25). God has spoken to the fathers; the Scripture is thus a word to Israel. So Paul can also say that he serves the "God of our fathers," since he believes "everything laid down by the law or written in the prophets" (24:14). In the historical résumé in 7:3,37, it is stated that God spoke directly to the fathers: God directs the history of Israel.

It is not to be wondered at that the Jews not only are named "sons" of Israel, but especially "sons of the prophets," or "of the covenant" (3:25). These phrases mark them as heirs of the prophets and the Scripture. But now the "true" sons of the prophets have title to Scripture, which of course means those who are endowed with the Spirit (2:17ff.). The Spirit is poured out upon sons and daughters (2:17). It is in itself noteworthy that the outpouring of the Spirit is not legitimized by its mere occurrence, but that it is interpreted with the aid of Scripture and thus described as God's Spirit (2:16: τοῦτό ἐστιν τὸ εἰρημένον ["this is the meaning . . ."]). The Spirit is poured out only upon Israel, upon the Twelve (2:1-4). In his Pentecost speech, Peter turns only to Israel (2:14,22,30). Only later are also the Gentiles added (11:15-17). Consequently, Israel and the Spirit are combined, a feature which also identifies the community as Israel once the Spirit is poured out (2:17ff.).[55]

Not only the prophets and David belong to the center of Scripture, but Israel as well. The issue is salvation for Israel and thus also the rebuilding of "the dwelling of David" (15:16).[56] Luke does not state what is meant by "the dwelling of David,"[57] but within the framework of Acts as well as within the context which makes sharp distinction between the dwelling of David and τὰ ἔθνη ("the Gentiles"), it may be interpreted as the Jewish-Christian community.[58] For Luke, Israel's claim to Scripture is self-evident,[59] because Israel is the people of God and thus also of the Scripture. And what takes place in the Gentile mission (15:7-9, 12) is now shown to be in accord with Scripture and only in this fashion also legitimized. Because it is prophesied in Scripture that the salvation of the Gentiles will be linked to the destiny of Israel, so too the Gentile mission is proved to be the legitimate concern of the people of God. Finally, Luke expresses Israel's title to Scripture by interpreting the resurrection as enthronement on the seat of David (2:30-31).

The impenitent Jews have forfeited this claim, for they fulfill the Scriptures (ἐπλήρωσαν and ἐτέλεσαν) by crucifying and burying Jesus (13:27-29). Within the New Testament this too is a unique interpretation of scripture fulfillment (but cf. Rom. 13:8).

Finally, the place of the Scripture is the synagogue, so that Scripture has its "home" in the house of Israel. Scripture does not exist for private reading. The only exception to this is the Ethiopian chamberlain (8:22ff.). Otherwise it is said that Scripture belongs to recitation and exposition in the synagogal worship of God as expressed in the many synagogue scenes (9:20; 13:5,14,27; 14:1; 17:1-2,10f.,17; 18:4, 19,20; and 19:8).[60] We may not interpret these scenes as a tactical pragmatism on the part of Paul. It is a tragedy that the people of God rejects the Messiah. And it does not help to hear the utterances of the prophets (13:7), for what is decisive is to understand that their utterances speak of Jesus. When the Jews do not recognize Jesus, they also do not understand the prophets (13:27).

When Paul visits the synagogue in Thessalonica (17:1-4), the reason does not lie in his missionary activity, but in Jewish faith and Paul's piety, κατὰ δὲ τὸ εἰωθὸς τῷ Παύλῳ ("according to Paul's custom"; cf. Luke 4:16). Paul is at home in the synagogue because the Scripture is recited there. In 17:11 also it is assumed that Israel's Scripture is involved; the church leads the Jews toward the Scripture. On the basis of Scripture, εἰ ἔχοι ταῦτα οὕτως ("if these things were so"; 17:11-12), the Jews come to faith. In Acts the Christians do not abandon the synagogue but are thrust out.[61]

It is chiefly the references to Scripture in the summaries that tell us of the content of that center (3:18; 10:43; 17:3; 18:28; 26:22-23; Luke 24:26,46). The summaries indicate that the subject is first of all the παθεῖν τοῦ Χριστοῦ, the suffering and death of the Messiah (3:18; 17:3; 26:22; Luke 24:26,46).[62] The utterances are fairly consonant. The subject is not suffering in itself. The question is whether Scripture gives witness that it was the Messiah who had to suffer and die according to the Scriptures. The identity of the suffering one is important (Acts 8:34). The question is whether the prophet himself is the suffering one, thus whether the suffering already belongs to history. Only "someone else" (v. 34) is Messiah, a feature which is also given the accent in 3:18; 17:3; 26:22; Luke 24:26 and 46. Witness to the towering significance of the Messiah's suffering death as furnishing content to the center of Scripture appears also in 13:29: the Jews have fulfilled (ἐτέλεσαν) all (πάντα) that was written of Jesus. The "all" in this passage, as is indicated in what follows, means simply suffering and death. Not only the summaries in general but also individual passages indicate suffering as the mark of the Messiah's identity (4:25; 5:30; 8:32).[63]

In the second place, the summaries deal with the resurrection, the exaltation of this very suffering Messiah! This aspect is variously formulated in the summaries (17:3; 26:22-23; Luke 24:24,46). Again, the problem of witnessing to the resurrection as such is clearly not the issue. Luke knows that the Jews believe in it—or at least most Jews (23:6ff.). At stake again is the question, "Who is the resurrected One?" Luke is most concerned to show that it is not David but his descendant, the Messiah-Jesus (2:25ff.; 13:33ff.).[64] The polemical account indicates that Luke is intent on showing that the story of Jesus is in harmony with Scripture; more, that the Scripture applies only to Jesus. It is emphasized that this Messiah witnessed to in Scripture can only be Jesus. This is stated directly in the summaries (17:3; 18:28), as well as indirectly (3:18,21; 10:42,43; 26:22,23; Luke 24:16,27; 24:44,46). Acts 24:14 indicates that the resurrection can also be understood as that "all" in Scripture.[65] Paul believes everything that the Law and prophets say, which is explained in more detail in verse 15—the resurrection of the dead.

It is stressed with especial clarity in 3:18ff. and 13:3ff. that it is David's son who must die and rise. What the death and resurrection really mean—the critical factor for Paul—retreats for Luke behind the fact *that* it has to do with the son of David.

For Luke, not only the death and resurrection of the Messiah are witnessed to in Scripture, but an entire series of phenomena such as the death of Judas and the subsequent choice of an apostle (1:20ff.); the outpouring of the Spirit (2:17ff.); the parousia (3:21); idolatry in the wilderness period (7:42-43); God and the temple (7:49-50); mission (13:47); the regulations of the Law (23:5); Israel's hardening (26:26); etc. Here too the Lukan πᾶς ("everything") probably applies—all that occurs in the community according to God's will is according to Scripture. Other topics such as death and resurrection do not have the same significance, as is indicated by the fact that they are not referred to in the summaries. Excepting the death and resurrection, they mention only the forgiveness of sins (10:43; Luke 24:45) and the mission (26:22; Luke 24:46). The first is construed as the result of the death and resurrection, the second as an interpretation of the resurrection. This can be seen from the fact that Acts 26:22 mentions the mission in place of the resurrection. And in addition, utterances concerning the opening of Scripture[66] are linked only to the theme of Jesus' suffering and resurrection (Acts 17:3; 8:31ff.; 18:28; Luke 24:26-27,32,45ff.). Other scripture references apparently do not require an ''opening''—which again points unequivocally to the center. This makes clear that the center of Scripture is also the center of the Christian message.

8

The Circumcised Messiah[1]

Translated by Roy A. Harrisville

In Chapters 1–2 of Luke's gospel, a prehistory tinted with legend, there is an historical account from Jesus' childhood that is entirely above suspicion: "And at the end of eight days, when he was circumcised, he was called Jesus, the name given by the angel before he was conceived in the womb" (Luke 2:21 RSV). Only Luke mentions this event. But this indisputable statement has caused exegetes a certain embarrassment—that is, if they concern themselves at all with this account. The historicity of the event as such is naturally not in question; the issue is rather that of explaining how it is that Luke and only he among the gospel authors tells of Jesus' circumcision. We do not expect that Luke intends to emphasize that Jesus is the circumcised Messiah.

The proposal is that we regard Luke 2:21 as an interpolation,[2] or that Luke makes such use of narrative technique as to indicate that he actually intends to state that the naming, not the circumcision, took place, and further, that the sentence structure gives evidence of this.[3] This is scarcely convincing, for if Luke wanted to state that Jesus was not circumcised, it would only be natural expressly to say so. Instead, we encounter a statement which immediately gives the impression that Jesus was actually circumcised. Most of the exegetes, however, have another explanation. They state that in Luke 2:21 the accent is on the giving of the name.[4] But we cannot avoid the problem even in this way. For, wherever the accent, mention of the circumcision is unmistakable. It is particularly puzzling that Luke, the supposed universalistically-minded Gentile Christian—he is still interpreted in this fashion—should tell of a circumcised Messiah. Of course, we could say that Jesus' circumcision is included here as a matter of course without significance,[5] or that verse 21 serves only to report the occasion.[6] This would make sense under certain conditions, if, for example, the statement derives from a period in which there were no Gentile Christians in the church. But elsewhere as well Luke reports disputes and conflicts in the church, and these deal precisely with circumcision. Whether Luke 2:21 is to be regarded as Luke's own, or as a tradition appropriated by him, in any event it was written down in a time when circumcision was the object of disputes in the church. For this reason, the report in Luke 2:21 had to raise tempers. We should also keep in mind that for a long time circumcision remained a problem in the church, that is, even after the recognition of the Gentile mission free of circumcision. This is attested to by the phenomenon of Jewish Christianity as such. In this connection, it is sufficient to refer to Justin's *Dialog with Trypho*.[7]

Further, the problem of Luke 2:21 cannot be solved by asserting that the passage is a Jewish-Christian appendix to the gospel. And the assumption that the material in the prehistory derives from Baptist sects and the like does not aid us further,[8] but merely gives rise to new and scarcely solvable problems. It may be that at present it is just this prehistory of Luke in Chapters 1 and 2 which represents the chief problem in Lukan exegesis.[9] How can the Gentile-Christian universalist—provided Luke is such—offer a portion of Jewish Christianity in such shape as an introduction to his work? Or, if the author of the third gospel is not himself responsible for Chapters 1 and 2, how is it possible to regard these two chapters as an appropriate introduction to the gospel? From whatever perspective, the author of Luke's gospel and of Acts must be interpreted differently than is usual in present-day research.

From the viewpoint of language and style,[10] Luke 2:21 betrays Lukan origin. And, it is true of the prehistory as a whole that Luke gave it his own stamp, provided he appropriated it *en bloc*, in which case he reworked the material and consciously and deliberately appropriated it. A series of exegetes is not persuaded that the mention of circumcision in Luke 2:21 is due to accident.[11] But even in this case it is not clear why Luke assigns a certain significance particularly to the circumcision of Jesus.[12] And, to my knowledge, no one has attempted to see or interpret Luke 2:21 within the framework of Luke's understanding of circumcision, that is, as is often given expression in Acts (Acts 7:8 [51]; 10:45; 11:2; 15:1,5; 16:3; 21:21).

It is not only present-day exegetes who have had difficulties with Luke 2:21, as the transmission of the text clearly indicates.[13] In the edition of Aland-Nestle, the text of this verse makes a poor showing from a linguistic point of view—καὶ ὅτε ἐπλήσθησαν ἡμέραι ὀκτὼ τοῦ περιτεμεῖν αὐτὸν καὶ ἐκλήθη τὸ ὄνομα αὐτοῦ Ἰησοῦς. The καὶ ("and") which precedes the ἐκλήθη ("was called") is grammatically troublesome. The sentence contains a temporal subordinate clause connected with a main clause by way of parataxis, or, the genitive of an infinitive used as noun in parataxis with a finite verb.[14] A succession of textual witnesses has not reproduced the intrusive καὶ— Cantabrigiensis, the chief Western witness; a few minuscule manuscripts;[15] several Old Latin manuscripts,[16] and also Koridethi and the Peshitta. This omission not only yields a clause which is grammatically correct, but also solves the theological problem of the text in approximately the fashion of most modern exegetes: the giving of the name replaces the circumcision.[17] When we recall the anti-Jewish character of Cantabrigiensis,[18] we scarcely err in the assumption that a theological correction is involved. The Sinaitic Syriac text is unobjectionably clear, since we find in it a construction with two finite verbs: ". . . he was circumcised, and he was called Jesus."[19] A few locate the original version here.[20] But the text is too complete and lucid to permit us to regard it as original. In addition, it has another, clearly secondary, element.[21] The version in Nestle–Aland is certainly the most original. Internal as well as external criteria speak for it. The intrusive and clumsy καὶ may be a Semitism, which perhaps suggests that Luke wishes to make two statements of equal weight—regarding circumcision and the giving of the name. Strictly speaking, it is not expressly stated that the circumcision took place, though it is difficult to avoid this impression. But the way to a proper interpretation of Luke 2:21 is made clear by the fact that the position of the verse is fixed by the context, and that the circumcision here is interpreted within the framework of other Lukan utterances regarding circumcision.

The tendency to play down or erase the statements concerning Jesus' circumcision is quite understandable. The New Testament apocryphal writings do not mention his circumcision. But in ancient church literature we encounter statements which indicate the significance of Jesus' circumcision for primitive Christianity. Epiphanius remarks that Ebionites[22] and Cerinthians[23] refer to Matthew 10:25 and summon their hearers: περιετμήθη γὰρ, φησὶν, ὁ Χριστός, καὶ σὺ περιτμήθητι ("For Christ was circumcised, it says, and you [sing.] should be circumcised").[24]

For Jewish-Christian sects, Jesus' circumcision proves that Christians are obliged to undergo circumcision and live according to the law.[25] Justin confirms this in his *Dialog with Trypho*. His Jewish partner in the *Dialog,* who also emerges as a kind of advocate for Jewish Christianity,[26] argues against Justin's understanding of the law by appeal to Jesus' circumcision.[27] At this point, Justin clearly runs into difficulty, because he cannot deny Jesus' circumcision.[28] Thus also his reply to Trypho is unsatisfactory.[29] Trypho uses Jesus' circumcision not only to show that Christians are obligated to the law, but he also asserts that instead of the virgin birth the true sign of Jesus' messiahship should rather be his circumcision and obedience to the law.[30] Consequently, Jesus' circumcision is not only representative of life according to the law, but has messianic significance.

For Luke as well this is decisive, and we turn to him again. In the prehistory, the perspective as a whole is restricted to Israel,[31] and by way of reference to the fulfillment of the promises to the one people of God (1:14,16,32,34,54,65,68,69,71-74; 2:25,32,34,38). Mention of Jesus' circumcision fits well with this. But Luke 2:21 appears in the narrower context of 2:21-39, where reference is made to a series of legal obligations—purification, presentation in the temple, sacrifice (vv. 22-24). Following the section on the prophetic utterances about Jesus in the temple at Jerusalem (vv. 25 and 28), Luke 2:21-39 is summed up in verse 39: καὶ ὡς ἐτέλεσαν πάντα τὰ κατὰ τὸν νόμον κυρίου ("And when they had performed everything according to the law of the Lord").[32]

Of chief concern in the Lukan prehistory is the fulfillment of the law.[33] Where the Messiah of Israel appears, there the law is satisfied.[34] Within the framework of 2:21-39, it would be strange indeed if mention of the circumcision signified a more or less accidental side issue. We arrive at a positive solution to this problem, as well as to that of the significance of circumcision in this passage, only when we include Luke's other utterances concerning circumcision. We need only mention here that the ceremonial aspect of the law—and thus also circumcision—is decisive for Luke's understanding of the law.[35]

Only with the reception of Gentiles into the community did circumcision become a problem in primitive Christianity. What is at issue is a typical problem of mission. This can be seen in the only New Testament author besides Luke who speaks of circumcision as a problem, that is, Paul.[36] Luke also perceives circumcision as a problem of mission, as is clear from his description of the apostolic council in Acts

15:1ff. It is further recognized as such in the discussion of the conversion of the first Gentile in Acts 10:45 and 11:2. The passages indicate quite clearly Luke's own attitude toward the question of
circumcision and obedience to the law: the Gentiles are saved as Gentiles, and without circumcision;[37] as Gentiles they share in the promises
of the people of God.

But this renders Luke 2:21 even more enigmatic. What purpose shall
it serve to remind the readers, especially where Jewish Christians are
involved, that Jesus was circumcised? But then Luke makes other
statements regarding circumcision, which are not determined by the
Gentile mission, but rather by the situation of Jewish Christians following the reception of Gentiles into the church. Precisely these statements make clear the significance of Luke 2:21 and its continuity within
the history of salvation in Chapters 1 and 2. In Acts 7:8, the covenant
with Abraham[38] is simply named the "covenant of circumcision"
(διαθήκη περιτομῆς). It is neither deprecated nor construed as provisional or surpassed. The linkage, Abraham-covenant-circumcision,
appears in the context as an expression for the promises of salvation
to Abraham and the people (vv. 6-7 and 17).[39] The subject is Israel's
deliverance from Egypt and the possibility of serving God unhindered.
For Luke, Abraham is the recipient of the saving promise (Luke 1:55;
1:72-73; 3:8; 13:16; 19:9; Acts 3:25; 7:2ff.; 7:17; 13:26,33). Actually,
Abraham is neither an individual entity nor a single person. His faith,
his piety, his obedience, and the like are not decisive. He is not the
type or model of the believer, but the personification of Israel, that is,
of the people to whom God has promised salvation (cf. the connection
between Israel and Abraham in Luke 1:54-55). Only four times does
Luke speak of the covenant (the διαθήκη). In three passages, the
covenant with Abraham is referred to expressly as the "covenant of
circumcision" (Luke 1:72). In these, the Jews are "children of the
covenant." The case is similar with the institution of the Lord's Supper
in Luke 22:19ff.—assuming that the longer text is original. The "new
covenant" is not new in the sense that it abrogates or is contrary to
an old or earlier covenant. What is involved is rather a renewal of the
covenant, and this renewal applies to Israel. Verses 19 and 20 must
be understood in this way, not merely because of their connection with
other statements concerning the covenant. Luke 22:29-30 in particular
forces us to this view.[40] According to Acts 7:8, circumcision is the
sign of the "covenant of promise," and it shows that salvation applies
to Israel as God's people. For this reason also the patriarchs were
circumcised (Acts 7:8b).

From this passage we recognize the link between Jesus' circumcision (Luke 2:21) and the promise to Israel which plays a decisive role in the prehistory of Luke's gospel. The connection between the statements regarding Abraham in Acts 7:8 and those in Luke 1:72f.[41] is unequivocal. The latter passage states that through the coming Messiah God will show mercy to the fathers of Israel and will remember his holy covenant, that is, the oath which he swore to Abraham concerning his freedom and right to serve God. The subject here is no doubt ''the covenant of circumcision,'' and it is clear that this covenant with its promises to Abraham is finally fulfilled through Jesus.

But we encounter difficulty when we use Acts 7:8 to interpret Luke 2:21. Does Acts 7 derive from Luke? If we must reply in the negative, new problems emerge. Why did Luke take up Acts 7 into his work, if he was not in agreement with it? I do not see that Acts 7 should be non-Lukan, or that it offers another theological view than that which we find elsewhere in Luke-Acts.[42] Luke also mentions circumcision in Acts 21:21, where there is no question of our having to do with Luke himself.

It is true also of Acts 21 that the issue is not the problematic of mission, that is, the reception of Gentiles into the church. In Acts 21:21, Paul is accused of teaching all the Jews in the Diaspora that they should not circumcise their children and no longer live according to the Law of Moses. This is depicted as apostasy from Moses (ἀποστασίαν ἀπὸ Μωυσέως). Luke is concerned to show that it cannot be maintained with any ounce of justification that Paul speaks against circumcision. On the contrary, Paul always fought for the law and circumcision.[43] Luke prepared for this assertion as early as in Acts 16:3 by the circumcision of Timothy. The affair of circumcision is so decisive for Luke that he describes it as the chief factor in the final agreement between Paul and the Jerusalem community in Acts 21. He asserts that where Jewish Christians are involved, Paul makes a plea for circumcision. As a result, the statement regarding Paul's struggle on behalf of circumcision is to some degree the obverse side of the coin of the council's resolution, namely, that circumcision is not necessary for Gentile Christians (Acts 15:1ff.). What follows in Acts 21:22ff. indicates that Paul viewed circumcision and the law as unconditionally necessary for Jewish Christians, and this because circumcision is the sign of the promise and the covenant. Not only Israel, but also the church claims title to the covenant and the promise. If Paul had wished to abolish circumcision and the promise, then all promise and title to the name *Israel* would have been lost to the church as well. Jesus himself was circumcised; he is the fulfiller of the covenant with Abraham. Thus for Luke, Paul could not possibly speak against circumcision.

It is important to Luke that Paul held fast to circumcision. It is no less important that Jesus himself was circumcised. Acts 7:8 and 21:21 indicate how decisive circumcision was for Luke. He does not write his Acts of the Apostles in order to show that the Gentiles need no circumcision. This matter had already been settled long since (Acts 15:1ff.). But the situation of Jewish Christians in this very situation is of concern. In the church, Jewish Christians represent the people of God, that is, the only people of God in existence. The Gentiles have received a share in the promises of this people of God. Luke states to the point of tedium that the promises belong to Israel (Luke 1:32-33,51-54,55,72-73; 13:16; 19:9; 22:29-30; Acts 2:22f., 36,39; 3:13ff.,24ff.; 4:10ff.,27; 5:30ff.; 10:26; 13:17ff.,32-33; etc.). The promises belong together with the "covenant of circumcision."

Jesus was circumcised after eight days. Within the framework of the prehistory this indicates that for Luke Jesus is the true bearer of the promises to Israel. He bears the "sign" of Israel's identity. So it is also important to Luke that we recognize that Jesus never preached or acted against the law of Moses (on this topic, cf. the summary statement in Acts 6:14).[44] Jesus spells salvation for Israel (and salvation also for the Gentiles via Israel). Jesus is Israel's Messiah also because he was circumcised. In the view of an early Christian or Jewish Christian, an uncircumcised Messiah is a self-contradiction. It is only long after Gentile Christians have gained a majority in the church and Jewish Christians feel threatened that the time is ripe for speaking of Jesus' circumcision. The discussion belongs to a situation in which the significance of circumcision is contested. Luke 2:21 fits smoothly with that interpretation which construes Luke 1 and 2 as prolegomena to the Lukan dual work. Jesus is the Jewish Messiah. He shall sit upon the throne of David and reign forever over the house of Jacob (Luke 1:32).[45] This prophetic promise will be completely fulfilled at the resurrection (Acts 2:30), and later at the parousia (Acts 3:21ff.). The scenery of the prehistory consists of David's house; David's city, Jerusalem; the temple; the law of Moses; etc. For Luke, Χριστός (Christ) is not a name, but a title.[46] Jesus' Messiahship is not determined by his suffering and death. Rather, despite his suffering and death Jesus is the Messiah, as given paradigmatic expression in Luke 24:21-27.[47] Because of his resurrection Jesus is that Messiah who has taken his seat on David's throne (cf. Luke 1:32f. and Acts 2:30ff.).

The promises to Israel are fulfilled in the only Israel of which Luke is aware, the Jewish Christians. Then, because the church is the direct continuation of the history of God's people, and itself the bearer of the promises, Luke must indicate that the Messiah Jesus is the genuine and true Messiah. Among other things, this is evidenced by the fact that he was circumcised according to the law. Luke 2:21 is scarcely a happenstance; it is not a "subordinate clause." Together with others, this passage indicates that the legitimacy and right of Jesus to speak and act in the name of the God of Israel for salvation on behalf of the people and the nations is beyond doubt.

9

The Daughters of Abraham: Women in Acts

Translated by Roy A. Harrisville

Luke is an especial friend of women. This can be seen in almost all commentaries on his gospel, and for the most part is simply accepted as fact without further discussion or explanation.[1] It is also linked to Luke's oft-mentioned preference for the poor and little people,[2] or on occasion to his so-called universalism.[3] But it is difficult to explain Luke's preference for women, and thus why he is their friend. It has been correctly stated that a certain embarrassment among expositors can be detected here.[4] The embarrassment has not lessened in most recent times, due to a fully justified struggle on behalf of woman's equality that has induced expositors to believe they can find an almost "modern" conception of woman's position in portions of the New Testament. In such instances appeal is made chiefly to Luke.[5] But as usual it is the one writing of Luke which is involved, that is, the gospel. Acts comes much less into view. And when we take more careful note, the women in Acts noticeably retreat, not only in comparison with the gospel, but in general. What is strange in this connection is the relation between the gospel and Acts, since the gospel usually lays the basis for Acts, that is yields the decisive impulses and presuppositions for Christology, soteriology, and ecclesiology as they are interpreted in Acts. How does it happen that in Acts the women are definitely overshadowed as compared with the gospel[6]—if such is the case?[7] And what is it that interests or moves Luke when he gives preference to

the woman in the gospel? Is it a general interest in woman as such? I
think not. The women in Luke's writings are important because they
are the daughters of Abraham. They are members of the people of
God, a people of such importance in Luke's ecclesiology because it
was to this very people that the promises of God were given. Only as
such are woman important to Luke.

We may limit ourselves here to a quite brief description of this theme
in the gospel. As is well known, in comparison with Matthew and
Mark, Luke furnishes many narratives in which women play a deciding
role. In the prehistory, women such as Mary, Elizabeth, and Anna are
almost the principal actors (Mary in Luke 1:26-38,46-56; 2:1-24,41-
52; Elizabeth in 1:39-45,57-60; Anna in 2:36-38). The Lukan special
material offers a series of narratives about women which also give
shape to the gospel's composition[8]—the narratives of Zechariah and
Mary (1:11f.,27-29,46-47); Simeon and Anna (2:25,36); the widow
and the father (7:12; 8:41); the lawyer and the sisters (10:25-37,38-
42); the importunate man and the importunate widow (11:5-7; 18:1-
8); the man and the woman healed on the Sabbath (13:10-17; 14:1-6);
the daughter and the son of Abraham (13:16; 19:9); the shepherd and
the woman (15:3-7,8-10), and the male and female witnesses (8:1,2f.;
22:22,24; in addition, cf. also 11:27; 15:8ff.; 21:1f.; 23:27ff.,49; and
24:10). Luke 8:1-3 is of quite special importance because it presents
us with the followers of Jesus. The Twelve enjoy first rank (cf. v. 1).
In addition, there is an entire succession of women who also accompany
Jesus on his journey. Three of the women are mentioned by name (vv.
2-3), but in addition there are "many others" (ἕτεραι πολλαί, v.
3).Thus among Jesus' followers are a few men and many women. Luke
does not state that this causes any great stir, since it is unusual and
unheard of that a teacher in Israel takes female disciples with him.[9]
And, are the women here actually understood to be disciples?[10] What
all these women do is of course stated in verse 3—they serve Jesus
(διηκόνουν) with their means. It is uncertain whether this statement
applies to all mentioned. Not all can be regarded as people of means.
It is also uncertain whether, as a few commentators suppose, the women
are active as preachers of the gospel after the fashion of the Twelve.[11]
Luke 8:1-3 is important for us, not as the expression of a particularly
liberal attitude on the part of Jesus who in quite unheard of fashion
includes women among his pupils. Rather, the passage is a totally
Lukan, redactional note,[12] which gives us a key to Luke's understanding
of women in the community and thus prepares for Acts.[13] I give no
credence to the current and scarcely disputed assertion that in Luke

8:1-3 Luke prepares for women as witnesses to the resurrection (24:1-12,22).[14] The women do not at all appear as such; only the Twelve are fit for that (Acts 1:2ff., 15-16). The women do not lack the prerequisites (Acts 1:21-22)—they walked with Jesus and had seen the empty grave (8:2-3; 24:1ff.). But they lack what is decisive for Luke respecting the apostolate—not that they are not men, but that they are not Jewish men. The Twelve are "the twelve on the thrones" of the twelve-tribe nation (Luke 22:30).[15] Obviously, no women may be seated there, for the patriarchs were of course all Israelite males. In 8:2-3, Luke intends to describe the appearance of the community of Jesus, and women's significance in it. But even in the life of Jesus as Luke portrays it in his gospel, women retreat from the public eye. They are not sent out, as are the Twelve or the seventy-two (Luke 9:1ff.; 10:1ff.). On the mount, Peter, James, and John are present (Luke 9:28ff.), and it is these three who constitute the inner circle about Jesus (5:1ff.; 9:54; 22:8ff.). At the Lord's Supper, only the apostles are present (22:15ff.). And the women do not belong to the "disciples" (cf. 22:11 and 39ff.).

Luke is naturally aware of the decisive role that women play in the earliest communities, especially in those outside Jerusalem, and now attempts to give this theological explanation. What he says in Luke 13:16 is most significant; the woman healed here is a daughter of Abraham. In precisely this way Luke justifies Jesus' healing of the woman.[16] What is decisive is not that she is a woman who suffers, but that she is an Israelite, a Jewess, one of the elect people who is suffering. According to Luke, salvation belongs first and above all to Israel (e.g., Acts 2:39; 3:25; 13:47; 15:16; etc., and in the prehistory, Luke 1:16-17,32-33,54-55,68ff.; 2:10f.; and 25:30-32,38). In the New Testament, the rare title, "daughter of Abraham,"[17] occurs only in Luke,[18] as is true also of the title, "son of Abraham" (Luke 19:9). Such a designation is unknown in the literature from this period, and attested to at a much later time than that of Luke.[19] I suspect that Luke himself coined the title, and by it intends to show the significance of women in the community. A woman who is infirm provides the starting point in Luke 13, and we note that the women in Luke 8:1-3 are also such as have been healed of various illnesses and weaknesses. In this way at least they give witness to Jesus' miracles.

The women in Luke's gospel are all Israelites, Jewesses. This is already evident from the fact that Luke describes Jesus as geographically and ethnically active only within the borders of Israel.[20] His presence at Gerasa is an exception (Luke 8:26-39), but there nothing is reported of women. Whether Luke intentionally omits the Gentile woman in Matthew 15:21-28 and Mark 7:24-30 cannot be said with certainty.[21] Thus, geographically speaking, where women are involved, only Jewesses appear in Luke's gospel. The exception is the widow of Zarephath in Luke 4:25f., who is nevertheless supposed to serve as warning to Israel from the Old Testament (1 Kings 17:1ff.). In many instances, accent is placed on the women as Israelites, thus in the case of Mary who all but personifies Israel (Luke 1:30-33,51-55; 2:10-11). Salvation applies to Israel, quite particularly to the poor, oppressed Israel, and expressly to Abraham and his posterity (Luke 1:55). It thus also applies to Elizabeth (Luke 1:5ff.) and to Anna (2:36ff.). In these instances Jewish descent as well as Jewish concern are noted. What is decisive is not that these persons are women but that they are Jewesses. It is evident from Luke 8:2-3 that the women who follow Jesus are Israelites. This is also true of the woman in Luke 13:10-17, explicitly described as such in verse 16. This is true also of the women on Jesus' way to the cross, of the daughters of Jerusalem (23:27f.). Elsewhere it is not expressly stated because it is superfluous, and the context continually makes clear that the women are all Jewesses, thus in Luke 7:11ff.; 10:38ff.; 15:8-10; and 18:1-8.

In itself, it is not strange that the women here are all Jewesses. Nor does this feature derive merely from Luke's conviction that Jesus is the Messiah of Israel, the people of salvation.[22] There is no "Messiah of the nations." Non-Jews must be incorporated into Israel in order to receive a share in salvation.[23] But in any case, Jesus' activity occurs on Jewish soil. For this reason the women in the other Gospels as well are predominantly Jewesses, and special mention is made whenever a Gentile woman appears (Mark 7:24-30; Matt. 15:21-28; John 4; etc.). But Luke accents what is Jewish. If this is self-evident in the gospel, the situation is quite different in Acts. For here the topic is the Christian community from Jerusalem to Rome. So it is striking here too that the women mentioned in Acts are chiefly Jewesses. In a few instances, so-called God-fearing women appear, that is, women already connected with the synagogue, and who for this reason are no doubt de facto regarded as Jewesses, which of course cannot be determined with certainty. What is certain, however, is that these God-fearing women appear as Jewesses from the religious point of view; they thus have a clear connection with Israel. Remarkably enough, "pure" Gentile women are absent, that is, women without any relation to the people of God, provided they are not to be reckoned among those in the reports of conversions in Acts 11:21,24 and 18:8. In any event, when women are expressly named in such reports, they are Jewesses and God-fearers.

The female members of the primitive community in Jerusalem are Jewish (Acts 1:14). In 5:14, the great majority of women converted are also Jews, since the conversion takes place in Jerusalem and the first Gentile does not appear till Acts 10. The women in the communities in Judea and Damascus are also Jewesses (8:3 and 9:2). Paul arrests men as well as women (cf. also Acts 22:4)—which in itself indicates the significance of women. Further, the women at Philippi are Jewesses (Acts 16:13f.), provided they do not belong to the God-fearers, which cannot be said with certainty. But such is unlikely, since Paul knows of no community which does not consist essentially of Jews. The four prophesying daughters of Philip as well as Priscilla are also Jewesses (21:8 and 18:2,26). There are Jewish widows in the communities (Acts 6:1; 9:39-41). Tabitha may also be a Jewess (Acts 9:36ff.). Her name is Jewish, and she is described in a Jewish formula of her activity, πλήρης ἔργων ἀγαθῶν καὶ ἐλεημοσυνῶν ("full of good works and acts of charity").[24] In addition, there are "God-fearing" women in Acts 17:4,10ff. The fact that Samaritan women are also baptized (Acts 8:12; cf. 8:3) is no exception, since for Luke Samaritans are also Jews, the "lost sheep," so to speak, "of the house of Israel."[25]

According to Luke, then, the women in the church are almost only Jewesses, daughters of Abraham. And it is clear that they comprise a considerable group within the community.[26] This is also stated in Luke's reports concerning mass conversions. In a few of these, there is direct or indirect reference only to men; thus in 2:41; 4:4; 6:1; and 7; in others, only to "many," "a great company," and the like (cf. 9:42; 17:12; 14:1). But in others there is also emphatic reference to women (5:14 and 17:12).[27] In addition, Acts 8:12; 9:2; and 16:13f. record that the women were a significant group. But as stated, they are chiefly devout Jewesses, which for Luke naturally coheres with the fact that the church is the restored Israel. It is obvious to Luke that others besides Jews also belong to the church, but he is less interested in them.

The question, however, concerns the significance of women in the church, the role which they actually play. After reading the gospel we are struck by the fact that in Acts women retreat to the background. Those narratives of women in the gospel of Luke which give shape to its composition are totally lacking in Acts. We can almost abstract the women from Acts without detecting any alteration in the character of the work. The women obviously make up the community, but do not exercise any leading function. As early as in Acts 1:14, "the women" whom we recognize from Luke 8:2-3; 23:55; and 24:1ff., together with the mother of Jesus and the Twelve, constitute the nascent community. The conversion reports noted above also witness to women in the community and as community. This is also true of the statement that in Judea, Damascus, and Samaria, Paul arrested and deported men and women (8:3; 9:2), which cannot be easily harmonized with the fact that the women retreat to the background. The same is true of the Samaritan women in Acts 8:12. In addition, the Jewish "community" in Philippi apparently consists only of women, which means that Paul is speaking exclusively to women at the place of prayer or in the synagogue (this is puzzling; cf. Acts 16:13).

The mention of many women, however, indicates that they are merely subordinate members of the community,[28] though we detect a certain tension here between Luke's material and his redaction.[29] Luke says nothing at all of subordination. What we find in Paul in 1 Corinthians 14, in the Deutero-Paulines, the Catholic and Pastoral Epistles of women's subordination does not at all appear in Luke. But it is quite clear that the women in Acts are subordinate, as may be seen from many aspects. Is this accepted by Luke as self-evident, or has he consciously given it shape?

In the speeches of Acts which constitute the essence of the work, a speech is never addressed to women. Only once does Acts mention that Paul speaks to or with women, in 16:13—καθίσαντες ἐλαλοῦμεν ταῖς συνελθούσαις γυναιξίν ("we sat down and spoke to the women who had come together"). But in this passage, no speech of Paul is transmitted. On two occasions, the speeches have no addressees (Acts 10:34 and 11:14). In the remainder, that is, in almost all the speeches of Acts, the audiences are addressed as "men, brethren." Perhaps one could also find women included under ἀδελφοί ("brothers"). But that is impossible where "men" (ἄνδρες) are the subject, and such occurs twelve times (1:16; 2:14; 3:12; [4:8]; 7:1; 13:16; 14:15; 15:7,13; 17:22;[30] 22:1; 23:1; and 28:17). Now, in certain respects this is only natural, if Luke is concerned to give an historically accurate report. For on streets and in public places obviously only or almost only men were present. The situation is more complex when Luke has his readers in view. But, of course, it is also true that the salutation "men" is used in connection with speeches or sermons in the community where women were also present. In 1:16, the congregation is addressed as "men and brethren" (ἄνδρες, ἀδελφοί), and despite Acts 1:14 which refers to the women who are together with men in the congregation. We find the same feature in the proceedings at the council in Jerusalem (Acts 15:7,13). Only men are addressed (cf. also 20:17 and 21:18).

Of course, this also indicates that only the men decide the affairs of the church. Even where we have to do with synagogal assemblies, in which the presence of women, and indeed "God-fearing" women, is noted, the audience is addressed only as "men" (ἄνδρες; Acts 13:16,26). A speech to Israelites opens with "men of Israel," or on occasion, "fathers" (2:14; 3:12; 7:1; and 22:1). The women are clearly present only through their husbands, as if represented by them. The great care with which Luke composes his speeches and their opening[31] suggests that we have to do with more than accidentals here. Preaching, of course, applies to "the sons of Israel" (9:15; 10:35). Salvation also applies to "the sons" (Acts 3:25), then naturally only through them to women.

Luke is quite aware of the women in the community, so that we are not dealing with chance here. Only men are addressed, and in the descriptions of the community life we find almost no woman mentioned, all of which indicates that Luke is consciously giving shape to his report. Without stating it in so many words, the woman is subordinate. Are women also less obligated than men in questions pertaining to the law, that is, in matters of ritual? So it would appear from Acts 15:10—"we" have been unable to keep the law, and the "we" are clearly the men of the community (Acts 15:7). In addition, "the fathers" are also named. The apostolic decree is directed to "brethren" (Acts 15:23). But its contents have also to do with women, though the men bear the responsibility.

Luke is aware that women have played a signal role, and clearly intends to temper this fact and to describe the Christian women as "daughters of Abraham," as pious Jewesses who live according to Jewish custom. This harmonizes with his conception of the church. He addresses the men and thus also indirectly the women. Nowhere do we detect that women are active in the services of worship. If there is an exception, it would naturally be Lydia at Philippi. But there is no reference to worship in this instance, and Lydia appears as Paul's landlady (Acts 16:15). From the role which temple and synagogue play as houses of worship for the Christian communities in Acts, it can easily be explained why women retreat to the background in respect of worship.

No woman assumes an office of leading position.[32] There is no woman among the twelve apostles. For Luke there cannot be, since the apostles are also the rulers of the restored nation of the twelve tribes.[33] And it would of course be impossible for Luke to depict the church or its formation as the "gathering of Israel"[34] and then to have

a woman among the new patriarchs. But women also do not belong
to the "elders"; they do not at all belong to the governing body of the
church. There is not a single woman among the missionaries of Acts.
Whereas Paul speaks of a whole series of female co-workers, engaged
with him in missionary activity or as teachers, thus, e.g., in Rom.
16:1-22, in Acts not a single woman is described as assisting Paul,
though Luke is aware of a great number of Paul's male co-workers.[35]
Priscilla too is no exception, since Paul of course lives with her *and*
her husband (Acts 18:1-2), and Priscilla *and* Aquila further assisted in
Apollo's instruction (Acts 18:26). In Acts, she is not a fellow worker
with Paul, as Paul himself presents her in Rom. 16:3 and 1 Cor. 16:19.
But we will return to Priscilla.

The women compose, as it were, the hearing community (cf. Mark
in Luke 10:38-42).[36] For the woman as well, the hearing of the word
of God is decisive. And if women not merely comprise the passive
community,[37] they are active above all in diaconate. Here we return
to Luke 8:1-3. After what is related in Acts, the verses cannot possibly
be interpreted to mean that here also women are active as missionaries,
that is, in proclamation. They clearly have diaconal tasks (διηκόνουν,
v. 3), or concretely put, they serve the community with their means
(ἐκ τῶν ὑπαρχόντων αὐταῖς). Luke is not referring here to a female
diaconate,[38] or to a diaconal office which women may also exercise.
Where the giving of aid is concerned, women who are active in diaconate are named by name,[39] not as a group or in any official sense.
In Acts 9:36-42, especially in verses 36 and 39, Tabitha is clearly to
be seen from this perspective.[40] Further, the mother of Mark also serves
in diaconate (Acts 12:12). The wealthy Lydia from Philippi is probably
also to be viewed in this fashion (Acts 16:13ff.), though it is not so
stated (v. 15). She actually appears to be the community leader, though
Luke cannot and does not intend to say so. Still further, in Acts 17:12,
mention is made of women of "high standing" at Berea who are
converted. These also serve the community with their means, but in
this instance no one is named. The sense is not of an office, but rather
of an action which is typical. Accordingly, the women mentioned in
Acts 1:14 must rather be viewed as deaconesses, if they exercise any
activity at all in the community. There is no reference to any leading
position or office. This is of course also obvious from Acts 6—the
only deacons in the community are males. Without more detailed explanation or reason it is clear that the seven can only be chosen from
among the men (ἄνδρας). They are a governing body. It is stated in
Acts that even the Twelve served at tables (Acts 6:2). Then follow the

seven who assume the office of deacon (6:3-5). It is clear that in Acts
we hear nothing in greater detail of the diaconal activity of the Twelve
or the seven. On the other hand, the seven appear to be missionaries
and community leaders. How this can be the case historically is of no
concern in this context. But it is important that the office and service
of the diaconate which is of such decisive moment to Luke are exercised
under the leadership of men, as is quite clearly expressed in Acts 6:1-
7. In this context also the women are confirmed as daughters of Abraham. Later in Acts we hear nothing of a male, diaconal activity, which
merely indicates that in Acts 6 as well Luke shapes his material in a
theological manner. Thus, the material which related lively activity on
the part of women in the community is interpreted by means of Acts
6 and other passages in such a way that none can take offense. There
is neither the entitlement of women to equal rights nor any emancipation
of women.

In only one instance is there reference to women's spiritual activity,
that is, in addition to what every member of the community exercises,
and this has to do with prophecy. After reading Luke 1–2, where we
encounter three women of prophecy (though the term "prophet" is
not used)—Mary, Elizabeth and Anna—we expect something of the
same in Acts. It is already evident from Acts 2 that the community is
actually a prophetic community, and that the prophetic marks the people
of God of the end-time. By means of scripture proof,[41] this passage
states that the community is and should be a community of prophets
(Acts 2:17). The proof consists of Joel 2:28, which is interpreted even
in rabbinic literature to mean that in the coming world all Israel should
be prophets.[42] Acts 2:17 by way of Joel 2:28 states that men as well
as women should appear as prophets.[43] This was certainly the case,[44]
as can be inferred not merely from 1 Corinthians 11. In Acts also this
is set forth in detail, but it is characteristic that the women are almost
totally absent here as well. In Acts we find frequent mention of prophets
of the church (11:27; 13:1; 15:23; and 21:10). The community is also
characterized as "sons [!] of the prophets" (Acts 3:25).[45] We encounter
descriptions in which missionaries or other community leaders exercise
a prophetic function. This is true of the speeches in Acts, almost all
of which can only be understood as prophetic (in addition, cf. Acts
3:20ff. and 19:6). But what is the woman's situation? Only once is
there mention of female prophets, that is, of the four daughters of
Philip in Acts 21:9. The prophets or persons in Acts who appear as
prophets are clearly all men; of the women named in Acts no prophetic
activity is reported. The four daughters in Acts 21:9 thus furnish the

exception. And of course this does not mean that they are less than daughters of Abraham. First of all, their prophetic activity as such is in accordance with Scripture (Acts 2:17). Second, Luke was probably also aware of Old Testament models, that is, of prophetic women.[46] But in this respect also the women are subordinate.

In Luke, the woman's situation is also expressed in another way. Not one single female from the Old Testament is mentioned in Acts, apart from the daughter of Pharaoh in Acts 7:21. In Acts, Luke gives two historical resumes (7:1-53 and 13:16-25), but the history which he narrates is altogether that of men.[47] The situation is different in Hebrews 11, and in other writings of the New Testament. We encounter a succession of women from the Old Testament, particularly in the epistolary literature.[48] Though in contrast to Paul, e.g., in 1 Cor. 11:3ff. and 2 Cor. 11:1-3, Luke does not offer any single statement of principle regarding the woman, and as noted does not expressly advocate subordination, the woman is clearly not in the same situation as the man.

Now Luke is aware that women played an important role in the communities.[49] But in Acts they appear as individuals with their own names and never as types representing woman's position in the church.[50] We have already mentioned Lydia,[51] Mary, and Tabitha. And now we return to Priscilla. In Acts 18:1-3, she is named together with her husband, Aquila. But here Aquila is clearly the person of importance. Paul lives with the couple, and his connection with them is due to his exercise of the same calling as Aquila. Acts 18:18 merely states that the two accompany Paul on his journey to Syria. How much is to be inferred from mention of Priscilla ahead of her husband in this passage cannot be determined with certainty.[52] We should perhaps not overemphasize the point. But nothing indicates that Priscilla was for Luke an active fellow worker of Paul. Nor can this be inferred from the third mention of Priscilla in Acts 18:26. Here it is stated that Priscilla and Aquila—and in this sequence—heard of Apollos and instructed him more precisely concerning the "Way." A certain teaching activity on the part of the couple is referred to here, but how this is to be further understood cannot be determined with certainty.[53] In Rom. 16:3-5, the two are mentioned as "fellow workers" (συνεργοί) of Paul; as leaders of the community, and are revered by "all the churches of the Gentiles" (cf. also 1 Cor. 16:19). What Paul says of the two is known also to Luke, but is lessened somewhat. We cannot infer from Acts that they cooperated with Paul in apostolic activity.

This fact is also of interest because Priscilla is the one woman among the many active with Paul mentioned by Luke. From this we can of course hazard an opinion regarding this woman's eminence. Luke is aware of an entire succession of Paul's male co-workers—Apollos, Aquila, Aristarchus, Barnabas, Mark, Silvanus, Stephen, Timothy, and Titus (?). This means that he knows and mentions all of Paul's most significant fellow workers. Consequently, it is strange that only the one woman is mentioned. Of course, from the historical perspective, the men are for Paul more active as missionaries than are the women. But apart from Priscilla, the entire series of women who are active as missionaries, a few of them actually journeying about, and who are given particular mention in Romans 16, is absent in Luke. It appears as if Luke is concerned to play down the role of women in the work of Paul, which may be linked to Luke's conception of Paul as the Pharisee, faithful to the law, who missionizes among the Jews and appears chiefly in their synagogues (Acts 13:14ff.; 14:1ff.; 16:3,13; 17:1f.,17; 18:4; 21:20ff.; 23:3ff.; 26:5ff.).[54]

Only one group of women plays a greater role in Luke—the widows. They are mentioned in the gospel in 2:37; 4:25f.; 7:12; 18:3,5; 20:47; and 21:2. Apart from the two latter passages, the material here is unique to Luke. The role of widows is repeated in Acts; 6:1 is of quite particular importance, but see also 9:39,41. Aside from Luke 2:37, the widows in these passages are especially needy; they are among the poorest. In addition, the Lukan widows are emphatically described as devout persons (Luke 2:37; 21:12). In Israelite, Jewish charity, widows also played a signal role.[55] The cultic community had the quite special task of caring for widows. Widows were naturally regarded as needy daughters of Abraham. The woman in Luke 13:9 is also in need, but is not described as a widow, and because she is in need, she is also called a daughter of Abraham. The widows in Acts are not administrators of charity, but merely recipients. The later office of widows in the church, commencing with the Pastorals, does not appear in Luke.[56] When Luke describes widows simply as a permanent element of the Christian community, and in particular as objects of works of love, the community is again acknowledged to be the true Israel. Widows are important to the community to the extent they evoke a reorganization of the community's charity (Acts 6:1ff.). Luke's entire concern for the poor is not concern for the poor as such, but for the poor in Israel. In this aspect as well the community is shown to be the heir of Israel. And it is striking that in Luke and Acts women are for the most part described as devout or as women in need. Then too, in the Lukan writings the only Christians of wealth are women, that is, Jewesses or God-fearers of means (Luke 8:3; Acts 12:12; 16:14; 17:4,12). But these spend their riches on the community. The importance of this last point is also indicated in the narrative of a contrary case, that of Sapphira in Acts 5:1ff.

In his gospel, Luke has a great quantity of material dealing with women. The material reflects a historical fact, that is, the great significance of women for earliest Christianity. In the New Testament, this is expressed chiefly in Paul. Note, for example, the list of his fellow workers in Romans 16, where an entire succession of women appears. When we compare the material in Luke's gospel with that in the other gospels, we note in addition a retrograde movement, which can also be detected in the epistolary literature of the New Testament. The influence of Jewish Christianity is making itself felt. But Luke's concern for women is not a concern for women as such, but for the Jewesses within the church, the daughters of Abraham. Luke's understanding of women in the church suits his understanding of the church as the Israel of the end-time. Women are a part of the people of Israel in the end-time, thus of the church. As such they also appear as devout Jewesses. Luke is not aware of an equal status of women in the church, though he does not at all contest it. What he says of women in the gospel has its continuation in Acts: women constitute the community, together with the men. But they have no leading or definite role; they are subordinate, though Luke uses no term for subordination. And because Luke wrote not merely a gospel, but also Acts, he can now interpret the material concerning women in the gospel in the book of the Acts: women are simply daughters of Abraham, devout Jewesses, who have found their proper place in the church.

Notes

Chapter 1: The History of Early Christianity and the Acts of the Apostles

1. E. Haenchen, "Die Apostelgeschichte als Quelle für die christliche Fruhgeschichte," in *Die Bibel und Wir* (Tübingen: Mohr, 1968), p. 312, maintains that Luke did not want to write the history of early Christianity. This is true, but only partly so, when Haenchen in the same place asserts that Luke "wollte eine bestimmte christliche Überlieferung wiedergeben, die er für authentisch hielt" (wanted to restore a specific Christian tradition that he considered authentic). To Luke there did not exist just one tradition but a series, a fact that forced him "to write an orderly account" of "all things" "which have been accomplished among us," even though he had "many" predecessors who wrote gospels (Luke 1:1-4).

2. It was an unjust criticism; see my article, "The Unknown Paul," Chapter 3 of this volume.

3 See the warnings against basing too much on the accusations against Stephen and his circle in order to reconstruct the preaching of the Hellenists in E. Haenchen, *The Acts of the Apostles*, trans. B. Noble and G. Shinn (Oxford: Blackwell, 1971), pp. 267f.; Gerhard Schneider, *Die Apostelgeschichte* 1 (HTKNT; Freiburg, 1980), pp. 406ff.

4 Among the later contributions: M. Hengel, "Die Ursprünge der christlichen Mission," *NTS* 18 (1971/72): 27; "Zwischen Jesus und Paulus, Die 'Hellenisten,' die 'Sieben' und Stephanus (Apg 6,1-15; 7,54—8,3)," *ZTK* 72 (1975): 151-206.

5. For attempts to weaken the statement about false witnesses see Otto Bauernfeind, *Die Apostelgeschichte* (THKNT 5; Leipzig: Deichert, 1939), p.110; L. Goppelt, *Jesus, Paul and Judaism* (New York: Nelson, 1964), p. 106f.; A. Harnack, *The Mission and Expansion of Christianity in the First Three Centuries*, 2nd ed. (New York: Putnam, 1908), 1:63; E. Preuschen, *Die Apostelgeschichte* (HNT IV/1; Tübingen, 1912), p. 38; G. Stählin, *Die Apostelgeschichte* (NTD 5; 12th ed., Göttingen, 1968), p. 102.

6. Franz Overbeck, *Kurze Erklärung der Apostelgeschichte*, 4th ed. (Kurzgefasstes exeg. HNT von W. M. L. deWette, I/4; Leipzig, 1870), p. 89.

7. On Stephen as a totally isolated figure in early Christianity see Marcel Simon, *St. Stephen and the Hellenists in the Primitive Church* (London: Longmans, Green, 1958), p. 98; against this is R. Scroggs, "The Earliest Hellenistic Christianity," in *Religions in Antiquity: Essays in Memory of E. R. Goodenough*, ed. J. Neusner (Leiden: Brill, 1968), pp. 176-206.

8. G. Schneider, op. cit., p. 516, holds that only the criticism of the law can with certainty be traced back to the controversies around the Hellenists, whereas the author of Acts is responsible for the sayings critical of the temple.

9. A. Harnack, op. cit., I: 55; N. A. Dahl, "The Story of Abraham in Luke-Acts," in L. E. Keck and J. L. Martyn eds., *Studies in Luke-Acts* (Nashville: Abingdon, 1966), pp. 87-98.

10. Representative of many exegetes is E. Haenchen, "Die Apostelgeschichte als Quelle," p. 322. It is curious that even the most recent exegesis labels Luke without hesitation or discussion as Gentile Christian, and without any definition of the meaning of the term. See the latest commentaries: Jürgen Roloff, *Die Apostelgeschichte* (NTD; 17th ed., Göttingen, 1981), p. 4; G. Schneider, op. cit., p. 111.

11. *Komm.* pp. xxxi, xxxiii, xxxv; cf. J.-Chr. Emmelius, "Tendenzkritik und Formengeschichte. Der Beitrag Franz Overbecks zur Auslegung der Apostelgeschichte im 19. Jahrhundert," *Forschungen zur Kirchen- und Dogmengeschichte* 27 (1975): 115ff.

12. A. v. Harnack, "Neue Untersuchungen zur Apostelgeschichte und zur Abfassungszeit der synoptischen Evangelien," *Beiträge zur Einleitung in das NT 4* (Leipzig: Hinrichs 1911), p. 78; "Die Apostelgeschichte," *Beiträge zur Einleitung in das NT 3* (1908), pp. 212, 219ff.; *Mission* 1: 63, n. 2.

13. We may say with H. Cadbury in *The Beginnings of Christianity*, ed. F. J. Foakes-Jackson and K. Lake (London: Macmillan, 1933), 5: 68f., that there is no idea of evolution in Acts, *in casu* the development of the missionary work. In spite of that, it is clear, and Cadbury even says so, that the divine plan for history was there from the beginning and that it develops gradually. And so the word *development* or even *evolution* is justified, if we do not think of immanent processes. The stylistic observation that Luke places small, impressive, and dramatic scenes next to each other and relatively independent of each other (so E. Haenchen, "Die Apostelgeschichte als Quelle für die christliche Frühgeschichte," p. 313) does not change the fact that Luke finds the occurrences connected, namely, as acts of God.

14. On Paul in Acts see J. Jervell, "Paul in the Acts of the Apostles," Chapter 4 in this volume; "The Unknown Paul," Chapter 3 in this volume; and, for a survey of the most recent literature, R. Maddox, *The Purpose of Luke-Acts* (FRLANT 16; Göttingen, 1982), pp. 66-90.

15. So already F. C. Baur, *Paulus* (Leipzig, 1845), pp. 10f., who maintained that the Paul of Acts is so different from the Paul of the Pauline letters that any trust in Luke as historically reliable comes "auf Kosten des moralischen Charakters des Apostels" (at the cost of the moral character of the apostle). This as opposed to M. Schneckenburger, *Über den Zweck der Apostelgeschichte* (1841), who says that the portrait of Paul in Acts, in spite of being apologetic and one-sided is historically accurate. And Schneckenburger shares the view of his teacher Baur regarding the place of Acts in the history of early Christianity. This shows that the very starting point, namely, operating with a contrast between Jewish and

Gentile Christianity is not decisive for the question about the trustworthiness of Acts; this is first of all exemplified by A. v. Harnack.

16. On the meaning of the notices on mass conversions see J. Jervell, *Luke and the People of God* (Minneapolis: Augsburg, 1972), pp. 44ff.

17. Luke knows of course of congregations not founded by Paul within his missionary territory, or he knows about Christians in places where Paul preached; so in Cyprus (Acts 11:19), Corinth (18:1-3), Ephesus (19:1ff.), Rome (18:15). It is, however, important for Luke to connect these and other places with Paul; see for other churches R. Maddox, op. cit., p. 69. It is thus clear to the readers of Acts what kind of preaching determines the congregations outside Jerusalem, on Paul's missionary field, namely, the preaching of Paul which is completely in line with that of Jerusalem. Maddox is right in stressing that Luke knew about a successful expansion of Christianity independent of Paul, but that is outside the special interest of Luke which clearly gives us the impression that Paul had founded most of the churches.

18. Andreas Lindemann, *Paulus im ältesten Christentum* (BHT 58; Tübingen: Mohr, 1979), finds the picture of Paul in Acts without the polemical traits. The Paul of Acts has absolute authority, and it is impossible to see that the author fights any "Bedrohung . . . dieses Bildes" (threat to this portrait). The absolute authority Paul has in Acts is theologically the authority of his preaching, which is in line with Jerusalem. But it is incomprehensible that Lindemann cannot see that Paul's authority is being threatened, which especially Acts 21:15ff. makes evident. When Lindemann (p. 67f.) maintains that Luke in his portrait of Paul seeks to recall "das zeitgenössische Heidenchristentum und die Herkunft aus der Predigt des Paulus" (contemporary Gentile Christianity and its roots in the preaching of Paul) we have to add that the same preaching stems from the Jewish Christian Pharisee, Paul.

19. Cf. E. Haenchen, "Die Apostelgeschichte als Quelle," p. 322: It has to do with a Gentile Christian theology, which is supposedly Luke's own theology as it was near the end of the first century.

20. Incomprehensible is the utterance of E. Haenchen in "Die Apostelgeschichte als Quelle," p. 322, in his interpretation of Acts 10–11: "Mag auch in den weiteren Kapiteln der Apg. die jerusalemische Gemeinde noch eine grosse Rolle spielen— im Grunde sieht man doch schon, dass das Judenchristentum eigentlich auf verlorenem Posten steht" (if in other chapters of Acts the Jerusalem church still plays a significant role, we can nonetheless already see in essence that Jewish Christianity actually is fighting a losing battle). But: "eine grosse Rolle" (a significant role)!

21. See note 17 above.

22. E. Haenchen, "Die Apostelgeschichte als Quelle," p. 322.

23. Cf. D. L. Tiede, *Prophecy and History in Luke-Acts* (Philadelphia: Fortress, 1980).

24. It is of course possible to talk about "theological history" as the genre of Luke-Acts and reckon with the fact that Luke in many cases is talking about "a past situation, which may be considerably different from that in which his readers stand"; so R. Maddox, op. cit., p. 18. That, however, does not change the fact that there is no "art for art's sake" in his dealing with history.

25. We will not here discuss why we see the "Hellenists" as Greek-speaking Jews from the diaspora. See G. Schneider, *Komm.*, pp. 406-416. H. J. Cadbury, *Beginnings* 5: 59ff., understood the Hellenists as Gentile Christians.

26. M. Hengel, "Mission," pp. 27ff., is representative of the newest trend.

27. So already Carl Weizsäcker, *Die apostolische Zeitalter der christlichen Kirche*, 3rd ed. (Tübingen: Mohr, 1902), pp. 51ff. and Harnack, *Mission*, 1: 61f., the latter with the reservation that the Hellenistic synagogues would be anything but liberal on questions of law. The explanation in M. Hengel, "Mission," pp. 28f., about the disappointment with the situation in the homeland for those who came from the diaspora, is artificial. And if there were a tendency to criticism of the law within Judaism it could not lead to a greater receptiveness for the message of Jesus.

28. For the different views on the Gentile mission see E. Käsemann, "Sentences of Holy Law in the New Testament," *New Testament Questions of Today* (Philadelphia: Fortress, 1969), pp. 66-81; "The Beginnings of Christian Theology," ibid., pp. 82-107; and "On the Subject of Primitive Christian Apocalyptic," ibid., pp. 108-137.

29. On the question of sources: It is possible that Luke had two different traditions or even two written sources, a collection of stories about Peter and a source about the Hellenists from Antioch, and that both claimed to tell about the origin of the Gentile mission; cf. M. Hengel, "Mission," p. 25.

30. The expression, "in the early days," in connection with the story about Cornelius (Acts 15:7) suggests that the Gentile mission was there from the beginning of the church. So Acts 10–11 is connected with the days of the founding of the church, and it is obvious that Luke does not intend to show any time interval between the first day of the church and the conversion of Cornelius. Such an understanding is found in F. F. Bruce, *The Acts of the Apostles*, 2nd ed. (London: Tyndale, 1952), p. 292, and K. Lake–H. J. Cadbury, *Beginnings*, 4: 172. F. Overbeck, op. cit., p. 225, and E. Haenchen, *Die Apostelgeschichte*, p. 427, maintain that the expression means to say that the decision was taken long ago. H. Conzelmann, *Die Apostelgeschichte* (Tübingen: Mohr, 1963), p. 202, and G. Stähling, *Die Apostelgeschichte*, p. 202, hold that the Cornelius story is depicted as the classical example. J. Roloff, *Die Apostelgeschichte*, p. 230, finds the meaning to be that the conversion of Cornelius happened through a divine plan for his salvation.

31. C. K. Barrett, *Luke the Historian in Recent Study* (London: Epworth, 1961), pp. 23f.

32. Helmut Koester, *Introduction to the New Testament* (Philadelphia: Fortress, 1982).

33. Some exegetes look on Galilee as the starting point for the mission among the Gentiles; so M. Hengel, "Mission," p. 27, n. 42, and H. Kasting, *Die Anfänge der urchristlichen Mission. Eine historische Untersuchung* (BEvt 55; München: Kaiser, 1969). For mission originating from Palestine in the very first days of the church, see O. Cullmann, "The Significance of the Qumran Texts for Research into the Beginnings of Christianity," in *The Scrolls and the New Testament*, ed. K. Stendahl (New York: Harper, 1957), pp. 18-32, and "L'opposition centre le Temple de Jerusalem," *NTS* (1958/59): 157-173.

34. H. Kasting, *Mission*, p. 109: The expectation of the immediate parousia did not permit any thoughts about a "programmatische Weltmission" (programmatic world mission). At the same time, the idea of the parousia meant that the time was near when the Gentiles should join the people of God, and this may have been the original cause for the mission among the Gentiles. Cf. E. Haenchen, *Die Apostelgeschichte*, p. 357.

35. So G. Klein, "Rezension von E. Haenchen," *Die Apostelgeschichte*, *ZKG* 68 (1957): 368; see H. J. Cadbury in *Beginnings*, 5: 59ff.: The Hellenists were

Gentiles. Against this E. Haenchen, "Die Apostelgeschichte als Quelle," p. 318, and *Die Apostelgeschichte*, p. 261, but with insufficient arguments: The hard discussion between Antioch and Jerusalem would not have taken place if Jerusalem already had accepted uncircumcised Gentiles. But Jerusalem had changed its ground, which we can see with Peter and Barnabas as examples (Gal. 2: llff.). The contention that the church would have been driven away from Jerusalem by the Jews if they had accepted Gentiles does not hold water. There was, for example, at that time a very active Jewish mission, and many "God-fearers" circulated in the synagogues.

36. That the Gentile mission was met with skepticism in Jerusalem we can see in Acts 11:1-3. But do we here find that the church did not have only circumcised members (see the expression οἱ ἐκ περιτομῆς)?
37. H. Koester, op. cit., 1:523.
38. Gal. 2:llff.; 2 Cor. 11:22ff.; 12:llf.; Rom. 15:20ff. And the same development is found in Acts 9:26ff. and, on the other hand, 21:15ff.

Chapter 2: The Mighty Minority

1. (1884), p. 445.
2. J. Jervell, *Luke and the People of God* (Minneapolis: Augsburg, 1972), pp. 44-49.
3. John 2:23; 7:31; 8:30; 10:41; 11:45; 12:11, 42.
4. J. Munck, *Paul and the Salvation of Mankind* (Richmond: John Knox, 1960), pp. 239ff.
5. E.g., Hans Conzelmann, "Heidenchristentum," RGG 3:141; L. Goppelt, *Christentum und Judentum im ersten und zweiten Jahrhundert* (Gütersloh, 1954), p. 149f.; Bo Reicke *The New Testament Era* (Philadelphia: Fortress, 1968), pp. 291f.
6. Gerhard Lohfink, *Die Sammlung Israels. Eine Untersuchung zur lukanischen Ekklesiologie* (STANT 39; Munich: Kösel, 1975).
7. Note 2; see also "The Circumcised Messiah," Chapter 8 in this volume; "Paul in the Acts of the Apostles," Chapter 4 of this volume; and "The Signs of an Apostle: Paul's Miracles," Chapter 5 of this volume.
8. Francois Bovon, *Luc le Theologien, Vingt-cinq ans de recherches (1950-1975)* (Neuchatel: Delachaux and Niestlé, 1978).
9. A. von Harnack, *The Mission and Expansion of Christianity* (New York: Putnam, 1908), 2:80.
10. Op. cit., pp. 228f.
11. E.g., A. v. Harnack, op. cit., p. 80.
12. E.g., A. v. Harnack, op. cit., p. 81.
13. S. G. F. Brandon, *The Fall of Jerusalem and the Christian Church* (London: S.P.C.K., 1951), p. 180: The Jewish Christians disappeared because they were "essentially one with the nation."
14. Most scholars reject E. Käsemann's "early catholicism" as a characterization of Acts ("New Testament Questions of Today," in *New Testament Questions of Today* [Philadelphia: Fortress, 1969], p. 22) but they still see Acts mostly as representative of the established church at the end of the first century.
15. J. Jervell, *Luke and the People of God*, pp. 143-145, 190-193.

16. A. v. Harnack, *Mission*, 2:74; M. Hengel, "Zwischen Jesus und Paulus," *ZTK* 72 (1975): 199; H. Kasting, *Die Anfänge der urchristlichen Mission* (*BEvT* 55; Munich: Kaiser, 1969), p. 116; E. Käsemann, *Exegetische Versuche und Besinnungen* 2 (1962), p. 113.

17. Cf. G. Barth, "Matthew's Understanding of the Law" in G. Bornkamm, G. Barth, and H. J. Held, *Tradition and Interpretation in Matthew* (Philadelphia: Westminster, 1963).

18. J. Jervell, "Das Volk des Geistes," in *God's Christ and His People*, ed. J. Jervell and W. A. Meeks (Oslo: Universitetsforlaget, 1978), pp. 91f.

19. J. Jervell, *Luke and the People of God*, pp. 41-74.

20. J. Jervell, *Luke and the People of God*, pp. 190-193.

21. M. Hengel, op. cit., p. 199.

22. A parallel is the Qumran sect being isolated within the people, still believing themselves to be the true Israel.

23. C. K. Barrett, "Things Sacrificed to Idols," *NTS* 11 (1965): 138-153.

24. J. Jervell, "Das Volk des Geistes," pp. 96ff.

25. For the following see my article, "The Letter to Jerusalem," in K. P. Donfried, ed., *The Romans Debate* (Minneapolis: Augsburg, 1977), pp. 61-74.

26. Esp. 3:1-8, 27-31; 4:1ff., 12, 16.

27. See note 25.

28. Above pp 26f.

29. A. v. Harnack, *Mission* 1: 101f.

30. For the following see the literature mentioned in notes 6–8.

31. Cf. my article, "The Circumcised Messiah," Chapter 8 in this volume.

32. See note 7.

33. Acts 13:13ff.; 14:1ff.; 16:13ff.; 17:1ff., 10ff.; 18:4ff., 19ff.; 19:8ff.

34. See my essay, "The Signs of an Apostle," Chapter 5 in this volume.

35. See Chr. Burchard, J. Jervell, J. Thomas, *Studien zu den Testamenten der zwölf Patriarchen* (*BZNW* 36; Berlin, 1969), pp. 55f., esp. n. 81.

36. In his Dialogue with Trypho.

37. *Theology of the New Testament* (New York: Scribner's, 1974), 2:15ff., 26ff.; *The Gospel of John* (Philadelphia: Westminster, 1971): Index, "Judaism."

38. N. A. Dahl, "The Johannine Church and History," in *Current Issues in New Testament Interpretation*, in honor of O. A. Piper (New York: Harper, 1962), pp. 124-142.

39. R. Leistner, *Antijudaismus im Johannesevangelium. Darstellung des Problems in der neueren Auslegungsgeschichte und Untersuchung der Leidensgeschichte* (Frankfurt: Peter Lang, 1974).

40. H. Odeberg, *The Fourth Gospel* (Chicago: Argonaut, 1968); N. A. Dahl, op. cit. (note 38).

41. E.g., Clark, Nepper-Christensen, Hebert, Strecker, Trilling, Walker.

42. Cf. G. Barth, op. cit. (above, n. 17).

43. On the tradition concerning the letter and the belief that it was written to Jewish Christians, see W. G. Kümmel, *Introduction to the New Testament* (Nashville: Abingdon, 1975), pp. 392 and 398ff.

44. The Pastorals seem to testify something like a turning point. One can still find an influential Jewish-Christian element in the church behind the Pastorals, but the Jewish Christians are regarded as adversaries (Titus 1:10, 14, 16; cf. 1 Tim. 1:4-7; 4:7; 2 Tim. 4:4). As to the gospel of Mark it is very hard to get a clear impression

of its attitude regarding Jewish Christians. According to some scholars, e.g., T. A. Burkill, *Mysterious Revelation* (Ithaca, N.Y.: Cornell, 1963), pp. 117-142, Mark is an anti-Jewish gospel. I cannot find evidence for this idea; see, e.g., 1:40-45; 12:28-34.
45. See *Studien* . . . (n. 35 above), pp. 30-61.
46. A. Schlatter, *Die Kirche Jerusalems vom Jahre 70-130* (Gutersloh: Bertelsmann, 1898); Eusebius, *Hist. eccl.* 4:5f.

Chapter 3: The Unknown Paul

1. The so-called *Redaktionsgeschichte* should have taught us to work out a neat analysis of the Pauline framework.
2. W. G. Kümmel, "Jesus und Paulus," in *Heilsgeschehen und Geschichte, Ges. Aufsätze 1933-64* (Marburger Theol. Stud. 3; Marburg: Elwert, 1965), pp. 430-465; E. E. Ellis and E. Grässer, eds., *Jesus und Paulus, Festschrift W. G. Kümmel z. 70. Geburtstag* (Göttingen, 1975).
3. For diverse modern attempts to determine the intention and significance of the letter to the Romans see K. P. Donfried, ed., *The Romans Debate* (Minneapolis: Augsburg, 1977), with essays by T. W. Manson, G. Bornkamm, K. P. Donfried, J. Jervell, R. J. Karris, W. Wiefel, M. L. Stirewalt Jr., W. Wuellner, G. Klein. See also W. Schmithals, *Der Römerbrief als historisches Problem* (Stud. zum NT 9; Gütersloh, 1975).
4. So G. Bornkamm, "The Letter to the Romans as Paul's Last Will and Testament," in K. P. Donfried, op. cit., pp. 17-31.
5. Jervell, "The Problem of Traditions in Acts," in *Luke and the People of God* (Minneapolis: Augsburg, 1972), pp. 19-40.
6. This is not a *captatio benevolentiae* or a literary formula of courtesy, of which we can furnish no evidence.
7. Cf. W. G. Kümmel, *Introduction to the New Testament*, rev. ed. (Nashville: Abingdon, 1975), p. 260. Kümmel himself, p. 261, maintains that 1 Thessalonians in its line of thought is genuinely Pauline.
8. So rightly, H. Schlier, *Der Römerbrief* (HTKNT 6; Freiburg-Basel-Wien, 1977), p. VII, holds that the letter to the Romans is one of the most difficult texts in the New Testament.
9. N. A. Dahl, "The Future of Israel," in *Studies in Paul* (Minneapolis: Augsburg, 1977), p. 137; B. A. Pearson, "1 Thessalonians 2:13-16, A Deutero-Pauline Interpolation," *HTR* 64 (1971): 97.
10. According to E. Käsemann, *Commentary on Romans* (Grand Rapids: Eerdmans, 1980), ad rem, there is no discrepancy between Galatians and Romans.
11. See notes 8 and 10.
12. Already 65 years ago, J. Weiss complained that in current exegesis what Paul had in common with the rest of the church has for us disappeared (*Earliest Christianity* [New York: Harper, 1959], 1: 3).
13. Representative of this is R. Bultmann, *Theology of the New Testament* (New York: Scribners, 1951-1955), 1: 262f.
14. So already Harnack, *Neue Untersuchungen zur Apostelgeschichte* (Beitr. z. Einleitung in das Neue Testament 4; Leipzig, 1911), pp. 42ff.

15. Ph. Vielhauer, "On the 'Paulinism' of Acts," *Studies in Luke-Acts*, ed. L. E. Keck and J. L. Martyn (Nashville: Abingdon, 1966), pp. 33-50.

16. J. Jervell, "Paul in the Acts of the Apostles," Chapter 4 in this volume; R. Maddox, *The Purpose of Luke-Acts* (FRLANT 126; Göttingen, 1982), pp. 66-91.

17. G. Eichholz, "Der ökumenische und missionarische Horizont der Kirche. Eine exegetische Studie zu Röm 1,8-15," in *Tradition und Interpretation* (Munich, 1965), pp. 85-98.

18. Unfortunately, it has not been discussed whether and under what circumstances the critical and correcting attitude of definition is a part of the process of tradition.

19. E. Güttgemanns, *Der leidende Apostel und sein Herr* (FRLANT 90; Göttingen, 1966); J. Jervell, "Der schwache Charismatiker," in *Rechtfertigung, Festschrift E. Käsemann* (Tubingen/Göttingen, 1976), pp. 185-198.

20. J. Jervell, "Der schwache Charismatiker," pp. 189f.

21. A recent important contribution that works this out is H. Hübner, *Das Gesetz bei Paulus*, 2nd ed. (FRLANT 119; Göttingen, 1980); see also "Nomos," in *Exegetisches Wörterbuch z. Neuen Testament*, ed. H. Balz and G. Schneider (Stuttgart, 1982), pp. 1168-1170; and U. Wilckens, "Zur Entwicklung des paulinischen Gesetzesverständnis," *NTS* 28, 2 (1982): 154-190.

22. It would be taking things too far to deal with the postcanonical conceptions of Paul. We are, however, wrong in thinking that Jewish Christianity as a whole and unanimously rejected Paul. In some of those circles Paul was accepted, e.g., by the Enkratites and the church of the *Epistula Apostolorum*.

23. R. Maddox, op. cit., pp. 40ff. tries to show against my observations in *Luke and the People of God*, pp. 133-185, that the common ground for Paul and the Pharisees is the doctrine of resurrection alone; in this way Maddox unduly plays down the importance of the law in Acts 21–28. And he has not observed that neither the Pharisees nor Luke can separate law from resurrection.

24. Cf. *Neue Untersuchungen zur Apostelgeschichte* (note 14), pp. 21ff.; *Lukas der Arzt* (Beitr. z. Einleitung in das Neue Testament I; Leipzig, 1907); *Die Apostelgeschichte* (Leipzig 1908), esp. pp. 159ff.

25. "On the 'Paulinism' of Acts" (note 15), pp. 33ff.; differently, S. Sandmel, *The First Christian Century in Judaism and Christianity* (New York: Oxford, 1969), p. 162: the Lukan Paul differs radically from the Pauline Paul "in doctrine, belief, and practice."

26. Ph. Vielhauer, op. cit., pp. 38ff.

27. For the theological problem in the legal process against Paul see J. Jervell, "Paul, the Teacher of Israel," in *Luke and the People of God*, pp. 153-184; R. Maddox, op. cit., pp. 76ff.

28. Above all by J. Munck, *Paul and the Salvation of Mankind* (Richmond: John Knox, 1959) and *Christ and Israel*.

29. Cf. H. Windisch, *Paulus und das Judentum* (Stuttgart, 1935), pp. 18ff.; he finds the Lukan Pharisee Paul even in the Pauline letters, even if the Lukan trend is to describe Paul as more Jewish than he actually was.

30. So already J. Weiss, op. cit., p. 168.

31. On the current discussion on the concept of the law in the Pauline letters see C. K. Barrett, "The Allegory of Abraham, Sarah, and Hagar in the Argument of Galatians," in *Rechtfertigung* (note 19), pp. 1-16; F. Hahn, "Das Gesetzesverständnis im Römer- und Galaterbrief," *ZNW* 67 (1976): 29-63; H. Hübner, op.

cit. (note 21); K. Kertelge, *'Rechtfertigung' bei Paulus*, 2nd ed. (Münster, 1971); G. Klein, "Sündenverstandnis und theologia crucis bei Paulus," in *Theologia crucis—signum crucis, Festschrift E. Dinkler* (Tübingen, 1979), pp. 249-82; E. P. Sanders, *Paul and Palestinian Judaism* (Philadelphia: Fortress, 1977); P. Stuhlmacher, "Das Gesetz als Thema biblischer Theologie," *ZThK* 75 (1978): 251-80; U. Wilckens, op. cit. (note 21).

32. See n. 13.

33. H. Conzelmann, *An Outline of the Theology of the New Testament* (New York: Harper and Row, 1969), pp. 247f.

34. On the speeches in Acts see M. Dibelius, "Die Reden der Apostelgeschichte," in *Aufsätze zur Apostelgeschichte* (FRLANT 60; Göttingen, 1961), pp. 120-62; U. Wilckens, *Die Missionsreden der Apostelgeschichte* (WMANT 5; Neukirchen, 1961).

35. For a survey of recent studies of Paul in Acts see R. Maddox, op. cit., pp. 66-90.

36. See Chapter 5 in this volume.

37. J. Jervell, "The Law in Luke-Acts," in *Luke and the People of God*, pp. 133-152.

38. Cf. H. Schlier, op. cit., p. 229 ". . . The law is a pneumatic word, a word determined by the Spirit"; "the law is according to its origin and nature and thereby even in its effect permeated and carried by the Spirit of God" (author's trans.).

39. The authority of the law is maintained in the letter to the Romans: H. Lietzmann, *An die Römer* (HNT 8; Tübingen, 1933), p. 113; O. Michel, *Der Brief an die Römer* (KEK 4, 4th ed.; Göttingen, 1966), p. 327, n. 2.

40. *Dikaioma*: E. Kasemann, *Commentary on Romans* (n. 10), pp. 51f.

41. H. Paulsen, *Überlieferung und Auslegung in Römer 8* (WMANT 43; Neukirchen, 1974), pp. 5ff., 197ff.

42. On Rom. 8:26ff. as glossolalia see E. Käsemann, *Commentary on Romans*, p. 241.

43. J. Jervell, "Paul in the Acts of the Apostles," Chapter 4 in this volume.

44. For one, G. Lohfink, *Die Sammlung Israels* (STANT 39; Munich, 1975); cf. R. Maddox, op. cit., pp. 31-65.

45. This is underlined in every description of the history of early Christianity, e.g., H. Conzelmann, *History of Primitive Christianity* (Nashville: Abingdon, 1973); L. Goppelt, *Die apostolische und nachapostolische Zeit*, "Die Kirche in ihrer Geschichte," 1A (2nd ed., Göttingen, 1966; see above chap. 1, n. 5).

46. For Bo Reicke, *The New Testament Era* (Philadelphia: Fortress, 1968), pp. 291f., this is so striking that he allows for Jewish mass conversions at the end of the first century.

47. A. Schlatter, *Gottes Gerechtigkeit: Ein Kommentar zum Römerbrief* (Stuttgart: Calwer, 1935), p. 9, found a constantly growing opposition against Paul because he fought the re-Judaizing of the church.

48. G. Eichholz, op. cit., p. 87, observes that Paul in the letter to the Romans in a striking way uses traditions of Jewish-Christian origin, traditions he highly values.

49. Chr. Ditzfelbinger, "Paulus und das Alte Testament," *Theol. Existenz heute*, N. F. 95 (1961), finds that the notion of the historical-empirical Israel as "Abraham's seed" is a common idea in early Christianity, but the concept in Galatians, where the church is the "seed of Abraham" is the actual Pauline idea.

50. In Romans the law is a sign even of the new, Christian way of life (8:3f.) and circumcision is a mark of justification by faith (4:11).
51. *Neue Untersuchungen* (note 14), pp. 42ff.
52. The thesis of Harnack, *Das Alte Testament in den paulinischen Briefen und in den paulinischen Gemeinden* (Sitzungsberichte A. B. Ph.h.Kl.; Berlin, 1928, 1929), pp. 124-141, later restated by H. Ulonska, *Paulus und das Alte Testament* (Münster, 1963), that Paul uses the Old Testament only when his adversaries force him into it, is to some extent correct. Paul interprets the Old Testament above all when dealing with the theme, Israel and the law of Moses. Cf. even H. Windisch, *Paulus und das Judentum*, pp. 57ff.
53. H. Conzelmann, *Outline*, p. 71, says that the history of Israel is no subject for Paul. This is only partly correct: it was no subject until Galatians and Romans.
54. Cf. note 51.
55. On Romans 7 and the apology for the law see W. G. Kümmel, *Römer 7 und die Bekehrung des Paulus* (Leipzig, 1929); this is criticized by E. Käsemann, *Comm.*, pp. 192ff.
56. B. Noack, "Current and Backwater in the Epistle to the Romans," *Studia Theologica* 19 (1965): 165.
57. Cf. even H. Windisch, *Paulus und das Judentum*, p. 33.

Chapter 4: Paul in the Acts of the Apostles: Tradition, History, Theology

1. In recent years things have changed in the study of Acts insofar as the dominating influence of scholars like Haenchen, Conzelmann, Vielhauer, etc., is clearly decreasing. Their points of view are highly estimated but not seen as the final solution. The new trend bears upon the problem in this essay too. See the remarks of E. Grässer in his foreword to the seventh edition of E. Haenchen's commentary on Acts (KEK 3; Göttingen, 1977), p. 8.
2. W. Gasque, *A History of the Criticism of the Acts of the Apostles* (Grand Rapids: Eerdmans, 1975); E. Grässer, "Acta-Forschung seit 1960," *ThR* 41 (1976): 141-194, 259-290, and 42 (1977): 1-68; Haenchen, *Apostelgeschichte*, pp. 124-141.
3. A more detailed presentation: J. Jervell, *Luke and the People of God* (Minneapolis, Augsburg, 1972), esp. pp. 133-184.
4. Chr. Burchard, *Der dreizehnte Zeuge, Traditions- und Kompositionsgeschichtliche Untersuchungen zu Lukas' Darstellung der Frühzeit des Paulus* (FRLANT 105; Göttingen, 1979).
5. K. Löning, *Die Saulustradition in der Apostelgeschichte* (NTANF; Münster, 1973).
6. V. Stolle, *Der Zeuge als Angeklagte. Untersuchungen zum Paulusbild des Lukas* (BWANT 102; Stuttgart, 1973).
7. H.-J. Michel, *Die Abschiedsrede des Paulus an die Kirche. Apg. 20, 17-38. Motivgeschichte und theologische Bedeutung* (STANT 35; Munich, 1973).
8. Cf. Chr. Burchard, "Paulus in der Apostelgeschichte," *ThLZ* 12 (1975): 881-895.
9. For the discussion of Luke's sources in Acts see J. Dupont, *Les sources du Livre des Acts. Etat de la question* (Bruges, 1960); W. Eltester, *Lukas und Paulus: Festschrift H. Hommel* (Tübingen, 1961), pp. 1-17; Haenchen, *Apostelgeschichte*,

pp. 38-48, 92-101, 124ff.; and A. J. Mattil Jr., *Luke as a Historian in Criticism since 1840* (Ann Arbor: University Microfilms, 1959).

10. Cf. Haenchen, *Apostelgeschichte*, p. 99.

11. See the interesting observations of O. Linton, "The Third Aspect. A Neglected Point of View. A Study in Gal. I-II and Acts IX and XV," *StTh* 3 (1950-51): 77-95.

12. See Chapter 3, note 15.

13. "Paulinism," p. 39; for literature on the question of Luke and Paul see Haenchen, *Apostelgeschichte*, pp. 702f. and 315f.

14. Cf. J. Jervell, "Der schwache Charismatiker," in *Rechtfertigung: Festschrift E. Käsemann* (Tübingen, 1976), pp. 185-198.

15. This has become almost a dogma among exegetes; cf. W. G. Kümmel, *Introduction to the New Testament*, rev. ed. (Nashville: Abingdon, 1975), pp. 147ff., 160ff.

16. Even if most scholars reject E. Käsemann's "early catholicism" as a characterization of Acts (*New Testament Questions of Today* [Philadelphia: Fortress, 1969], p. 22), so lately Haenchen, *Apostelgeschichte*, p. 62, they see Acts mostly as representative of the established church at the end of the first century.

17. See note 12.

18. On Romans as the last phase of Paul's theology see J. Jervell, "The Letter to Jerusalem," in *The Romans Debate*, ed. Karl P. Donfried (Minneapolis: Augsburg), pp. 50-60.

19. The study of Ph. Vielhauer (above, n. 12) has played an immense role in the understanding of the Paul of Acts. For another view see my book, *Luke and the People of God* (Minneapolis: Augsburg, 1972). For the new trend in the understanding of Luke's theology in general, different from the view of Haenchen, Conzelmann, Vielhauer, et al., see G. Lohfink, *Die Sammlung Israels* (STANT 39; Munich, 1982).

20. As it is taken for granted that Acts describes Paul above all as a missionary to the Gentiles, Acts 17 plays among scholars a far more decisive role for the understanding of Luke's idea about Paul than it actually deserves. If we anywhere in Acts are confronted with tradition without a strong Lukan recasting of the source it must be in the Areopagus scene. The very thought that Luke primarily shows Paul as "the teacher of Israel" (see my *Luke and the People of God*, pp. 153ff.) puts some important questions to our exegesis.

21. This part of Luke's Paul is often presented to us as a contradiction to the way Paul in his own letters is guided in his missionary activity; some scholars do not even observe that we have actually the same features in Paul's letters, but in a different form; see below, pp. 73f.

22. On these chapters in general, see G. Lohfink, *Sammlung*, pp. 17-32; on the combination of Spirit/law/prophecy see "The Circumcised Messiah," Chapter 8 in this volume.

23. On Acts 7 as an inherent part of Luke's theology, see N. A. Dahl, "The Story of Abraham in Luke-Acts," *Studies in Luke-Acts*, ed. L. Keck and J. L. Martyn (Nashville: Abingdon, 1966), pp. 139-158.

24. Cf. A. von Harnack, *Neue Untersuchungen zur Apostelgeschichte* (Beitr. z. Einleitung in das Neue Testament IV; Leipzig, 1911), pp. 21ff.

25. *Lukas der Arzt* (Beitr. z. Einleitung in das Neue Testament I; Leipzig, 1907); *Die Apostelgeschichte* (Leipzig, 1908), esp. pp. 159ff.; *Neue Untersuchungen zur Apostelgeschichte*, pp. 21ff.

26. For the latest discussion see Haenchen, *Apostelgeschichte*, pp. 125ff. (presenting the views of Barrett, Dupont, Eltester, Mattill).
27. J. Munck, *Paul and the Salvation of Mankind* (Richmond: John Knox, 1959), pp. 36ff., 247ff.; *Christ and Israel. An Interpretation of Romans 9–11* (Philadelphia: Fortress, 1967).
28. Cf. K. H. Rengstorf, "Paulus und die römische Christenheit," StEv 2 (TU 87; Berlin, 1964): 447ff.; and my commentary on the Romans, *Gud og hans fiender* (Oslo, 1973), pp. 274ff.
29. Cf. Munck, *Christ and Israel*, pp. 116ff.
30. See my article, "The Letter to Jerusalem" (note 18 above).
31. Harnack, *Untersuchungen*, pp. 42ff.
32. On the history of the interpretation of Romans 9–11 see Chr. Müller, *Gottes Gerechtigkeit und Gottes Volk, Eine Untersuchung zu Römer 9–11* (FRLANT 86; Göttingen, 1964); E. Käsemann, *Commentary on Romans* (Grand Rapids: Eerdmans, 1980), ad rem.
33. See note 18 above.
34. See my essay mentioned in note 14.
35. Cf. "The Law in Luke-Acts," in J. Jervell, *Luke and the People of God*, pp. 133-152.
36. *Untersuchungen*, pp. 42ff.

Chapter 5: The Signs of an Apostle: Paul's Miracles

1. B. Bauer, *Die Apostelgeschichte, eine Ausgleichung des Paulinismus und des Judenthums innerhalb der christlichen Kirche* (Berlin, 1850), pp. 7ff.
2. Cf. the more recent works: Ch. Burchard, *Der dreizehnte Zeuge. Traditions- und kompositionsgeschichtliche Untersuchungen zu Lukas' Darstellung der Frühzeit des Paulus* (FRLANT, 105; Göttingen, 1979); K. Löning, *Die Saulustradition in der Apostelgeschichte* (Münster, 1973); H. J. Michel, *Die Abschiedsrede des Paulus an die Kirche Apg 20, 17-38. Motivgeschichte und theologische Bedeutung* (STANT 35; Munich, 1973); V. Stolle, *Der Zeuge als Angeklagter, Untersuchungen zum Paulusbild des Lukas* (BWANT 102, Stuttgart-Berlin-Köln-Mainz, 1973). In addition, cf. J. Jervell, "The Law in Luke-Acts," *Luke and the People of God* (Minneapolis: Augsburg, 1972), pp. 133-151; "Paul: The Teacher of Israel. The Apologetic Speeches of Paul in Acts," *Luke and the People of God*, pp. 153-183; "Paul in the Acts of the Apostles: Tradition, History, Theology," Chapter 4 in this volume.
3. "On the 'Paulinism' of Acts" (see chap. 3, n. 15).
4. For literature on the question of Luke and Paul, cf. E. Haenchen, *Die Apostelgeschichte* (KEK 3; Göttingen, 1977[7]), pp. 315f. and 702f.; in addition cf. the most recent survey of Lukan research in the last 25 years in F. Bovon, *Luc le théologien. Vingt-cinq ans de recherches (1950-1975)* (Paris, 1978); on the question of Luke and Paul cf. especially pp. 370-378.
5. On the question of miracle in Acts, cf. H. Conzelmann, *Die Apostelgeschichte*, p. 32; T. W. Crafer, *The Healing Miracles in the Book of Acts* (London, 1939); M. Dibelius, *Aufsätze zur Apostelgeschichte*, ed. by H. Greeven (FRLANT 60; Göttingen, 1968), cf. pp. 18ff.; Haenchen, *Apostelgeschichte*, pp. 121f., 238ff., 538ff., and also Haenchen's index; J. A. Hardon, "The Miracle Narratives in the

Acts of the Apostles,'' *CBQ* 16 (1954): 303-318. In addition, cf. Bovon, *Luc*, pp. 211ff. on ''Le Saint-Esprit,'' and the index on ''Signes.''

6. Haenchen, *Apostelgeschichte*, pp. 122f., cf. p. 241.
7. Haenchen, ibid. p. 122.
8. Ibid.
9. E. Käsemann, ''Die Legitimität des Apostels. Eine Untersuchungen zu II Korinther 10-13,'' *ZNW* 41 (1942): 33-71, reprinted in K. H. Rengstorf, *Das Paulusbild in der neueren deutschen Forschung* (Darmstadt, 1969), pp. 475-521.
10. Haenchen, *Apostelgeschichte*, p. 540.
11. Whether the ''superlative'' apostles are to be interpreted here as the Jerusalem apostles (thus Käsemann, op. cit., pp. 41ff., and C. K. Barrett, ''Paul's Opponents in II Corinthians,'' *NTS* 17 [1970-71]: 233-254, 242ff.) is not decisive for us in this context.
12. Haenchen, *Apostelgeschichte*, p. 540.
13. A. v. Harnack, *Neue Untersuchungen zur Apostelgeschichte*, pp. 21ff.; in addition, by the same author, *Lukas der Arzt* and *Die Apostelgeschichte*, especially pp. 159ff. (see chap. 4, nn. 24-25).
14. Vielhauer, ''Paulinism,'' pp. 39ff.
15. Cf. e.g., Burchard, *Zeuge*, p. 178. We note, e.g., in Bovon, *Luc*, that in more recent research the question of miracle in Acts has not aroused much interest among exegetes. In Bovon's survey of research, miracle in Acts plays no role. Cf. e.g., the ''Index Analytique,'' pp. 451ff., especially ''Signes,'' p. 456.
16. On the question of Paul's working miracles as indicated in his letters, cf. J. Jervell, ''Der schwache Charismatiker,'' in J. Friedrich, W. Pöhlmann, and P. Stuhlmacher, eds., *Rechtfertigung: Festschrift für E. Käsemann*, pp. 185-198.
17. On the summaries, cf. P. Benoit, ''Remarques sur les 'sommaires' des Actes 2, 42 a 5,'' *Aux sources de la tradition chretienne* (Festschrift for M. Goguel) (Neuchatel-Paris, 1950), pp. 1-10; H. J. Cadbury, ''The Summaries in Acts,'' in *The Beginnings of Christianity*, K. Lake–H. J. Cadbury, eds., 5:392-402; H. Zimmermann, ''Die Sammelberichte der Apostelgeschichte,'' *BZ* 5 (1961): 71-82.
18. On the genre of the farewell speeches, cf. J. Munck, ''Discours d'adieu dans le Nouveau Testament et dans la littérature biblique,'' *Sources* (see note 17), pp. 155-170. On Acts 20:17-35 in particular, cf. Michel, *Abschiedsrede*.
19. On the trial chapters, cf. Stolle, *Zeuge*; Jervell, ''Teacher,'' pp. 153-184.
20. Of course, we cannot forget that the Pentecost narrative and speech are not merely to be construed as overtures to Peter.
21. Cf. J. Jervell, ''James: The Defender of Paul,'' *Luke and the People of God*, pp. 185-207, 188-199.
22. On the ''Jewish'' Paul of Acts, cf. Harnack, *Untersuchungen*; H. Windisch, *Paulus und das Judentum*, pp. 18ff.
23. Cf. below.
24. On the style of miracle stories in Acts, cf. Dibelius, *Aufsätze*, pp. 18ff.
25. Dibelius, *Aufsätze, pp. 120-162;* U. Wilcken, *Die Missionsreden der Apostelgeschichte*, 3rd ed. (WMANT; Neukirchen, 1974).
26. Cf. below.
27. Conzelmann, *Apostelgeschichte*, p. 41; Haenchen, *Apostelgeschichte*, pp. 121f.; B. Reicke, *Glaube und Leben der Urgemeinde. Bemerkungen zu Apg 1-7* (ATANT 32; Zürich, 1957), pp. 89-96; E. Trocme, ''Le 'Livre des Actes' et l'Histoire'' (Paris, 1957), pp. 30, 81, 183, 195.

28. On this subject, cf. Jervell, "Charismatiker," pp. 185-198.
29. The question whether or not a *healing* miracle is involved here (cf. Haenchen, *Apostelgeschichte*, p. 476) is without significance in this context.
30. On the theme of the "growth of the Word" in Acts, cf. N. A. Dahl, "Ordets vekst," *NTT* 67 (1966): 32-46.
31. Thus Haenchen, *Apostelgeschichte*, p. 430.
32. On this topic, cf. J. Jervell, "Das Volk des Geistes," in *God's Christ and His People*, ed. J. Jervell and W. A. Meeks (Festschrift for N. A. Dahl) (Oslo-Bergen-Tromsö, 1977), pp. 87-106.
33. On the "uneasiness" in research over against this story cf. Haenchen, *Apostelgeschichte*, pp. 538ff.
34. On this topic, cf. Jervell, "Charismatiker," pp. 185-198.
35. The expression, "sign of an apostle," is often regarded as a stereotyped and widespread formula; cf. R. Bultmann, *The Second Letter to the Corinthians* (Minneapolis: Augsburg, 1984), p. 231; H. D. Betz, *Der Apostel Paulus und die sokratische Tradition. Eine exegetische Untersuchung zu seiner 'Apologie' 2 Korinther 10-13* (Tübingen 1972), p. 70f.; Käsemann, *Legitimität*, p. 35; K. H. Rengstorf, "Σημεῖα, κτλ.," *TDNT*, 7:199-268, 259; W. Schmithals, *Das kirchliche Apostelamt. Eine historische Untersuchung* (FRLANT 81; Göttingen, 1961), p. 26. But I find no evidence for this. Why cannot Paul himself have invented the label?
36. Haenchen, *Apostelgeschichte*, p. 122.
37. Thus Betz, *Tradition*, p. 71 (on Rom. 15:19); G. Bornkamm, *Paulus*, (Stuttgart-Berlin-Köln-Mainz, 1969[2]), p. 92; Schmithals, *Apostelamt*, p. 27, and others.
38. Thus especially E. Güttgemanns, *Der leidende Apostel und sein Herr* (see chap. 3, n. 19), pp. 164f., 303.
39. It is incomprehensible that Betz can assert in *Tradition*, p. 71, that there is no clear witness to Paul's miraculous activity; cf. also Schmithals, *Apostelamt*, p. 27. Is it possible to deny that Paul himself lays claim to his own miraculous activity? If we answer yes, then how is Paul's claim to be understood?
40. Who the "superlative apostles" actually are is without significance for us (cf. n. 11). But what is important is how miracle is to be understood here.
41. Without any justification at all, Betz, *Tradition*, p. 71, denies that Galatians 3 has to do with miracles performed by Paul. How then is the connection between verses 2 and 3 to be understood? In the context, Paul is of course speaking of the Galatians making a beginning in the righteousness of faith.
42. The notion that in context and form the passage in 2 Cor. 12:2ff. occupies a unique position within the whole of Paul's epistles cannot be used to deny to Paul all claim to miracle, as does Betz in *Tradition*, p. 71. First of all, 12:12 is not unique to the whole of Paul's epistles, and second, the question of the problem of occasional writings is in this instance overlooked.
43. W. Grundmann, *Der Begriff der Kraft in der neutestamentlichen Gedankenwelt* (BWANT 60; Stuttgart, 1932), p. 99, denies that miraculous power is at issue here. Rather, he states, what is involved is a pneumatic power from God. In my opinion, Grundmann does not make clear how this is to be understood in contrast to the power to work miracles.

44. D. Georgi, *Die Gegner des Paulus im 2. Korintherbrief. Studien zur religiösen Propaganda in der Spätantike* (WMANT 11; Neukirchen, 1964), p. 229, note 7; Güttgemanns, *Apostel*, pp. 154ff.; Käsemann, *Legitimität*, pp. 34f.; W. Schmithals, *Die Gnosis in Korinth. Eine Untersuchung zu den Korintherbriefen* (FRLANT 66; Göttingen, 1956), p. 174; *Apostelamt*, pp. 27f.; U. Wilckens, *Weisheit und Torheit. Eine exegetisch-religionsgeschichtliche Untersuchung zu I Kor. 1–2* (Tübingen, 1959), p. 218.

45. H. Windisch, *Paulus und Christus. Ein biblisch- religionsgeschichtlicher Vergleich* (UNT 24; Leipzig, 1934), pp. 276f., has indicated the contrast between Paul's pneumatic self-consciousness and the massive resistance which he encountered.

46. On this subject, and particularly on ἀσθένεια in Paul as illness, cf. my article, "Charismatiker," especially pp. 191ff.

47. This is clear from such passages as 1 Cor. 9:1; 14:18; 15:7f.; 2 Cor. 5:13; 12:2ff.; Gal. 1:12,16; 2:2; etc. On this subject, cf. also Windisch, *Christus*, p. 180; E. Benz, *Paulus als Visionär. Eine vergleichende Untersuchung der Visionsberichte des Paulus in der Apostelgeschichte und in den paulinischen Briefen* (Mainz, 1952); H. Saake, "Paulus als Ekstatiker. Pneumatologische Beobachtungen zu 2 Kor. 12, 1-10," *Nov T 15* (1973): 153-160; A. T. Lincoln, "Paul the Visionary," *NTS* 25 (1979): 204-220.

Chapter 6: Sons of the Prophets: The Holy Spirit in the Acts of the Apostles

1. E. Schweizer, "πνεῦμα," *TDNT* 6: 404-415; J. A. Fitzmyer, *The Gospel According to Luke, 1-9* (Anchor Bible; New York: Doubleday, 1981), p. 230.

2. Fr. Bovon, *Luc le théologien* (Neuchatel/Paris, 1978), p. 234.

3. G.W.H. Lampe, "The Holy Spirit in the Writings of St. Luke," in *Studies in the Gospels. Essays in Memory of R. H. Lightfoot* (Oxford, 1955), pp. 160-165; W. B. Tatum, "The Epoch of Israel," *NTS* 13 (1966/67): 185, refers to "the centrality of the Spirit in the thought of St. Luke"; for other scholars see Tatum, p. 185, n. 4.

4. Only Luke among New Testament authors uses this phrase.

5. See further pp. 114f.

6. G. Schneider, *Die Apostelgeschichte 1* (see Chap. 1, n. 4), p. 258, rightly speaks of an "ausgesprochen ekklesiologische Ausrichtung der lukanischen Geistesauffassung" (expressly ecclesiological alignment in the Lukan conception of the Spirit).

7. On the Lukan combination of Spirit and kingdom see J. D. G. Dunn, "Spirit and Kingdom," *Expository Times* 82 (197-71): 36-40, esp. 38; H. v. Baer, *Der Heilige Geist in den Lukanschriften* (BWANT 39; Stuttgart, 1926), pp. 81f.; S. S. Smalley, "Spirit, Kingdom and Prayer in Luke-Acts," *NTS* 15 (1973): 63f.; H. H. Wendt, *Die Apostelgeschichte* (Meyers Krit. Ex. Comm. III, 5; Göttingen, 1913), pp. 69f.

8. This is a widespread notion in commentaries and monographs, a result of the idea that the church has replaced the old, empirical Israel and that Luke is writing only to Gentiles. There are some exceptions; H. v. Baer, op. cit., pp. 81f., sees the connection between the coming of the Spirit and the restoration of Israel, and Jesus denies that he immediately (*jetzt gleich*) will rebuild Israel. The nationalistic

idea is there, but confined by the concept of the world mission in 1:8; see further
G. Lohfink, *Die Sammlung Israels* (see chap. 3, n. 44), p. 79; A. Schlatter,
Erläuterungen zum Neuen Testament 1 (1928), "Apostelgechichte," pp. 5f.; Th.
Zahn, *Die Apostelgeschichte des Lucas I (1-12)* (Leipzig, 1919), pp. 30f.

9. The idea is the restoration of the twelve tribes of Israel and the leaders on Israel's
thrones (see Luke 22:29-30); see on the idea of the apostolate in Luke-Acts, J.
Jervell, *Luke and the People of God*, pp. 75-112.

10. Acts 15:16 is interpreted by E. Haenchen, *Apostelgeschichte*, p. 431, to mean
"die in der Auferstehung gipfelnde Jesusgeschichte" (the story of Jesus that cul-
minates in his resurrection). This interpretation is taken up without adding new
arguments by H. Braun, *Qumran und das Neue Testament* II (Tübingen, 1966),
p. 320; among recent commentaries, G. Schneider, *Komm.* I, p. 182f.; cf. further
J. Roloff, *Die Apostelgeschichte*, p. 232: v. 16 means that the apostles "aus dem
alten Gottesvolk das wahre Israel der Endzeit gesammelt" (have gathered the true
Israel of the end-time out of the old people of God); so also G. Lohfink, op. cit.,
pp. 58ff. The exegesis of Haenchen and others runs contrary to the tone of the
expression; see my *Luke and the People of God*, pp. 51ff.

11. J. Roloff, *Komm.*, p. 23, on Acts 1:6-8: The Spirit is given to the members of
the church at the end-time; the members, however, are not identical with the
empirical Israel.

12. Cf. n. 9.

13. J. Fitzmyer, op. cit., p. 231: "The reconstitution of the Twelve (1:15-26) is the
necessary preparation for the outpouring of the Spirit." That is correct, but Fitzmyer does not say what the reconstitution of the Twelve means in relation to Israel.

14. A. George, "L'Esprit Saint dans l'oeuvre de Luc," *RB* 85 (1978): 506-507: The
Spirit manifests itself primarily collectively.

15. Cf. V. C. Pfitzner, " 'Pneumatic' Apostleship? Apostle and Spirit in the Acts of
the Apostles," in *Wort in der Zeit: Festgabe für K. H. Rengstorf* (Leiden, 1980),
pp. 220f.

16. Apart from *epangelia* used in connection with the Spirit it refers in 7:17 to the
right worship and exodus, in 13:23 to the savior for Israel, and in 26:6 to the
resurrection.

17. H. v. Baer, op. cit., p. 68, wonders why the story about the baptism of Jesus
(Luke 3:21-22) and the temptation (4:1-14), both dominated by Jesus' possession
of the Spirit, are separated by the genealogy (3:21-28). Baer gives no answer.
The genealogy demonstrates that Jesus is the Messiah of Israel, and so again we
have the notion of the Spirit connected to Israel.

18. On Moses see below, pp. 117f.

19. M. Bachmann, *Jerusalem und der Tempel. Die geographisch-theologischen Ele-
mente in der lukanischen Sicht des Jüdischen Kultzentrums* (BWANT 109; Stuttgart, Berlin, Köln, Mainz, 1980).

20. J. Roloff's definition in his commentary, p. 23, that Luke can only conceive of
the Spirit as a witness to Jesus is too narrow.

21. So the work and words of the "historical" Jesus are to be understood in Luke's
gospel. The fact that only Jesus has the Spirit during his life (so H. Conzelmann
The Theology of St. Luke [New York: Harper, 1961]) does not speak against this.
But Conzelmann does not take Luke 1-2 into consideration; see below p. 100.

22. On the relation between Spirit and law see pp. 116-119.

23. A. George, op. cit., pp. 513-515.

24. On the words of the Spirit see below p. 108.

25. On the rabbinic idea of Israel as the people of the Spirit, and that Israel as long as they had the Scriptures was not without the energy of the Spirit see Fr. Büchsel, *Der Geist Gottes im Neuen Testament* (Gütersloh, 1926), pp. 130f.

26. Acts 2:30 is interesting as it shows what the prophecy above prophecies is to Luke, namely, that one of David's descendants should sit on his throne, and it is precisely this that is fulfilled in the resurrection of Jesus.

27. On the notion of "opening the Scriptures" see my essay, "The Center of Scripture in Luke," chap. 7 in this volume.

28. The meaning in Acts 13:27 is not that they did not know the words of the prophets, but they did not know Jesus; that is: "him" (τοῦτον) is the direct object for "recognize" (ἀγνοήσαντες), and "the voices" or "words" (τὰς φωνάς) for ἐπλήρωσαν; so G. Schneider, *Komm.* II, p. 135; A. Wikenhauser, *Komm.*, pp. 93, 95; K. Lake in *Beginnings* IV, p. 153. Otherwise, H. Conzelmann, *Komm.* p. 77; O. Bauernfeind, Komm., p. 175; E. Haenchen, *Komm.*, p. 394; J. Roloff, *Komm.*, p. 206; G. Stählin, *Komm.*, p. 179—against the wording of the text.

29. On this idea see D. Georgi, *Die Gegner des Paulus im 2. Korintherbrief*, (Neukirchen-Vluyn, 1954), pp. 114ff.; R. Leivestad, "Das Dogma von der prophetlosen Zeit," *NTS* 19 (1973): 295; P. Schäfer, *Die Vorstellung vom Heiligen Geist in den rabbinischen Literatur* (STANT 28; Munich, 1972), pp. 89ff., 112ff., 143ff.

30. It is well known that the eschatological time of salvation in Jewish thought is determined by a particular "Gottesmacht des Geistes" (display of God's power by the Spirit); H. v. Baer, op. cit., p. 142, with references to Joel 2:28-29 (RSV); Ezek. 36:26; 4 Esra 13, and Test. Levi 18.

31. W. B. Tatum, op. cit. (n. 3), insists on the role of the Spirit in the "period of Israel," the period of preparation, that is, in the infancy narratives (Luke 1–2).

32. On the Spirit in Luke 1–2 see A. George, op. cit., p. 514, n. 38; G. W. H. Lampe, op. cit., p. 160; W. B. Tatum, op. cit.; J. A. Fitzmyer, *Comm.* I, p. 229. G. Friedrich, προφήτης, TDNT 6: 835f., remarks that all these persons have a relation to the temple; temple and prophecy belong together.

33. H. v. Baer, op. cit., pp. 45ff., 55; M. A. Chevallier, *L'Esprit et le Messie dans le Bas-judaism et le Nouveau Testament* (Paris: 1958), p. 86; G. Friedrich, op. cit., pp. 838-842.

34. It is artificial to talk about the Spirit in Luke 1–2 as the prophetic Spirit in contrast to the messianic Spirit from Luke 3 forwards, as W. B. Tatum, op. cit., p. 191. What is the supposed contrast between them, especially when Luke has a Prophet-Messiah (Acts 3:22ff.; 7:37)? This exegesis is occasioned by Tatum's three-epoch scheme. How is it possible to find that Jesus was "not seized by the Spirit as an external power" (Tatum, ibid.)?

35. G. W. H. Lampe, op. cit., p. 165; W. B. Tatum, op. cit., p. 189.

36. Op. cit., p. 167.

37. We will not here raise the question about the possible sources and traditions used in Luke 1–2. The latest contributions are those of J. A. Fitzmyer, *Comm.*, pp. 309ff. and E. Schweizer, "Zum Aufbau von Lukas 1 und 2," in *Neues Testament und Christologie im Werden* (Göttingen, 1982), pp. 11-32. Both reckon with multiple sources and traditions, but the narratives were "in large part freely composed by Luke" (Fitzmyer) and Luke rewrites and penetrates "übernommene . . . Traditionen mit seinem Stil" (in his own way the traditions he took over) (Schweizer, p. 27). Important in our context is that Luke uses the same expression, τὸ

ἅγιον πνεῦμα in Luke 1–2 as he does, with rare exceptions, throughout the gospel and Acts. Nor is this expression typical for the Septuagint of the intertestamental literature. If Luke used sources or traditions he has reworked and rewritten them, at least for the notions about the Spirit in Luke 1–2; see H. v. Baer, op. cit., p. 54; A. v. Harnack, *Lukas der Arzt*, pp. 138-152.

38. References to the Spirit as active in the history of Israel cannot for Luke mean only "the period of Israel" as restricted to what we have in the infancy narratives of Luke 1–2; see J. A. Fitzmyer, *Comm.* I, p. 228; W. B. Tatum, op. cit., p. 186. It is not correct to use Luke 1–2 as a source for Luke's notion about the "epoch of Israel," or to characterize that epoch. It is the end of that epoch, not the whole of it, with a special task to identify Mary's child as the Messiah of the Scriptures. It is misleading to talk about the epoch of Israel, because the church is even an epoch of Israel, the Messiah-epoch. That Israel before Christ even has different epochs according to Luke is evident from Acts 7.

39. Only Luke 22:20, the eucharistic words, has the expression "the new covenant" (ἡ καινὴ διαθήκη). But this part of the text from the Last Supper is probably not a genuine part of Luke's gospel. Apart from the expression here, there is nothing in Luke's understanding of the gospel that would testify to the idea of a new covenant in contrast to the old. This would make sense in the context of Paul's contrast of law and faith, or in Matthew's understanding of the church having replaced Israel (21:43), but not to Luke, who could at most speak of a renewed covenant.

40. The Spirit being operative in the "period of Israel": J. A. Fitzmyer, *Comm.* I, pp. 228f.

41. Fr. Bovon, op. cit., p. 234 finds this understanding secured by exegesis; A. George, op. cit., p. 512; H. Conzelmann, *Die Apostelgeschichte*, p. 23f.; J. A. Fitzmyer, *Comm.* I, 231; G. Friedrich, προφήτης, 849; V. C. Pfitzner, op. cit., p. 223; J. Roloff, *Komm.*, p. 53; E. Schweizer, πνεῦμα, 410; W. B. Tatum, op. cit., p. 191.

42. W. B. Tatum, op. cit., p. 191. This is contrary to Acts, where only some few individuals act as prophets, but all have the Spirit, manifested in various ways.

43. This text is cited in Jewish sources; see Num. Rabbah 15:25: In this world only few persons prophesy; in the coming world the whole people of Israel will become prophets.

44. C. K. Barrett, "Light on the Holy Spirit from Simon Magus (Acts 8:4-25)," in J. Kremer, ed., *Les Actes des Apôtres. Traditions, redaction, theologie* (BETL XLVIII; Gembloux, 1979), pp. 281-295.

45. It should be observed that the Spirit is not the energy in the Christian life, giving people faith and salvation; see E. Schweizer, πνεῦμα, 410.

46. R. N. Longenecker, *The Christology of Early Jewish Christianity* (SBT, sec. ser. 17; London, 1970), pp. 37f., sees this Moses-prophet Christology as typical for Jewish Christians and for Jewish-Christian writers in the early church; cf. E. Hennecke and W. Schneemelcher, *New Testament Apocrypha* (Philadelphia: Westminster, 1963-1965), 2:164f., 174f.

47. This is the way Luke argues, and not, as J. Roloff, *Komm.*, p. 53, thinks, that the gift is for the church which is no longer part of the empirical Israel. Luke, of course, knows of only one Israel.

48. G. W. H. Lampe, op. cit., p. 172: "So far as his words and deeds are concerned, Jesus is virtually identical with the Spirit"; J. Fitzmyer, *Comm.* I, p. 230: The

Spirit in Acts 16:7 is a "substitute for the risen Christ himself, when he is no
longer physically present to his followers." This does not hold water. More correct
is Fr. Bovon, op. cit., p. 234: It is common to the exegetes that they have difficulties in detecting the connection between the exalted Christ and the Spirit.

49. Cf. K. Lake, "The Holy Spirit," in *The Beginnings of Christianity* I, V, pp. 109f.

50. J. Jervell, *Luke and the People of God*, pp. 113-132; further, R. J. Coggins, "The
Samaritans and Acts," *NTS* 28 (1982): 423-434, esp. 431-434.

51. The Gentiles are never on equal footing with the Jews. Acts 10:34-35 cannot be
understood so that the Gentiles and the Jews always have been in the same situation.
Such an interpretation would have to ignore the use of the Scriptures in Acts and
the history of Israel. And it would have to overlook the words in the speech
following vv. 34-35. The situation of the Gentiles has changed; they now have
part in the promises to Israel.

52. *Aufsätze zur Apostelgeschichte*, ed. H. Greeven (FRLANT 60; Göttingen, 1951),
pp. 96-107.

53. J. Roloff, *Komm.*, p. 230.

54. J. Jervell, *Luke and the People of God*, pp. 65ff.

55. One difference between Jews and Gentiles is the Spirit; this difference is removed
when God gives the Spirit to the Gentiles; see J. Roloff, *Komm.*, p. 230.

56. There are no parallels to this expression within the New Testament, and it shows
at least the importance of the relation between the prophets and the Jews to Luke.
There are no parallels in late Judaism; the ones in H. Strack–P. Billerbeck, *Kommentar zum Neuen Testament aus Talmud und Midrasch* (Munich, 1956), 2:627,
are not really parallels; so, correctly, G. Schneider, *Komm.* I, p. 330, n. 127.

57. G. Schneider, *Komm.* I, p. 330.

58. It is somewhat misleading when J. Roloff, *Komm.*, p. 253 and G. Stählin, *Die
Apostelgeschichte*, p. 226, understand Acts 17:11 so that the Jews would confirm
"der Richtigkeit seines Schriftbeweises" (the correctness of his scripture proofs)
(Roloff). What they do confirm is not Paul's exegetical technique, but whether
the gospel is actually there verbatim in the Scriptures.

59. H. v. Baer, op. cit., pp. 65, 69; it may be misleading to understand Luke 4:21
as J. A. Fitzmyer does, *Comm.* I, p. 230: "What Isaiah spoke of centuries before,
now sees fulfillment in a new sense today." But the idea to Luke is that Jesus
fulfilled the promise of Isaiah in the old—and only—sense.

60. Cf. my essay, "The Center of Scripture in Luke," Chapter 7 in this volume.

61. It is remarkable that this idea is not to be found in the lengthy description of the
legal process against Paul in Acts 21–28. Perhaps we have it in Acts 4:8,6,10
and Chapter 7. But the wisdom (σοφία) of 6:10 is mentioned already in 6:3 about
the seven, before any persecution is told of. If Luke wanted to avoid any doubt
about the attitude of the church to the Scriptures, we can understand his silence.
Of course Luke 12:12 is a word of Jesus, which Luke faithfully quotes without
using it, at least not very extensively.

62. Representative: H. Schlier, *Ekklesiologie des Neuen Testaments* (Mysterium Sal-
utis 4:1; Einsiedeln, 1972), p. 124; A. George, op. cit., p. 522.

63. Op. cit., p. 234.

64. The same idea is found in John 7:13,26, etc. For the special contrast between
παρρησία and what is secret or hidden see John 7:4; 10:24; 11:14,54). For Luke
the situation is different; nothing in the Jesus event is hidden, something that is
important for his exegesis of the Old Testament.

65. G. Delling, ". . . Als er uns die Schrift aufschloss," in *Das Wort und die Wörter: Festschrift G. Friedrich* (Stuttgart, 1973), p. 87, maintains that "the Word of God" (λόγος τοῦ θεοῦ) for Luke is not the Scriptures, but the gospel. But this is not significant as the gospel verbatim is to be found in the Scriptures.

66. Cf. H. Schlier, op. cit., p. 128.

67. The Spirit performing miracles is probably to be found even in Acts 7:35; 11:21; 13:11 in the references to God's "finger" or "hand"; cf. Luke 11:20 where Luke ascribes the exorcisms to the "finger of God" instead of "the Spirit of God" (see also Acts 4:28, 30); see G. W. H. Lampe, op. cit., p. 192; H. v. Baer., op. cit., p. 125.

68. So rightly G. Schneider, *Die Apostelgeschichte* 2: 264, and G. Stählin, *Komm.*, p. 254, against H. Conzelmann, *Komm.*, p. 111; J. Roloff, *Komm.*, p. 53 and A. Loisy, *Les Actes des Apôtres* (Paris, 1920), ad loc.

69. Acts 13:9-12 does not belong to this context. Paul is filled with the Holy Spirit and curses Elymas (13:8). The exact words of the curse are quoted in 13:10-11a. Then v. 11b shows the effect of the curse, and this effect is here probably seen as the work of the Spirit. ἐκπλήσσω (Acts 13:12) is used regularly in the synoptic gospels to express the reaction when people see miracles (Matt. 7:28; 13:54; Mark 1:22; 6:2; 7:33; 11:18; Luke 2:48; 4:32; 9:43).

70. When Paul in spite of the words of the Spirit goes to Jerusalem, it shows an unprecedented attitude towards the prophecies in the Scriptures. There is a great difference! The problems for the exegetes with Acts 21:4 are clear; J. Roloff, *Komm.*, p. 309, alludes to the "honest convictions" of the Christians from Tyre: G. Schneider, *Komm.* II, p. 303: the Spirit did not forbid Paul to go to Jerusalem, but revealed what was going to happen to him there; E. Haenchen, *Komm.*, p. 574, avoids the saying; H. Conzelmann, *Komm.*, pp. 120f.: It is not a command from the Spirit, but conclusions drawn by the disciples caused by the revelation of what would happen to Paul; G. Stählin, *Komm.*, p. 273: This is an honest warning, not implied in the words of the Spirit; O. Bauernfeind, p. 241: Paul misheard the true content of the words: K. Lake, *The Acts of the Apostles*, in *Beginnings* IV, 266: Paul paid no attention; "did he doubt their inspiration?"

71. So A. George, op. cit., p. 529, but at the same time he finds a "conception materielle," pp. 528f. Otherwise Fitzmyer, *Comm.* I, p. 228: The Spirit is "mainly an impersonal active force."

72. J. A. Fitzmyer, *Comm.* I, p. 231.

73. As a Samaritan he is considered a Jew (see n. 50).

74. The last of the great prophets are for Luke probably the persons in Luke 1–2. To assert that after these prophets there is prophecy only in the church is not to say that there is no prophecy in Israel, because the church is Israel, the legitimate continuation of the history of the prophet's Israel. The disobedient, nonbelieving Jews simply follow in the footsteps of their fathers, who opposed the Spirit (Acts 7:51).

75. Apart from Luke we find this in the New Testament only in Heb. 3:7; 10:15; 1 Peter 1:10-11; 2 Peter 1:21; Matt. 22:43 and in parallels.

76. Fr. Bovon, op. cit., pp. 237ff.; H. Conzelmann, *Komm.*, p. 27; E. Lohse, "Die Bedeutung des Pfingstberichtes im Rahmen des lukanischen Geschichtswerkes," *EvT* 13 (1953/54), pp. 422- 436; further, πεντηκοστή, TDNT 6, 46-49; J. Potin, *La fête juive de la Pentecôte* I-II (Lectio Divina 65, Paris 1971); E. Schweizer,

πνεῦμα, 408. Important texts: Jub. 6; lQS 1ff.; Philo *Decal* 9:32ff.; 11:44-46; *De vita contemplativa* 7:65-68; b. Talmud Yoma 4.

77. So with O. Bauernfeind, *Komm.*, p. 35; J. Bonsirven, *Le Judaïsme palestinien au temps de Jesus-Christ* II (Paris, 1935), p. 123; G. Kretschmar, "Himmelfahrt und Pfingsten," *ZKG* 66 (1954/55): 209-253; E. Schweizer, πνεῦμα, 408f.

78. Cf. E. Haenchen, *Komm.*, pp. 175ff.; E. Lohse, "Die Bedeutung des Pfingstberichtes," pp. 422ff.; πεντηκοστή, 46-49 (for the last two see n. 76); G. Schneider, *Komm.* I, pp. 246ff.; and above all W. L. Knox, *The Acts of the Apostles* (Cambridge University Press, 1948).

79. Representative: H. Conzelmann, *The Theology of St. Luke*, pp. 145ff., 212f.

80. E. Haenchen, *Komm.*, p. 562: Paul traveled to Jerusalem because he was a pious Jew; H. v. Baer, op. cit., p. 90. But H. H. Wendt, *Die Apostelgeschichte*, finds it unbelievable that Paul wanted "wieder das jüd. Fest in jüd. Weise mitzufeiern" (again to celebrate the Jewish festival in the Jewish way). E. Lohse, πεντηκοστή, 50, asks on the basis of 1 Cor. 16:8 whether there was at that time a Christian Pentecost in Ephesus or Corinth. He finds it possible that the church originally took part in the Jewish Pentecost.

81. J. Jervell, *Luke and the People of God*, p. 140.

82. On the law as prophecy see Luke 24:27,44; Acts 3:22; 7:35ff.; 24:14; 26:22; 28:23; ceremonial aspects: Luke 2:22,23,24,27,39; 5:14; 20:28; Acts 6:14; 7:8; 15:1,5; 18:15; 21:21; 22:3; 24:28; etc. Above all the law to Luke is a ceremonial law; see J. Jervell, *Luke and the People of God*, p. 139.

83. The outpouring of the Spirit is centered in Jerusalem; so H. v. Baer, op. cit., p. 78; G. Friedrich, προφήτης, 837. In late Judaism the Spirit is tied to the temple and Jerusalem (Sir. 48:10; 1 Macc. 4:46f.). On the temple as the place for the Spirit in rabbinism see P. Schäfer, op. cit., pp. 73-88; 135-139.

84. The commentaries in general notice that Spirit and law are mentioned together, without any attempt to explain the relation between them and to Stephen's speech as a whole; H. Conzelmann, *Komm.*, p. 50, and E. Haenchen, *Komm.*, p. 277, do not interpret Acts 7:53; G. Schneider, *Komm.*, 1:469; v. 53 "wertet das bisher konkret aufgeführte Verhalten . . . als Gesetzesübertretung" (deems the actual conduct up to that point as transgression of the law); G. Stählin, *Komm.*, p. 111: "wohl in erster Linie an das 5.Gebot gedacht" (no doubt primarily thinks of the fifth commandment"); O. Bauernfeind, *Komm.*, p. 119; A. Wikenhauser, *Die Apostelgeschichte* (RNT 5; Regensburg, 1951), p. 58; J. Roloff, *Komm.*, p. 12: Moses, the prophets, and Jesus "haben Israel den heiligen Gotteswillen, dem Gesetz unterstellt" (subjected Israel to God's holy will—to the law); when they killed them, they rejected the law. Cf. even K. Lake, *Beginnings* 4:83. H. H. Wendt, *Komm.*, p. 150: Their not keeping the law is more than the murder of "the Just One."

85. The coming prophet-Messiah in late Judaism was supposed to have Mosaic features; see R. N. Longenecker, op. cit., p. 33, with literature. On the Samaritans, see M. Gaster, *The Samaritans* (London: Milford, 1925), pp. 90f.; J. McDonald, *The Theology of the Samaritans* (Philadelphia: Westminster, 1964), pp. 160, 198, 216f., 361-63. For the idea of the coming Prophet see 1 Macc. 4:46; Sir. 48:10f.; Gen. Rabbah 71:9; 99:11; 4 Ezra 6:26; 7:28.

86. G. Stahlin, *Komm.*, p. 111: Above all, the fifth commandment; cf. J. Roloff, *Komm.*, p. 128. Stählin overlooks the fact that 7:51-53 is the conclusion to be drawn from the speech as a whole.

87. In Judaism we have combined the eschatological outpouring of the Spirit and the complete obedience of the law; so, e.g., Test. Judah 24; Orac. Sibyl. III 573. The Spirit and prophecy were given at Sinai according to Exod. Rabbah 5:12; 28:12.
88. J. Jervell, *Luke and the People of God*, pp. 138-141.
89. It may be misleading with J. A. Fitzmyer, *Comm.* I, p. 229 to refer to Luke's concept of the "new Spirit."

Chapter 7: The Center of Scripture in Luke

1. In what follows, the theme is treated primarily from the viewpoint of Acts.
2. According to F. Overbeck, *Kurze Erklärung der Apostelgeschichte* (HNT, de Wette I/4⁴; Leipzig, 1870), pp. 416f., Paul here denies "any distinction between his faith and the Old Testament . . . he maintains that his attitude toward the entire content of the Old Testament is no different from that of Jews in general." This is correctly seen, but overlooked in research.
3. Thus as early as in the prolog to his gospel, 1:3.
4. H. Conzelmann, *The Theology of St. Luke* (New York: Harper and Row, 1961), p. 158, writes that for Luke γραφή is not a title for the entire canon. But Luke's use of πᾶς, κτλ., precisely implies what is later described as γραφή. Luke does not view Scripture only in its totality, but also in its variety.
5. In J. Ernst, ed., *Schriftauslegung* (Paderborn, 1972), pp. 345-347, A. Sand maintains that the Scripture plays no role in Luke, but has been dispensed with in the community's missionary preaching. If this is true, how we are to explain the many references to Scripture in Acts which are independent of the tradition and original in their exposition remains a riddle.
6. G. Delling's remark in ". . . als er uns die Schrift aufschloss," contained in H. Dalz and S. Schulz, *Das Wort und die Wörter, Festschrift für G. Friedrich* (Stuttgart, 1973), p. 81, to the effect that for Luke the phrase "God's Word" does not denote the Old Testament but rather the message of salvation in Jesus, is correct, but of no material import. The message contains nothing which is not already present in Scripture; cf. below.
7. Strangely enough, these are almost overlooked in research.
8. These are not described as quotations.
9. We have no parallel to this in the New Testament, though we encounter summaries which are similar, that is, in Hebrews 11, a section which in somewhat formal sense borders on the collections of examples in I Clement. Acts 7 and 13, however, are not collections of examples, since what is decisive in these chapters is the history as such.
10. Matt. 22:40; 26:56; John 1:45; 5:39,46; 20:9; Rom. 1:2-3; 3:21; 16:26; 1 Cor. 15:3f.; Heb. 1:1.
11. E. Haenchen, *Die Apostelgeschichte*, p. 206, states that the community regards the prophets as a great unity which preached Messiah's suffering according to God's will. This is also stated in the commentaries by Bauernfeind, 65; Loisy, p. 233, and Wendt, p. 105. Where is the evidence for this?
12. Luke does not refer to "all the Scriptures," but designates all Scriptures as "prophets," indicating the overriding significance of the prophetic.

13. As is well known, we encounter summaries of the law in Rom. 13:9 and Gal. 5:14; or of the "law and the prophets" in Matt. 22:40. Rom. 1:2 regards the prophetic writings as a preaching of Christ beforehand, and in 1 Cor. 15:3, Jesus' death and resurrection are a summary of the content of Scripture. John, e.g., 5:39, is nearest to Luke, but the mystical exposition of Scripture in John has little in common with Luke.

14. The fact that in the New Testament Luke alone and with such emphasis refers to the Psalms is connected with the fact that he regards David as their author; for Luke, David is the central figure in the Scripture; cf. below.

15. In this connection, I evaluate Acts quite differently from T. Holtz, *Untersuchungen über die alttestamentlichen Zitate bei Lukas* (Berlin, 1968), and B. Lindars, *New Testament Apologetic* (London, 1961).

16. T. Holtz, op. cit., pp. 60-130, is of a different opinion.

17. These forms cannot be compared with the rabbinic-scribal ויומר ("and he said"), etc., as already indicated by the great variation in Luke's formulas of introduction. Add to this the importance of the Spirit in Luke's scriptural quotations.

18. But cf. Heb. 10:7, where the γέγραπται ("it is written") appears within a quotation—and is thus itself a quotation.

19. Cf. also 10:5, 8, where Christ, and 9:20, where Moses speaks.

20. In this passage, the ἐν Δαυίδ ("through David") cannot be intended in the local sense, as construed by Blass, Debrunner, and Rehkopf, *Grammatik des neutestamentlichen Griechisch* (Göttingen, 1976), para. 219, n. 1, but rather appears in place of the instrumental dative.

21. Thus also Heb. 1:1: ἐν τοῖς προφήταις ("by the prophets"; cf. also 1:2: ἐν υἱῷ, "by a Son") does not mean "in the prophetic books," but rather "through the prophets." Luke's manner of quoting differs from that of Hebrews which never indicates where a passage in Scripture appears. The human instruments are not important. They are, however, for Luke, since he intends to indicate the continuity of the prophets of Scripture with those of the community.

22. Cf. below.

23. For the center defined with respect to content, cf. below.

24. Cf. K. Lake–H. J. Cadbury, *The Beginnings of Christianity* 4:38.

25. Elsewhere, as in Acts 7:8f., Luke names "the twelve patriarchs."

26. In the New Testament only Luke calls David a "prophet," though it is common knowledge that David spoke "in the Spirit," Matt. 22:43 and parallels.

27. Cf. Acts 1:16 in comparison with 1:20, where Psalms 69 and 109 are cited.

28. T. Holtz, op. cit., p. 55, is of the opinion that Luke erroneously cites David as the author of Psalm 2. But it is clear that Luke regards David as author of all the Psalms. Cf. also the commentaries of Bauernfeind and Wendt on the passage. J. Roloff, *Die Apostelgeschichte*, p. 206, asserts that next to Psalm 110, Psalm 2 is the Old Testament text most frequently cited in the New Testament as a Christological scripture-proof. Be that as it may, Luke's exposition of Psalm 2 (Acts 4:25ff. and 13:33) in terms of Jesus' death and resurrection is unique to the New Testament.

29. E. Haenchen, op. cit., p. 223, thinks that τοῦ πατρὸς ἡμῶν ("our father") and διὰ πνεύματος ἁγίου ("by the Holy Spirit") are later additions, since God does not speak through the Spirit, but rather through the prophets. For Luke, however, this is no alternative. God speaks through the Spirit when speaking through the

prophets. Thus, of course, God also speaks through the prophets of the community via the Spirit (Acts 13:1ff.)!

30. Besides Luke, only Heb. 3:7 and 10:15 link the Spirit's speaking to a quotation from Scripture.

31. Holtz, op. cit., p. 11, writes that the addition of the καὶ προφητεύσουσιν is an error, since the Spirit's outpouring in Acts 2 is manifest in glossolalia, not in prophetic speech. First of all, Holtz seems to separate glossolalia and prophecy here in non-Lukan, Pauline fashion (1 Cor. 14). Second, the alleged addition is not conceivable as an error. Third, in Luke's interpretation of Scripture the prophetic element is the alpha and omega.

32. Cf. below.

33. It is striking that Luke refers either to Scripture prophets or to prophecy linked to the community, thus e.g., in Luke 1:76; 2:25ff.,36ff.; 4:24; 7:16,28; 9:8; 11:49; Acts 2:17ff.; 13:1; 15:32; 21:10; etc. But it is never stated that there are prophets in the synagogue, although the Jews are the sons of the prophets (Acts 3:25).

34. On this topic, cf. D. Juel, "Social Dimensions of Exegesis. The Use of Psalm 16 in Acts 2," *CBQ* 43 (1981): 543-556.

35. So the concern is not to show that the quotation is altogether suitable as a means of proof; thus M. Rese, *Alttestamentliche Motive in der Christologie des Lukas* (*SNT* 1; Gütersloh, 1969), p. 77. Luke does not doubt the evidential force of the passage, but rather wants to make clear that it can only have to do with Jesus.

36. Regarding the argument that the three quotations in vv. 33-35 were originally— that is, in Jewish exposition—oriented to David, cf. E. Lövestam, "Son and Saviour. A Study of Acts 13:32-37," *CNT* 18 (1961): 11ff. Cf. also T. Holtz, op. cit., pp. 140ff.

37. On the Lukan Paul as charismatic, cf. J. Jervell, "Paul in the Acts of the Apostles: Tradition, History, Theology," Chapter 4 in this volume.

38. According to Holtz, op. cit., pp. 135f., what is involved here is a Lukan reworking of the tradition. Holtz derives his main support for this view from 1 Clem. 18:1. In my opinion, it is more appropriate to regard v. 22 as an original Lukan construction, keeping in mind Luke's quite original portrayal of David.

39. Or, is it simply a matter of the rabbinic method of quotation, according to which the proofs from Scripture submitted are cited with a ויומר ("and he said"), thus here with an εἴρηκεν, λέγει ("he has said, it says")? Thus M. Rese, op. cit., p. 135. Here, however, the Scripture is clearly cited as the indisputable authority of God.

40. The passage is clearly to be understood in this sense, if τὰ ὅσια Δαυίδ τὰ πιστά ("the holy and sure blessings of David") are to be construed as the scriptural promises of David, a view strongly suggested by the context. Cf. in particular J. Roloff, op. cit., p. 207.

41. Cf. D. Juel, op. cit.

42. On this topic, cf. G. Delling, op. cit., pp. 75ff.

43. H. Conzelmann, *Die Apostelgeschichte*, pp. 56f. writes that v. 34 formulates a basic problem of the primitive Christian hermeneutic, and he makes reference to Justin's Dialogs, passim. Cf. also J. Roloff, op. cit., p. 141. This is probably correct, but in the New Testament only Luke defines the problem. In Acts 8:34 it is the same problem as in Chapters 2 and 13. Does it reflect a discussion with the synagogue?

44. On Acts 18:28, cf. E. Haenchen, op. cit., p. 527, who remarks that the phrase "well versed (mighty) in the Scriptures" (v.24) means to possess the gift of the Spirit which enables one to uncover the hidden Christian meaning of the Old Testament. But for Luke the Scriptures do not at all have such hidden meaning.

45. On this subject, cf. E. Haenchen, op. cit., p. 398, and my criticism in *Luke and the People of God*, pp. 55ff.

46. The significance of the prophetic for Luke can also be seen in Luke 13:28. To the tradition in Matt. 8:11-13, Luke has added "Abraham and Isaac and Jacob," and "all the prophets."

47. As M. Rese correctly sees, op. cit., pp. 93f.

48. On this topic, cf. J. Jervell, "The Unknown Paul," Chapter 3 in this volume.

49. The combination of law and the worship of God appears also in Acts 6:13; 21:28; and 25:8.

50. On this subject, cf. J. Roloff, op. cit., p. 208; J. Jervell, *Luke and the People of God*, pp. 133-151.

51. Contra H. Conzelmann, *The Theology of St. Luke*, pp. 159ff.

52. Cf. above.

53. It may be correct that Luke all throughout gives positive evaluation to the mediation of the law through angels, cf. E. Haenchen, op. cit., p. 227; G. Schneider, *Die Apostelgeschichte* 1:464. Nevertheless, we may not overlook the inferiority of the law in comparison with the prophetic.

54. In Luke, "the fathers" are evaluated positively as well as negatively; positively in 3:13,25; 5:30; 7:12; 13:17; 22:14; and 26:6, and negatively in 7:38,45,51-63; 15:10; and 28:25.

55. The peculiar significance of Israel in connection with prophecy lies also in the fact that Luke—again alone in the New Testament—describes David as "our father," that is, father of the Jews (4:25). Not only the Messiah is the son of David, but also the people of Israel. David is emphatically described as father of the Messiah in Luke 1:32.

56. The words in the quotation from Amos are cited as "the words of the prophets" (v. 16), though the "I" speaking in the text can only be understood as God himself. This indicates how obviously Luke construes the words of the prophets as God's own.

57. Cf. the altered situation in the Qumran texts: CD 7:16 and 4Q Flor 1:12. In these texts, Amos 9:11, but not 9:12, is interpreted.

58. Cf. a different judgment in E. Haenchen, op. cit., p. 431. On this position, cf. my critique in *Luke and the People of God*, pp. 51ff.

59. Holtz, op. cit., pp. 24f., asserts that v. 16 does not derive from Luke who merely cites v. 17, since the Jewish Christians had directed the prophecy toward themselves. Luke, however, did not follow suit. Holtz gives no reason for this other than that Luke's theology is sharply distinguished from a Jewish-Christian theology. Why?

60. To this is also connected the fact that Luke understands the words of the Scripture as spoken, as oral; cf. below. In the New Testament, only Luke makes any mention of the reading of Scripture on the Sabbath (13:27; 15:21; Luke 4:16); but cf. 2 Cor. 3:15.

61. In Acts, Luke gives no criticism of the synagogue as institution, which, e.g., would correspond to the words concerning the temple in v. 7.

62. On the concept of the prophets as a greater unity which proclaimed Messiah's suffering, cf. above, note 10. But we should not forget that Luke is not merely interested in individual writings, but also in individual prophets. In addition, in Luke's reference to "the prophets" he has in mind not only the prophets but all the writings of the Old Testament. Just as the rabbis regarded Scripture as a whole as Torah, so Luke regarded it as prophecy, and thus as a witness to Christ. In this sense we may speak of "a great unity."

63. No direct quotation is given here. But the reference is clearly to Deut. 21:22 (LXX); thus also E. Haenchen, op. cit., p. 245, who maintains that the Christians had interpreted Deut. 21:22 of Jesus' crucifixion. "The Christians" here are Luke and Paul, since κρεμάννυμι ("hang"), applied to Jesus' death, appears only in Luke (four times) and in Paul (Gal. 3:13). The combination of κρεμάννυμι and ξύλον ("tree") occurs only in Acts 5:30; 10:39; and Gal. 3:13.

64. Only the resurrection can be the subject of this exposition of Psalm 2:7 as, in my opinion, v. 34 clearly shows. It is clear that the use of Psalm 2 here is quite peculiar and unique to the New Testament. In Acts 4:25-26, Luke refers Ps. 2:1-2 to Jesus' death. For this reason, it is easy to understand that in Acts 13:33ff. he also finds the resurrection in Psalm 2.

65. In the references to Scripture in Acts, the life of Jesus before his death is never treated. This too is in harmony with the content of the kerygmatic formulas (the exceptions are Acts 2:22 and 10:37).

66. Cf. above.

Chapter 8: The Circumcised Messiah

1. First published under the title, "Den omskarne Messias," in *SEÅ* 37-38 (1972-73): 145-155.

2. Cf. H. Sahlin, *Der Messias und das Gottesvolk. Studien zur protolukanischen Theologie* (ASNU 12, Uppsala, 1945), pp. 240f. Sahlin writes that 2:21 is an interpolation because it is the only biographical verse in Luke 1-2.

3. J. Weiss, W. Bousset, and W. Heitmüller, *Die Schriften des Neuen Testaments* I (Göttingen, 1917[3]), p. 412. Cf. also the commentaries by H. Schürmann and L. Brun on Luke 2:21.

4. Thus in the commentaries by Brun, G. B. Caird, B. S. Easton, W. Grundmann, W. J. Harrington, F. Hauck, E. Klostermann, Schürmann. Luke 1:60-63 indicates that the naming of the Baptist is decisive for reasons other than the naming of Jesus. Matt. 1:21 gives evidence of a quite different reflection upon the name than occurs in Luke. Now, this does not mean that for Luke the giving of the name is unimportant, for it is the fulfillment of an angel's word. But this gives us no right to play off the giving of the name against the circumcision—the tendency of the commentaries. On the understanding of the "name" as an element in Jewish-Christian Christology, cf. R. N. Longenecker, *The Christology of Early Jewish Christianity* (SBT 2, 17; London, 1970), pp. 41-46.

5. In his commentary, Easton writes that the circumcision "is taken for granted."

6. In his commentary on Luke 2:21, Schürmann states that obedience to angels is more important than obedience to the Law.

7. Justin, *Dialog*, 46ff.

8. On the various attempts at solving the problem of sources, etc., cf. R. McL. Wilson, "Some Recent Studies in the Lucan Infancy Narratives" in SE 1:235-253; H. H. Oliver, "The Lucan Birth Stories and the Purpose of Luke-Acts" in *NTS* 10 (1963-64): 202-226, 205ff. Most recent works include C. Burger, *Jesus als Davidssohn* (FRLANT 98; Göttingen, 1970), pp. 127ff.; W. Wink, *John the Baptist in the Gospel Tradition* (SNTSMS 7; Cambridge, 1968), pp. 58ff.

9. Cf. G. Lohfink, *Die Sammlung Israels* (STANT; Munich, 1975), esp. pp. 17-32.

10. This can be seen in (1) the καὶ ὅτε; (2) the construction τοῦ with the infinitive to denote intent; (3) the term πίμπλημι together with ἡμέραι and the like, and (4) the verb συλλαμβάνειν. Cf. A. Plummer's commentary on the passage.

11. Cf. the commentaries by E. E. Ellis, Plummer, K. H. Rengstorf, Th. Zahn. In addition, cf. K. Bornhäuser, *Die Geburts- und Kindheitsgeschichte Jesu* (Gütersloh, 1930), pp. 112f., and B. Weiss, *Das Leben Jesu* 1 (Stuttgart-Berlin, 1902⁴),
p. 235.

12. Ellis writes that Jesus is identified with his people; Bornhäuser, that Jesus is received by the people and obliged to obey the law; and T. W. Manson that the fulfillment of the law is calculated to show that "Christianity is the fulfillment of Judaism." Plummer writes that Jesus, the son of Abraham, is obedient to God's will by fulfilling the law; Rengstorf that Jesus is taken up into the people of God, because circumcision gives a share in God's covenant with Abraham and his generation, and Zahn that Jesus is obedient to the law (by way of reference to Gal. 4:4).

13. The newer editions do not give sufficient evidence of this. We refer to C. Tischendorf's *Editio octava critica major* and to A. Merx, *Die vier kanonischen Evangelien nach ihrem ältesten bekannten Text* II/1 (Berlin, 1905), p. 205.

14. On this construction, cf. F. Blass, A. Debrunner, and F. Rehkopf, *Grammatik des neutestamentlichen Griechisch* (Göttingen, 1976¹⁴), para. 442, 7.

15. Mss. 13, 69, 124, 346.

16. Not e and q.

17. Cf. above, n. 3.

18. E. J. Epp, *The Theological Tendency of Codex Bezae Cantabrigiensis in Acts* (SNTSMS 3; Cambridge, 1966), pp. 41ff. In D we find an introduction to Acts 11:2 which intends to show that it is not the primitive community as such, but merely a group of Judaizers in the communities which criticizes Peter for having fellowship with the uncircumcised.

19. Cf. Merx, op. cit., p. 205.

20. Merx, op. cit.; thus also W. Bauer, *Das Leben Jesu im Zeitalter der neutestamentlichen Apokryphen* (Darmstadt, 1967 [= Tübingen, 1909]), p. 74.

21. The Sinaitic Syriac text has παιδίον, "child," instead of αὐτόν, "him." So also Cantabrigiensis and others.

22. Epiphanius, *Pan.* [*Haer*]. 30, 36, 3. On the embarrassment of Epiphanius regarding Jesus' circumcision, cf. Epiphanius, op. cit., 30, 26, 8ff.

23. Epiphanius, *Pan.* [*Haer*]. 38, 5, 2. The fact that Epiphanius' description of Cerinthus is unhistorical (Cerinthus as contemporary of the original apostles and representative of an explicit Judaism) does not alter what is historically accurate here— the decisive significance of Jesus' circumcision for Jewish Christians.

24. The quotation is an Ebionitic utterance from Epiphanius, *Pan.* [*Haer*]. 30, 26, 2. On the Ebionites, cf. also Irenaeus, *Adv. haer.* 1, 26, 2: *et circumciduntur, ac*

perseverant in his consuetudinibus, quae sunt secundum legem. Cf. also Hippolytus, *Ref.* 7, 34, 1. Irenaeus and Epiphanius remark that in this regard Jewish
Christians make use of the gospel of Matthew or portions thereof. Luke's gospel,
and particularly 2:21, are not mentioned in the quotations.

25. Origen, of course, also attests to this in his *Hom. in Lucam* XIV. In this passage,
    he stresses that we should not permit ourselves to be circumcised because of the
    circumcision of Jesus, since the latter occurred for our sakes. Jesus' death, res-
    urrection, and circumcision took place on our behalf. At this juncture, Origen
    refers to Romans 6.
26. Cf. Justin, *Dial.* 46ff., where circumcision is described as a chief concern for
    Jewish Christianity.
27. Justin, *Dial.* 67:5.
28. Justin, *Dial.* 67:5-6. On Justin's negative evaluation of circumcision, cf. *Dial.*
    16:2 and 24:8ff. Circumcision belongs to the things which Moses commanded
    "for the hardness of your heart." For Justin, the sins of the Jewish people are at
    issue here. It is not surprising that he has great difficulty with Jesus' circumcision.
29. Justin, *Dial.* 67:6, writes that Jesus was not circumcised in order to be justified
    by the law, but because it was God's will for him. He adds that the parallels to
    Jesus' circumcision are his incarnation and death on the cross for the sins of Israel.
    Cf. also Origen, *Hom. in Lucam* XIV. In a later period also we note difficulties
    with circumcision, thus, e.g., in Cyril of Alexandria, *Comm. in Lucam* 129-132.
    In Ambrose and Theophylact we find the later "standard answer": Jesus was
    placed under the law in order to redeem us from its curse. Cf. Ambrose, *Expos.
    in Lucam*, II, 1299f., and Theophylact, *Ennaratio in Evangelium Lucae*, II, 282.
30. Justin, *Dial.* 63, 1ff.; 67, 1ff. Obviously, Justin does not state that Trypho thinks
    that in Luke 2 as well Jesus' Messiahship can be derived from his obedience to
    the law. This is all taken to be purely hypothetical—if it were possible to prove
    the messiahship of Jesus, it would be so by means of the law and not by the virgin
    birth. It is clear, however, that Justin's description intends to refer to a Jewish-
    Christian attitude.
31. This is especially clear in R. Laurentin, *Structure et theologie de Luc I-II* (Paris,
    1964), pp. 102ff. But the perspective in Luke is his variant on the phrase, "to
    the Jew first . . .," that is, through Jewish Christians who comprise the purified
    and restored Israel, salvation comes to the Gentiles. Cf. my work, "Das gespaltene
    Israel und die Heidenvölker," in *StTh* 19 (1965): 68-96.
32. Cf. Th. Zahn, *Das Evangelium des Lucas* (Leipzig-Erlangen, 1920³⁻⁴), on the
    passage.
33. In Luke, Jerusalem, the law, the cultus, and prophecy play a decisive role in the
    prehistory. The situation is different in Matthew, in which everything hinges on
    the Scripture being fulfilled.
34. G. B. Caird, *The Gospel of St. Luke* (London, 1968), p. 63, thinks that the interest
    in the law in 2:21 is inexplicable, since Luke can scarcely have had "a deep
    personal interest in the details of Jewish ceremonial." Cf. also Sahlin, *Messias*,
    p. 242, n. 1, who writes that Luke, the Gentile Christian, cannot intend to em-
    phasize that Jesus was subject to the Jewish Law.
35. J. Jervell, "The Law in Luke-Acts," in *Luke and the People of God*, pp. 133-
    154.
36. Rom. 2:25; 3:1; 4:10,12; 15:8; Gal. 2:3; 5:2ff., 11; 6:15; Phil. 3:3; Col. 2:11.
    The passages in Romans indicate a certain similarity with the statements in Acts.

This coheres with the fact that in Romans Paul is concerned with the meaning of circumcision for Jewish Christians, while in Galatians he regards it more as a problem of mission. Cf. J. Jervell, "The Letter to Jerusalem," in *The Romans Debate*, pp. 61-74.

37. On circumcision as a condition for salvation in Judaism, cf. Strack and Billerbeck, 3:263f.; 4:37-40, 1063-70.
38. On the figure of Abraham in Luke-Acts, cf. N. A. Dahl, "The Story of Abraham in Luke-Acts," in L. E. Keck and J. L. Martyn, eds., *Studies in Luke-Acts* (Nashville: Abingdon, 1966), pp. 139-158.
39. On the successive fulfillment of the promise within an historical development, cf. E. Lohse, "Lukas als Theologe der Heilsgeschichte," in *EvT* 14 (1954): 254-275, 256ff.; Dahl, op. cit., pp. 152ff.
40. On this subject, cf. "The Twelve on Israel's Throne," in my book, *Luke and the People of God*, pp. 75-112.
41. On this connection, cf. Dahl, op. cit., pp. 146ff.
42. Dahl, op. cit., pp. 149ff.
43. On the interpretation of Paul in Acts, cf. J. Jervell, "Paul: The Teacher of Israel," in *Luke and the People of God*, pp. 153-184. The essay is in essence concerned with an analysis of Chapters 21ff. On Luke's description of Paul, cf. further C. Burchard, *Der dreizehnte Zeuge* (FRLANT 103; Göttingen, 1970) and "Paulus in der Apostelgeschichte," in *TLZ* 100 (1975): 881-895; K. Löning, *Die Saulustradition in der Apostelgeschichte;* V. Stolle, *Der Zeuge als Angeklagter* (BWANT 102; Stuttgart-Berlin-Köln-Mainz, 1973).
44. This corresponds with the description in Luke's gospel. Jesus never speaks or acts against the Law; cf. Jervell, "Law," pp. 27ff. The future ἀλλάξει ("will change") in Acts 6:14 is striking: (One day) Jesus will overturn the ordinances which Moses handed down to us. Perhaps the future called for in v. 14a requires the same tense in v. 14b. In any event, it is clearly stated that Jesus altered nothing of the law.
45. On this passage, cf. F. Hahn, *Christologische Hoheitstitel* (FRLANT 83; Göttingen, 1974⁴), p. 247, who underscores what is Jewish in these statements. Burger, op. cit., p. 135, takes a somewhat different position.
46. Luke 2:11,26; 4:41; 9:20; 22:67; 23:2,35,39; 24:26; Acts 2:36; 3:18,20; 8:5; 9:22; 17:3; 18:5; 28:31. Cf. also Acts 4:27 and 10:38; cf. Hahn, op. cit., p. 224, n. 1.
47. The frequent schematic utterances are characteristic of Acts: You crucified—God raised (2:23ff., 36; 3:13,14; 4:10; 5:30; 10:39f.; 13:28ff.). This is also a Christology "despite the cross."

Chapter 9: The Daughters of Abraham: Women in Acts

1. R. Bultmann, *The History of the Synoptic Tradition*, rev. ed. (New York: Harper & Row, 1968), p. 367, finds "a sentimental feature" in this.
2. R. Bultmann, ibid.; Jeremias, *New Testament Theology* (New York: Scribner's 1971), 1:226ff.; L. Morris, *The Gospel According to St. Luke* (Grand Rapids: Eerdmans, 1974), pp. 40f.; J. Schmid, *Das Evangelium nach Lukas*, 4th ed. (RNT 3; Regensburg, 1960), p. 21.
3. K. H. Rengstorf, *Das Evangelium des Lukas*, 14th ed. (Göttingen, 1969), p. 4.
4. J. Ernst, *Das Evangeliums nach Lukas* (Regensburg, 1977), pp. 17f. Here in Luke Ernst believes he sees a reflection of the experiences of the apostolic period; cf.

also E. Schweizer, *The Good News According to Luke* (Atlanta: John Knox, 1984), pp. 58f.

5. Cf. e.g., R. J. Cassidy, *Jesus, Politics, and Society. A Study of Luke's Gospel* (Maryknoll, N.Y.: Orbis, 1978). Cassidy finds, e.g., that Luke's portrayal of Jesus and the women is "extremely progressive": according to Luke, Jesus gives women a new identity and a new social status. This may be correct where Jesus is concerned, but the Lukan portrayal is scarcely tenable. Cf. A. Oepke, "γυνή," *TDNT* 1:784, who is of another opinion.

6. J. Leipoldt, *Die Frau in der Antiken Welt und im Urchristentum*, 2nd ed. (Gütersloh, 1955), p. 166, believes that "in Acts we detect the same concerns," that is, as in the Gospel. Thus also A. v. Harnack, *Die Mission und Ausbreitung des Christentums in den ersten drei Jahrhunderten* (1924⁴), 4:592ff.; G. Stählin, *Die Apostelgeschichte*, 4:87; J. Roloff, *Die Apostelgeschichte*, p. 28 (see chap. 1, nn. 5 and 10).

7. One indication of this fact is that in indexes to works on Acts, in commentaries and descriptions of theology, the key word *woman* is most often lacking; e.g., in E. Haenchen, *Die Apostelgeschichte* 1. For the older works, cf. F. J. Foakes-Jackson–Lake, *The Beginnings of Christianity* I-V.

8. Cf. K. H. Rengstorf, *Mann und Frau im Urchristentum*, (Arbeitsgemeinschaft für Forschung des Landes Nordrhein-Westfalen, 1953), p. 17.

9. K. H. Rengstorf, *Mann und Frau*, p. 21: Jesus' own practice in Luke 8:1ff. underscores the revolutionary logion in Mark 10:11ff. Cf. also E. Schweizer, op. cit., p. 93.

10. The momentous passage in Luke 8:1-3 is often accented without any explanation or foundation. Cf. W. Grundmann, *Das Evangelium nach Lukas* (THKNT 3; Berlin, 1964), p. 174; H. Schürmann, *Das Lukas Evangelium* I (HTKNT 3; 1969), pp. 445ff.

11. Among others, cf. J. Leipoldt, op. cit., pp. 126ff.

12. J. Jeremias, op. cit., p. 226, note 3, writes that Luke 8: 1-3 has been shaped by Luke, but that the names derive from ancient tradition.

13. E. Schweizer, op. cit., p. 93, states that "by this formulation Luke will have had in mind female service in the communities known to him."

14. In contrast to many, cf. H. Conzelmann, *Die Apostelgeschichte*, p. 23 (on Acts 1:14).

15. J. Jervell, *Luke and the People of God*, pp. 75-112.

16. Thus A. Schlatter, *Das Evangelium des Lukas* (Stuttgart, 1931), p. 326; E. Haenchen, *Der Weg Jesu* (Berlin, 1968²), pp. 126ff.

17. On the concept in Rabbinism, cf. H. Strack and P. Billerbeck, *Kommentar* 2:200; A. Schlatter, *Lukas*, p. 327.

18. This designation is most often noted without any explanation, thus e.g., in W. Grundmann, op cit., p. 280; J. Schmid, op. cit., p. 236; E. E. Ellis, *The Gospel of Luke* (Greenwood, S. C.: Attic, 1966), p. 186. A. Schlatter, op. cit., thinks that Luke 13:10-17 was connected with Luke's infancy stories; G. Schneider, *Das Evangelium nach Lukas* (Ökum. Taschenbuchkomm. z. N.T. 3:2; Gütersloh, 1977), p. 300, writes that the phrase indicates that the woman is of more value than house pets; cf. also K. H. Rengstorff, *Komm.*, p. 171, who states that the designation is altogether unusual, but indicates that for every Jew the woman should be a "neighbor."

19. The designation first appears in the fourth century, though we find a similar expression as early as in the third century— "daughters of Abraham, Isaac, and Jacob." In these instances the subject is Israel as the daughters of Abraham.

20. H. Conzelmann, *The Theology of St. Luke* (New York: Harper and Row, 1961), p. 31; E. Loymeyer, *Galiläa und Jerusalem* (FRLANT 34; Göttingen, 1936), pp. 44f.; V. Taylor, *Behind the Third Gospel* (Oxford: Clarendon, 1926), p. 91.

21. Here, of course, we are dealing with "the great omission," thus with Mark 6:45— 8:26.

22. J. Jervell, "The Circumcised Messiah," Chapter 8 of this volume.

23. J. Jervell, *Luke and the People of God*, pp. 41-74.

24. J. Leipoldt, op. cit., pp. 152f.; G. Stählin, op. cit., p. 145.

25. J. Jervell, *Luke and the People of God*, pp. 113-132.

26. J. Leipoldt, op. cit., p. 156, speaks of a surplus of women in the communities.

27. Cf. G. Stählin, op. cit., p. 87; E. Haenchen, *Komm.*, p. 238, note 5, inquires whether this mention of the woman alongside the men means that till now Luke intends to report only the conversion of men. At the least it indicates who the chief persons of the community are.

28. F. V. Filson, *A New Testament History* (Philadelphia: Westminster, 1965), p. 266, thinks that "Luke, in both his Gospel and the Acts mentions women who exercised leadership in the church." Where do we find this?

29. To all appearances, what J. Leipoldt, op. cit., p. 191, asserts is correct, that a worsening of woman's status in the community occurred due to Jewish influence. It is clear that after A.D. 48, and even after A.D. 70, Jewish Christianity took on greater and greater strength in the church, cf. my essay, "The Mighty Minority," Chapter 2 in this volume.

30. Of course, we find a woman mentioned in Acts 17:34—Damaris. This should really mean that women were also among the hearers of Paul in Athens. But it does not agree with Luke's portrait in v. 18, or with the addressees in v. 22; cf. G. Stählin, op. cit., p. 239. In any event, it indicates how Luke gives shape to his material here. In Athens, a devout Jewess or woman in the community would of course not appear in public with men.

31. Cf. J. Jervell, *Luke and the People of God*, p. 50.

32. F. V. Filson, n. 28 above; J. Leipoldt, op. cit., p. 157, is also incorrect when he states that the women in the community "are not only present, but play a role."

33. J. Jervell, *Luke and the People of God*, pp. 75-112.

34. G. Lohfink, *Die Sammlung Israels* (STANT 39; Munich, 1975).

35. Cf. below, pp. 155f.

36. H. Lietzmann, *Geschichte der Alten Kirche* (Berlin, 1932), p. 150, writes: "In general, the Christian woman in worship gatherings will have been relegated to a strictly passive role, corresponding to good custom among Gentiles and Jews." This is correct in respect of Luke, but not at all of Paul, as is indicated not merely in 1 Corinthians 11, but also by Paul's many female co-workers; cf. especially the list in Romans 16.

37. We may not speak of women's independent activity in the congregations; thus E. Haenchen, *Komm.*, p. 160.

38. G. Stählin makes this statement without support, op. cit., p. 145 (on Acts 9:36); cf. J. Roloff to the contrary, op. cit., p. 161.

39. This is true apart from the so-called women of means who, however, have no office at all or exercise any regular function.

40. A. Oepke, op. cit., p. 787; J. Roloff, op. cit., p. 161.
41. Leipoldt, op. cit., p. 150, writes that the Christians define their self-consciousness on the basis of the Old Testament, as is true especially of Joel 3:1 (2:28, ET) in Acts 2:17ff.
42. Cf. Num. R. 15:25; Tanch. B 28; Midr. Ps. 14,6; cf. Strack and Billerbeck 2:615.
43. J. Leipoldt, op. cit., p. 75, states that in the Old Testament prophetesses recede to very great extent in comparison with male prophets; cf. also 83: "In the Jewish world, prophetesses are scarcely possible."
44. Rabbinism reckons with seven prophetesses in Scripture; Strack and Billerbeck 2:140; 4:20f.
45. "The fathers" (οἱ πατέρες) play a great role in Acts; cf. 3:25; 7 passim; 13:17, 32; 26:6; 28:25. Obviously, there is no analogous reference to "mothers," though such is not entirely impossible, due to the female figures in the Old Testament. "The elders" (οἱ πρεσβύτεροι) in Acts were of course also only men.
46. E. Schweizer, op. cit., p. 93.
47. This is also the case in the early Jewish historical resumes, Sir. 44–49; Wisd. 10; 1 Macc. 2; Pss. 78; 105; 106; 135; 136; Ezek. 20. In 2 Bar. 59:1 Miriam is mentioned. The exception here is the Book of Jubilees which mentions a series of women.
48. Sarah in Rom. 4:19; 9:9; 1 Peter 3:6; and Heb. 11:1; Rebecca in Romans 9–10; Rachel in Matt. 2:18; Hagar in Gal. 4:24-25; and Eve in 2 Cor. 11:3 and 1 Tim. 2:13.
49. A. v. Harnack, op. cit., pp. 59f., speaks of an "antifeminist strain which came into its own in Acts and threads through the entire second century (over against a strain decidedly friendly towards women), and which penetrated the tradition of the Pauline letters."
50. Clearly, "the women" in Luke 8:2 and Acts 1:14 do not play a role in the communities but rather as a community.
51. Whether Luke is also aware of the other women from Philippi, thus Euodia and Syntyche in Phil. 4:2, cannot be determined. In any case, he mentions only Lydia, whom Paul, however, does not mention—that is, provided Lydia is not a cognomen. But women share in the founding of the Philippian community, as both Luke and Paul make clear. Cf. also A. v. Harnack, op. cit., p. 693, n. 2.
52. There is no justification for regarding Priscilla as "spiritually superior" to Aquila, and to offer this as Luke's opinion, as does J. Leipoldt, op. cit., p. 166. For this opinion, cf. also J. Roloff, op. cit., p. 275, as well as most commentaries.
53. A. v. Harnack, op. cit., p. 594, thinks he is able to infer from Acts that Priscilla was active as a missionary "in her own right." He also believes she was the woman who instructed Apollos, an idea which already appears in Chrysostom, *De virg.* 47. As such, this may be historically correct, but cannot at all be inferred from Acts 18:18, 26, as Harnack supposes.
54. On the other hand, according to the Pauline epistles, women have full share in the offices of the community and in its worship life, thus H. Koester, *Introduction to the New Testament* (Philadelphia: Fortress, 1980), 2:124ff.
55. Strack and Billerbeck, 2:643-647; 4:536-558; J. Jeremias, *Jerusalem at the Time of Jesus* (Philadelphia: Fortress, 1977), pp. 31-34; A. Strobel, "Armenpfleger 'um des Friedens willen,'" *ZNW* 63 (1972): 271-276; K. Lake in *Beginnings*

5:140-151—all on a discussion of Acts 6:1. Cf. further E. Haenchen, *Komm.* on the passage; S. W. Baron, *A Social and Religious History of the Jews*, 2nd ed. (New York: Columbia, 1952), 2:269-274; H. Bolkestein, *Wohltätigkeit und Armenpflege im vorchristlichen Altertum* (Utrecht, 1939), pp. 401-417.

56. 1 Tim. (3:8) 5:3ff., 9ff.